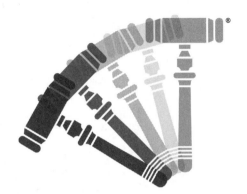

D1370987

Casenote™ Legal Briefs

ADMINISTRATIVE LAW

Keyed to Courses Using

Funk, Shapiro, and Weaver's
Administrative Procedure and Practice

Fourth Edition

Wolters Kluwer

Law & Business

AUSTIN   BOSTON   CHICAGO   NEW YORK   THE NETHERLANDS

This publication is designed to provide accurate and authoritative information in regard to the subject matter covered. It is sold with the understanding that the publisher is not engaged in rendering legal, accounting, or other professional services. If legal advice or other expert assistance is required, the services of a competent professional person should be sought.

> — From a Declaration of Principles adopted jointly by a Committee of the American Bar Association and a Committee of Publishers and Associates

© 2011 Aspen Publishers. All Rights Reserved.
www.AspenLaw.com

No part of this publication may be reproduced or transmitted in any form or by any means, electronic or mechanical, including photocopy, recording, or any information storage and retrieval system, without permission in writing from the publisher. Requests for permission to make copies of any part of this publication should be mailed to:

Aspen Publishers
Attn: Permissions Dept.
76 Ninth Avenue, 7th Floor
New York, NY 10011-5201

To contact Customer Care, e-mail customer.service@aspenpublishers.com, call 1-800-234-1660, fax 1-800-901-9075, or mail correspondence to:

Aspen Publishers
Attn: Order Department
P.O. Box 990
Frederick, MD 21705

Printed in the United States of America.

1 2 3 4 5 6 7 8 9 0

ISBN 978-0-7355-0799-9

About Wolters Kluwer Law & Business

Wolters Kluwer Law & Business is a leading provider of research information and workflow solutions in key specialty areas. The strengths of the individual brands of Aspen Publishers, CCH, Kluwer Law International and Loislaw are aligned within Wolters Kluwer Law & Business to provide comprehensive, in-depth solutions and expert-authored content for the legal, professional and education markets.

CCH was founded in 1913 and has served more than four generations of business professionals and their clients. The CCH products in the Wolters Kluwer Law & Business group are highly regarded electronic and print resources for legal, securities, antitrust and trade regulation, government contracting, banking, pension, payroll, employment and labor, and health-care reimbursement and compliance professionals.

Aspen Publishers is a leading information provider for attorneys, business professionals and law students. Written by preeminent authorities, Aspen products offer analytical and practical information in a range of specialty practice areas from securities law and intellectual property to mergers and acquisitions and pension/benefits. Aspen's trusted legal education resources provide professors and students with high-quality, up-to-date and effective resources for successful instruction and study in all areas of the law.

Kluwer Law International supplies the global business community with comprehensive English-language international legal information. Legal practitioners, corporate counsel and business executives around the world rely on the Kluwer Law International journals, loose-leafs, books and electronic products for authoritative information in many areas of international legal practice.

Loislaw is a premier provider of digitized legal content to small law firm practitioners of various specializations. Loislaw provides attorneys with the ability to quickly and efficiently find the necessary legal information they need, when and where they need it, by facilitating access to primary law as well as state-specific law, records, forms and treatises.

Wolters Kluwer Law & Business, a unit of Wolters Kluwer, is headquartered in New York and Riverwoods, Illinois. Wolters Kluwer is a leading multinational publisher and information services company.

Format for the Casenote Legal Brief

Nature of Case: This section identifies the form of action (e.g., breach of contract, negligence, battery), the type of proceeding (e.g., demurrer, appeal from trial court's jury instructions), or the relief sought (e.g., damages, injunction, criminal sanctions).

Fact Summary: This is included to refresh your memory and can be used as a quick reminder of the facts.

Rule of Law: Summarizes the general principle of law that the case illustrates. It may be used for instant recall of the court's holding and for classroom discussion or home review.

Facts: This section contains all relevant facts of the case, including the contentions of the parties and the lower court holdings. It is written in a logical order to give the student a clear understanding of the case. The plaintiff and defendant are identified by their proper names throughout and are always labeled with a (P) or (D).

Palsgraf v. Long Island R.R. Co.

Injured bystander (P) v. Railroad company (D)

N.Y. Ct. App., 248 N.Y. 339, 162 N.E. 99 (1928).

NATURE OF CASE: Appeal from judgment affirming verdict for plaintiff seeking damages for personal injury.

FACT SUMMARY: Helen Palsgraf (P) was injured on R.R.'s (D) train platform when R.R.'s (D) guard helped a passenger aboard a moving train, causing his package to fall on the tracks. The package contained fireworks which exploded, creating a shock that tipped a scale onto Palsgraf (P).

🏛 RULE OF LAW
The risk reasonably to be perceived defines the duty to be obeyed.

FACTS: Helen Palsgraf (P) purchased a ticket to Rockaway Beach from R.R. (D) and was waiting on the train platform. As she waited, two men ran to catch a train that was pulling out from the platform. The first man jumped aboard, but the second man, who appeared as if he might fall, was helped aboard by the guard on the train who had kept the door open so they could jump aboard. A guard on the platform also helped by pushing him onto the train. The man was carrying a package wrapped in newspaper. In the process, the man dropped his package, which fell on the tracks. The package contained fireworks and exploded. The shock of the explosion was apparently of great enough strength to tip over some scales at the other end of the platform, which fell on Palsgraf (P) and injured her. A jury awarded her damages, and R.R. (D) appealed.

ISSUE: Does the risk reasonably to be perceived define the duty to be obeyed?

HOLDING AND DECISION: (Cardozo, C.J.) Yes. The risk reasonably to be perceived defines the duty to be obeyed. If there is no foreseeable hazard to the injured party as the result of a seemingly innocent act, the act does not become a tort because it happened to be a wrong as to another. If the wrong was not willful, the plaintiff must show that the act as to her had such great and apparent possibilities of danger as to entitle her to protection. Negligence in the abstract is not enough upon which to base liability. Negligence is a relative concept, evolving out of the common law doctrine of trespass on the case. To establish liability, the defendant must owe a legal duty of reasonable care to the injured party. A cause of action in tort will lie where harm,

though unintended, could have been averted or avoided by observance of such a duty. The scope of the duty is limited by the range of danger that a reasonable person could foresee. In this case, there was nothing to suggest from the appearance of the parcel or otherwise that the parcel contained fireworks. The guard could not reasonably have had any warning of a threat to Palsgraf (P), and R.R. (D) therefore cannot be held liable. Judgment is reversed in favor of R.R. (D).

DISSENT: (Andrews, J.) The concept that there is no negligence unless R.R. (D) owes a legal duty to take care as to Palsgraf (P) herself is too narrow. Everyone owes to the world at large the duty of refraining from those acts that may unreasonably threaten the safety of others. If the guard's action was negligent as to those nearby, it was also negligent as to those outside what might be termed the "danger zone." For Palsgraf (P) to recover, R.R.'s (D) negligence must have been the proximate cause of her injury, a question of fact for the jury.

▶ ANALYSIS
The majority defined the limit of the defendant's liability in terms of the danger that a reasonable person in defendant's situation would have perceived. The dissent argued that the limitation should not be placed on liability, but rather on damages. Judge Andrews suggested that only injuries that would not have happened but for R.R.'s (D) negligence should be compensable. Both the majority and dissent recognized the policy-driven need to limit liability for negligent acts, seeking, in the words of Judge Andrews, to define a framework "that will be practical and in keeping with the general understanding of mankind." The Restatement (Second) of Torts has accepted Judge Cardozo's view.

Quicknotes
FORESEEABILITY A reasonable expectation that change is the probable result of certain acts or omissions.

NEGLIGENCE Conduct falling below the standard of care that a reasonable person would demonstrate under similar conditions.

PROXIMATE CAUSE The natural sequence of events without which an injury would not have been sustained.

Party ID: Quick identification of the relationship between the parties.

Concurrence/Dissent: All concurrences and dissents are briefed whenever they are included by the casebook editor.

Analysis: This last paragraph gives you a broad understanding of where the case "fits in" with other cases in the section of the book and with the entire course. It is a hornbook-style discussion indicating whether the case is a majority or minority opinion and comparing the principal case with other cases in the casebook. It may also provide analysis from restatements, uniform codes, and law review articles. The analysis will prove to be invaluable to classroom discussion.

Issue: The issue is a concise question that brings out the essence of the opinion as it relates to the section of the casebook in which the case appears. Both substantive and procedural issues are included if relevant to the decision.

Holding and Decision: This section offers a clear and in-depth discussion of the rule of the case and the court's rationale. It is written in easy-to-understand language and answers the issue presented by applying the law to the facts of the case. When relevant, it includes a thorough discussion of the exceptions to the case as listed by the court, any major cites to the other cases on point, and the names of the judges who wrote the decisions.

Quicknotes: Conveniently defines legal terms found in the case and summarizes the nature of any statutes, codes, or rules referred to in the text.

Aspen Publishers is proud to offer *Casenote Legal Briefs*—continuing thirty years of publishing America's best-selling legal briefs.

Casenote Legal Briefs are designed to help you save time when briefing assigned cases. Organized under convenient headings, they show you how to abstract the basic facts and holdings from the text of the actual opinions handed down by the courts. Used as part of a rigorous study regimen, they can help you spend more time analyzing and critiquing points of law than on copying bits and pieces of judicial opinions into your notebook or outline.

Casenote Legal Briefs should never be used as a substitute for assigned casebook readings. They work best when read as a follow-up to reviewing the underlying opinions themselves. Students who try to avoid reading and digesting the judicial opinions in their casebooks or online sources will end up shortchanging themselves in the long run. The ability to absorb, critique, and restate the dynamic and complex elements of case law decisions is crucial to your success in law school and beyond. It cannot be developed vicariously.

Casenote Legal Briefs represents but one of the many offerings in Aspen's Study Aid Timeline, which includes:

- *Casenote Legal Briefs*
- *Emanuel Law Outlines*
- *Examples & Explanations* Series
- *Introduction to Law* Series
- Emanuel *Law in a Flash* Flash Cards
- Emanuel *CrunchTime* Series

Each of these series is designed to provide you with easy-to-understand explanations of complex points of law. Each volume offers guidance on the principles of legal analysis and, consulted regularly, will hone your ability to spot relevant issues. We have titles that will help you prepare for class, prepare for your exams, and enhance your general comprehension of the law along the way.

To find out more about Aspen Study Aid publications, visit us online at *www.AspenLaw.com* or email us at *legaledu@wolterskluwer.com*. We'll be happy to assist you.

Get this Casenote Legal Brief as an AspenLaw Studydesk eBook today!

By returning this form to Aspen Publishers, you will receive a complimentary eBook download of this Casenote Legal Brief and AspenLaw Studydesk productivity software.* Learn more about AspenLaw Studydesk today at *www.AspenLaw.com/Studydesk.*

Name	Phone ( )
Address	Apt. No.
City	State	ZIP Code
Law School	Graduation Date Month _____ Year _____

Cut out the UPC found on the lower left corner of the back cover of this book. Staple the UPC inside this box. Only the original UPC from the book cover will be accepted. (No photocopies or store stickers are allowed.)

Attach UPC inside this box.

Email (Print legibly or you may not get access!)
Title of this book (course subject)
ISBN of this book (10- or 13-digit number on the UPC)
Used with which casebook (provide author's name)

Mail the completed form to:

Aspen Publishers, Inc.
Legal Education Division
130 Turner Street, Bldg 3, 4th Floor
Waltham, MA 02453-8901

* Upon receipt of this completed form, you will be emailed a code for the digital download of this book in AspenLaw Studydesk eBook format and a free copy of the software application, which is required to read the eBook.

For a full list of eBook study aids available for AspenLaw Studydesk software and other resources that will help you with your law school studies, visit *www.AspenLaw.com.*

Make a photocopy of this form and your UPC for your records.

For detailed information on the use of the information you provide on this form, please see the PRIVACY POLICY at *www.AspenLaw.com.*

A. Decide on a Format and Stick to It

Structure is essential to a good brief. It enables you to arrange systematically the related parts that are scattered throughout most cases, thus making manageable and understandable what might otherwise seem to be an endless and unfathomable sea of information. There are, of course, an unlimited number of formats that can be utilized. However, it is best to find one that suits your needs and stick to it. Consistency breeds both efficiency and the security that when called upon you will know where to look in your brief for the information you are asked to give.

Any format, as long as it presents the essential elements of a case in an organized fashion, can be used. Experience, however, has led *Casenotes* to develop and utilize the following format because of its logical flow and universal applicability.

NATURE OF CASE: This is a brief statement of the legal character and procedural status of the case (e.g., "Appeal of a burglary conviction").

There are many different alternatives open to a litigant dissatisfied with a court ruling. The key to determining which one has been used is to discover *who is asking this court for what.*

This first entry in the brief should be kept as *short as possible.* Use the court's terminology if you understand it. But since jurisdictions vary as to the titles of pleadings, the best entry is the one that addresses who wants what in this proceeding, not the one that sounds most like the court's language.

RULE OF LAW: A statement of the general principle of law that the case illustrates (e.g., "An acceptance that varies any term of the offer is considered a rejection and counteroffer").

Determining the rule of law of a case is a procedure similar to determining the issue of the case. Avoid being fooled by red herrings; there may be a few rules of law mentioned in the case excerpt, but usually only one is *the* rule with which the casebook editor is concerned. The techniques used to locate the issue, described below, may also be utilized to find the rule of law. Generally, your best guide is simply the chapter heading. It is a clue to the point the casebook editor seeks to make and should be kept in mind when reading every case in the respective section.

FACTS: A synopsis of only the essential facts of the case, i.e., those bearing upon or leading up to the issue.

The facts entry should be a short statement of the events and transactions that led one party to initiate legal proceedings against another in the first place. While some cases conveniently state the salient facts at the beginning of the decision, in other instances they will have to be culled from hiding places throughout the text, even from concurring and dissenting opinions. Some of the "facts" will often be in dispute and should be so noted. Conflicting evidence may be briefly pointed up. "Hard" facts must be included. Both must be *relevant* in order to be listed in the facts entry. It is impossible to tell what is relevant until the entire case is read, as the ultimate determination of the rights and liabilities of the parties may turn on something buried deep in the opinion.

Generally, the facts entry should not be longer than three to five *short* sentences.

It is often helpful to identify the role played by a party in a given context. For example, in a construction contract case the identification of a party as the "contractor" or "builder" alleviates the need to tell that that party was the one who was supposed to have built the house.

It is always helpful, and a good general practice, to identify the "plaintiff" and the "defendant." This may seem elementary and uncomplicated, but, especially in view of the creative editing practiced by some casebook editors, it is sometimes a difficult or even impossible task. Bear in mind that the *party presently* seeking something from this court may not be the plaintiff, and that sometimes only the cross-claim of a defendant is treated in the excerpt. Confusing or misaligning the parties can ruin your analysis and understanding of the case.

ISSUE: A statement of the general legal question answered by or illustrated in the case. For clarity, the issue is best put in the form of a question capable of a "yes" or "no" answer. In reality, the issue is simply the Rule of Law put in the form of a question (e.g., "May an offer be accepted by performance?").

The major problem presented in discerning what is *the* issue in the case is that an opinion usually purports to raise and answer several questions. However, except for rare cases, only one such question is really the issue in the case. Collateral issues not necessary to the resolution of the matter in controversy are handled by the court by language known as *"obiter dictum"* or merely *"dictum."* While dicta may be included later in the brief, they have no place under the issue heading.

To find the issue, ask *who wants what* and then go on to ask *why did that party succeed or fail in getting it.* Once this is determined, the "why" should be turned into a question.

The complexity of the issues in the cases will vary, but in all cases a single-sentence question should sum up the issue. *In a few cases,* there will be two, or even more rarely, three issues of equal importance to the resolution of the case. Each should be expressed in a single-sentence question.

Since many issues are resolved by a court in coming to a final disposition of a case, the casebook editor will reproduce the portion of the opinion containing the issue or issues most relevant to the area of law under scrutiny. A noted law professor gave this advice: "Close the book; look at the title on the cover." Chances are, if it is Property, you need not concern yourself with whether, for example, the federal government's treatment of the plaintiff's land really raises a federal question sufficient to support jurisdiction on this ground in federal court.

The same rule applies to chapter headings designating sub-areas within the subjects. They tip you off as to what the text is designed to teach. The cases are arranged in a casebook to show a progression or development of the law, so that the preceding cases may also help.

It is also most important to remember to *read the notes and questions* at the end of a case to determine what the editors wanted you to have gleaned from it.

HOLDING AND DECISION: This section should succinctly explain the rationale of the court in arriving at its decision. In capsulizing the "reasoning" of the court, it should always include an application of the general rule or rules of law to the specific facts of the case. Hidden justifications come to light in this entry: the reasons for the state of the law, the public policies, the biases and prejudices, those considerations that influence the justices' thinking and, ultimately, the outcome of the case. At the end, there should be a short indication of the disposition or procedural resolution of the case (e.g., "Decision of the trial court for Mr. Smith (P) reversed").

The foregoing format is designed to help you "digest" the reams of case material with which you will be faced in your law school career. Once mastered by practice, it will place at your fingertips the information the authors of your casebooks have sought to impart to you in case-by-case illustration and analysis.

B. Be as Economical as Possible in Briefing Cases

Once armed with a format that encourages succinctness, it is as important to be economical with regard to the time spent on the actual reading of the case as it is to be economical in the writing of the brief itself. This does not mean "skimming" a case. Rather, it means reading the case with an "eye" trained to recognize into which "section" of your brief a particular passage or line fits and having a system for quickly and precisely marking the case so that the passages fitting any one particular part of

the brief can be easily identified and brought together in a concise and accurate manner when the brief is actually written.

It is of no use to simply repeat everything in the opinion of the court; record only enough information to trigger your recollection of what the court said. Nevertheless, an accurate statement of the "law of the case," i.e., the legal principle applied to the facts, is absolutely essential to class preparation and to learning the law under the case method.

To that end, it is important to develop a "shorthand" that you can use to make marginal notations. These notations will tell you at a glance in which section of the brief you will be placing that particular passage or portion of the opinion.

Some students prefer to underline all the salient portions of the opinion (with a pencil or colored underliner marker), making marginal notations as they go along. Others prefer the color-coded method of underlining, utilizing different colors of markers to underline the salient portions of the case, each separate color being used to represent a different section of the brief. For example, blue underlining could be used for passages relating to the rule of law, yellow for those relating to the issue, and green for those relating to the holding and decision, etc. While it has its advocates, the color-coded method can be confusing and time-consuming (all that time spent on changing colored markers). Furthermore, it can interfere with the continuity and concentration many students deem essential to the reading of a case for maximum comprehension. In the end, however, it is a matter of personal preference and style. Just remember, whatever method you use, underlining must be used sparingly or its value is lost.

If you take the marginal notation route, an efficient and easy method is to go along underlining the key portions of the case and placing in the margin alongside them the following "markers" to indicate where a particular passage or line "belongs" in the brief you will write:

N   (NATURE OF CASE)
RL   (RULE OF LAW)
I   (ISSUE)
HL   (HOLDING AND DECISION, relates to
      the RULE OF LAW behind the decision)
HR   (HOLDING AND DECISION, gives the
      RATIONALE or reasoning behind the
      decision)
HA   (HOLDING AND DECISION, APPLIES
      the general principle(s) of law to the facts
      of the case to arrive at the decision)

Remember that a particular passage may well contain information necessary to more than one part of your brief, in which case you simply note that in the margin. If you are using the color-coded underlining method instead of marginal notation, simply make asterisks or checks in the margin next to the passage in question in the colors that indicate the additional sections of the brief where it might be utilized.

The economy of utilizing "shorthand" in marking cases for briefing can be maintained in the actual brief writing process itself by utilizing "law student shorthand" within the brief. There are many commonly used words and phrases for which abbreviations can be substituted in your briefs (and in your class notes also). You can develop abbreviations that are personal to you and which will save you a lot of time. A reference list of briefing abbreviations can be found on page xii of this book.

C. Use Both the Briefing Process and the Brief as a Learning Tool

Now that you have a format and the tools for briefing cases efficiently, the most important thing is to make the time spent in briefing profitable to you and to make the most advantageous use of the briefs you create. Of course, the briefs are invaluable for classroom reference when you are called upon to explain or analyze a particular case. However, they are also useful in reviewing for exams. A quick glance at the fact summary should bring the case to mind, and a rereading of the rule of law should enable you to go over the underlying legal concept in your mind, how it was applied in that particular case, and how it might apply in other factual settings.

As to the value to be derived from engaging in the briefing process itself, there is an immediate benefit that arises from being forced to sift through the essential facts and reasoning from the court's opinion and to succinctly express them in your own words in your brief. The process ensures that you understand the case and the point that it illustrates, and that means you will be ready to absorb further analysis and information brought forth in class. It also ensures you will have something to say when called upon in class. The briefing process helps develop a mental agility for getting to the *gist* of a case and for identifying, expounding on, and applying the legal concepts and issues found there. The briefing process is the mental process on which you must rely in taking law school examinations; it is also the mental process upon which a lawyer relies in serving his clients and in making his living.

Abbreviations for Briefs

acceptance	acp	offer	O
affirmed	aff	offeree	OE
answer	ans	offeror	OR
assumption of risk	a/r	ordinance	ord
attorney	atty	pain and suffering	p/s
beyond a reasonable doubt	b/r/d	parol evidence	p/e
bona fide purchaser	BFP	plaintiff	P
breach of contract	br/k	prima facie	p/f
cause of action	c/a	probable cause	p/c
common law	c/l	proximate cause	px/c
Constitution	Con	real property	r/p
constitutional	con	reasonable doubt	r/d
contract	K	reasonable man	r/m
contributory negligence	c/n	rebuttable presumption	rb/p
cross	x	remanded	rem
cross-complaint	x/c	res ipsa loquitur	RIL
cross-examination	x/ex	respondeat superior	r/s
cruel and unusual punishment	c/u/p	Restatement	RS
defendant	D	reversed	rev
dismissed	dis	Rule Against Perpetuities	RAP
double jeopardy	d/j	search and seizure	s/s
due process	d/p	search warrant	s/w
equal protection	e/p	self-defense	s/d
equity	eq	specific performance	s/p
evidence	ev	statute	S
exclude	exc	statute of frauds	S/F
exclusionary rule	exc/r	statute of limitations	S/L
felony	f/n	summary judgment	s/j
freedom of speech	f/s	tenancy at will	t/w
good faith	g/f	tenancy in common	t/c
habeas corpus	h/c	tenant	t
hearsay	hr	third party	TP
husband	H	third party beneficiary	TPB
injunction	inj	transferred intent	TI
in loco parentis	ILP	unconscionable	uncon
inter vivos	I/v	unconstitutional	unconst
joint tenancy	j/t	undue influence	u/e
judgment	judgt	Uniform Commercial Code	UCC
jurisdiction	jur	unilateral	uni
last clear chance	LCC	vendee	VE
long-arm statute	LAS	vendor	VR
majority view	maj	versus	v
meeting of minds	MOM	void for vagueness	VFV
minority view	min	weight of authority	w/a
Miranda rule	Mir/r	weight of the evidence	w/e
Miranda warnings	Mir/w	wife	W
negligence	neg	with	w/
notice	ntc	within	w/i
nuisance	nus	without	w/o
obligation	ob	without prejudice	w/o/p
obscene	obs	wrongful death	wr/d

Table of Cases

CHAPTER 1

Practicing Administrative Law

Quick Reference Rules of Law

Fund for Animals, Inc. v. Rice

Public interest group (P) v. Government agency (D)

85 F.3d 535 (11th Cir. 1996).

NATURE OF CASE: Action seeking injunction against agency decision.

FACT SUMMARY: Fund for Animals (P) challenged the Fish and Wildlife Service's (FWS's) (D) decision to issue a permit for a landfill on a site Fund for Animals (P) claimed would threaten endangered species.

🏛 RULE OF LAW
[No rule is provided; the case in the casebook gives only the facts and issues to show an example of an administrative law case.]

FACTS: Sarasota County applied for a permit with the United States Army Corps of Engineers (Corps) (D) to build a landfill. The Corps (D) could only grant a permit if the proposed project was consistent with the rules of the Environmental Protection Agency (D) and did not adversely affect a species covered under the Endangered Species Act. Accordingly, the FWS (D) was required to conduct an environmental assessment of Sarasota's proposed landfill. The FWS (D) gave its approval to the project but the Fund for Animals (the Fund) (P) complained that it hadn't considered the affect on the endangered Florida panther and Eastern Indigo snake. The FWS (D) then issued a Biological Opinion that addressed concerns regarding those species and concluded that the project was unlikely to jeopardize the panther and snake. The opinion did include recommendations for certain preservation measures. The Fund (P) then filed suit against all of the agencies involved with approving the permit. After some modifications, the permit was approved on April 13, 1995, and the Fund (P) amended their complaint and sought injunctive relief. The district court ruled against the Fund (P) and it appealed.

HOLDING AND DECISION: (Dubina, J.) The district court did not act arbitrarily or capriciously in approving the permit for the Sarasota project or in relying on the Biological Opinion of the FWS (D). Affirmed.

▌ ANALYSIS

This is a standard case in terms of the parties involved. Government agencies usually make decisions that affect private parties differently. When it reaches the stage of litigation, one party seeks to overturn the decision and another desires to uphold it.

Quicknotes

INJUNCTIVE RELIEF A court order issued as a remedy, requiring a person to do, or prohibiting that person from doing, a specific act.

Rulemaking

Quick Reference Rules of Law

Telecommunications Research & Action Center v. Federal Communications Commission

Consumer group (P) v. Government agency (D)

750 F.2d 70 (D.C. Cir. 1984).

NATURE OF CASE: Action challenging agency's failure to make a decision.

FACT SUMMARY: The Federal Communications Commission (FCC) (D) had not made a decision five years after being petitioned to decide whether AT&T had overcharged its customers.

🏛 RULE OF LAW
Unreasonable agency delays are subject to interlocutory appeals and may warrant mandamus under certain circumstances.

FACTS: The Telecommunications Research & Action Center (TRAC) (P) petitioned the FCC (D) in 1979 to decide whether AT&T had overcharged its customers. After periodically claiming that a decision was forthcoming, the FCC (D) still had not decided the issue five years later. TRAC (P) filed suit to compel the FCC (D) to decide and, while the case was pending, the FCC (D) indicated that it would resolve the matter by November 1984.

ISSUE: Are claims of unreasonable agency delays subject to interlocutory appeals?

HOLDING AND DECISION: (Edwards, J.) Yes. Unreasonable agency delays are subject to interlocutory appeals and may warrant mandamus under certain circumstances. Generally, appeals can only be taken of final actions by agencies. By waiting for final action, an administrative agency will have developed a factual record and piecemeal appeals are avoided. However, the agency's expertise and preparation of a factual record is not a factor where the agency never takes action. Thus, claims of unreasonable delay must be subject to interlocutory appeal. Furthermore, statutes expressly require agencies to decide matters within a reasonable time. "[T]he first stage of judicial inquiry is to consider whether the delay is so egregious as to warrant mandamus." There is no single standard for this determination, but the time agencies take to make decisions must be governed by a rule of reason. The key factors include any express congressional requirements, the effect of the delay on other agencies, and the resulting prejudice to interested parties. A delay can be unreasonable even without impropriety behind the delay. In the present case, the delays are very serious but the FCC (D) has assured the court that a final decision is imminent. Accordingly, the court will not resort to mandamus, but will retain jurisdiction over the case until the FCC (D) does decide the issue.

▶ ANALYSIS

The court acknowledged that delay in agency proceedings can deprive parties of important economic opportunities. However, the court plainly stated that decisions affecting health and welfare would be judged more closely in terms of delay. Even where the law lays out a timetable, agencies often ignore the deadlines and must be sued in order to prompt decisions.

Quicknotes

INTERLOCUTORY APPEAL The appeal of an issue that does not resolve the disposition of the case, but is essential to a determination of the parties' legal rights.

MANDAMUS A court order issued commanding a public or private entity, or an official thereof, to perform a duty required by law.

Arkansas Power & Light Co. v. Interstate Commerce Commission

Utility company (P) v. Government agency (D)

725 F.2d 716 (D.C. Cir. 1984).

NATURE OF CASE: Appeal from agency rejection of petition for rulemaking.

FACT SUMMARY: Arkansas Power & Light Co. (P) petitioned the Interstate Commerce Commission (ICC) (D) to collect certain data so that it could review rates that railroads charged for certain shippers.

🏛 RULE OF LAW
Courts will compel agencies to institute rulemaking proceedings only in extremely rare circumstances.

FACTS: Arkansas Power & Light Co. (P) and other utility companies wanted review of rates that "captive" shippers were charged by railroads. They petitioned the ICC (D) to institute rulemaking to collect data so that the rates could be approved. The ICC (D) concluded that development of a nationwide database was unnecessary, not required by statute and too burdensome. The ICC (D) decided to retain a system whereby companies could obtain the needed data on an individual basis for rate approvals. Arkansas Power & Light (P) filed suit to compel the rulemaking and collection of a database.

ISSUE: Will courts commonly compel agencies to institute rulemaking proceedings?

HOLDING AND DECISION: (Edwards, J.) No. Courts will compel agencies to institute rulemaking proceedings only in extremely rare circumstances. Review of agency decisions is limited to ensuring that the agency has adequately explained the facts and policy concerns it relied on and that the facts have some factual basis. In the present case, the ICC (D) clearly decided that there were important reasons for not instituting rulemaking to collect data from all carriers. The reasons had a factual basis and were not arbitrary. Accordingly, there is absolutely no basis for the court to step in and compel agency action in this matter. The ICC's (D) decision not to engage in rulemaking is affirmed.

▶ ANALYSIS

The ICC (D) apparently believed that making decisions on rates was best handled on an individual case basis. The agency (D) thought that the plaintiff utility companies would have adequate information available without an established database for the entire nation. Given the narrow standard of review, this explanation was more than adequate for the court.

Quicknotes

RULEMAKING The promulgation of a rule governing a particular activity by an administrative agency, acting within the scope of its power pursuant to statute.

Massachusetts v. EPA

Coalition (P) v. Government agency (D)

549 U.S. 497 (2007).

NATURE OF CASE: Review of denial of rulemaking petition by agency.

FACT SUMMARY: Coalition of state and local governments and private organizations (collectively "coalition") (P) petitioned the Environmental Protection Agency (EPA) (D) to regulate greenhouse gas emissions pursuant to the Clean Air Act (CAA).

🏛 RULE OF LAW

Agency action is arbitrary and capricious when the agency fails to base its denial of the rulemaking petition in the statute at issue, offering no reasoned explanation for its refusal to reach a determination on the substantive matter of the petition.

FACTS: A coalition of state and local governments and private organizations (collectively "coalition") (P) petitioned the EPA (D) to regulate greenhouse gas emissions from new motor vehicles pursuant to the CAA. Upon requesting and receiving more than 50,000 public comments on the issues raised in the rulemaking petition, the EPA (D) denied the petition. Specifically, the EPA (D) concluded that the CAA did not authorize it to issue regulations to address global climate change, and, even if the EPA (D) did have the authority to set greenhouse gas emissions standards, it would decline to do so because such regulation would conflict with other administration priorities.

ISSUE: Is agency action arbitrary and capricious when the agency fails to base its denial of the rulemaking petition in the statute at issue, offering no reasoned explanation for its refusal to reach a determination on the substantive matter of the petition?

HOLDING AND DECISION: (Stevens, J.) Yes. Agency action is arbitrary and capricious when the agency fails to base its denial of the rulemaking petition in the statute at issue, offering no reasoned explanation for its refusal to reach a determination on the substantive matter of the petition. Here, the EPA (D) erred in concluding that the CAA did not authorize it to issue mandatory regulations to address global climate change. Indeed, the CAA requires the EPA (D) either to determine that greenhouse gases do not contribute to climate change or to provide a reasonable explanation as to why it cannot or will not exercise its discretion to determine whether said gases contribute to climate change. And notwithstanding the EPA's (D) broad discretion in choosing how to efficiently allocate limited resources to carry out its delegated responsibilities, it is the intent of Congress to constrain agency discretion in pursuing priorities of the President. As such, and without reaching

the question of whether policy concerns can inform the EPA's (D) actions upon making an endangerment finding, if the EPA (D) ultimately makes such a finding, it is clear that the denial of the rulemaking petition was arbitrary and capricious. Remanded for further proceedings.

▶ ANALYSIS

The initial petitioners in *Massachusetts v. EPA*, a group of private organizations, were joined, prior to review in the D.C. Circuit, by the intervenor Massachusetts and other state and local governments. In dissent here, Chief Justice Roberts writes of his concern that a state has little or no authority to bring suit against the federal government, and that the majority has devised a new doctrine of state standing to support its result. Furthermore, Article III standing requirements, argues the Chief Justice, should not be relaxed because asserted injuries are pressed by a State. In other words, the complaint of Massachusetts that it faces impending loss of coastal land does not meet the particularized injury requirement set forth in *Lujan v. Defenders of Wildlife*, 504 U.S. 555 (1992). In short, the dissent concludes, the relaxation of Article III standing requirements improperly expands the role of courts.

■═■

Quicknotes

RULEMAKING The promulgation of a rule governing a particular activity by an administrative agency, acting within the scope of its power pursuant to statute.

■═■

American Hospital Assn. v. Bowen

Trade organization (P) v. Government agency (D)

834 F.2d 1037 (D.C. Cir. 1987).

NATURE OF CASE: Appeal from declaration that certain agency guidelines were invalid.

FACT SUMMARY: The American Hospital Association (AHA) (P) claimed that the Department of Health and Human Services (HHS) (D) had issued rules and regulations regarding Peer Review Organizations (PROs) without following proper notice and comment procedures.

🏛 RULE OF LAW
The requirement of notice and an opportunity for comment does not apply to interpretative rules, general statements of policy, or rules of agency organization, procedure, or practice.

FACTS: When Congress amended the Medicare system and established PROs to monitor providers of Medicare services, HHS (D) promulgated regulations after notice and comment. HHS (D) also issued, without notice or comment, a large number of documents setting forth procedures, which were not published as regulations. When the AHA's (P) request that HHS (D) promulgate a complete set of regulations governing all aspects of the PRO program was ignored, the AHA (P) sued, requesting the court to declare that various transmittals and directives were invalid because they failed to comply with § 553 of the Administrative Procedure Act (APA). The district court ruled that some rules were invalid. HHS (D) appealed, claiming a transmittal mapping out an enforcement strategy for the PROs with whom HHS (D) contracted was a procedural rule and therefore exempt from the notice and comment requirement under the APA.

ISSUE: Does the requirement of notice and an opportunity for comment apply to interpretative rules, general statements of policy, or rules of agency organization, procedure, or practice?

HOLDING AND DECISION: (Wald, C.J.) No. The requirement of notice and an opportunity for comment does not apply to interpretative rules, general statements of policy, or rules of agency organization, procedure, or practice. The requirements set forth in the transmittal were classic procedural rules. The bulk of the regulations in the transmittal set forth an enforcement plan for HHS's (D) agents in monitoring the quality of and necessity for certain operations. Enforcement plans developed by agencies directing their enforcement activity are entitled to considerable deference. Reversed.

◗ ANALYSIS

The court reasoned that the manual in question did not place any new burdens on hospitals. Nor was a new standard of review mandated. The new rules were therefore found to be merely procedural and were exempt from the notice and comment requirement that applied to substantive rules.

Quicknotes

ADMINISTRATIVE PROCEDURE ACT Provides the standard for judicial review of agency rules.

NOTICE AND COMMENT PERIOD The period of time, established by the Administrative Procedures Act, for an administrative agency to publish a proposed regulation and receive public comment on it.

PROCEDURAL RULE Rule relating to the process of carrying out a lawsuit and not to the substantive rights asserted by the parties.

Air Transport Association of America v. Department of Transportation

Trade association (P) v. Federal agency (D)

900 F.2d 369 (D.C. Cir. 1990).

NATURE OF CASE: [Not stated in the casebook excerpt.]

FACT SUMMARY: In December of 1987, Congress enacted a series of amendments to the Federal Aviation Act relating to civil penalties.

🏛 RULE OF LAW
The promulgation of regulations governing the adjudication of administrative civil penalty actions is not exempt from the requirements of notice and comment.

FACTS: Because the prior method of handling disputed penalties resulted in few prosecutions, Congress sought to close the holes in the Federal Aviation Administration's (FAA) (D) safety net by raising the maximum penalty and giving the FAA the power to prosecute penalty actions administratively. Of the amendments to the Federal Aviation Act pertaining to civil penalties, one raised the maximum penalty for a single violation of aviation safety standards to $10,000. Another established a "demonstration program" authorizing the FAA (D) to prosecute and adjudicate administrative penalty actions involving less than $50,000. Approximately nine months after Congress enacted the amendments, the FAA (D) promulgated the Penalty Rules, establishing a schedule of civil penalties and a comprehensive adjudicatory scheme providing for formal notice, settlement procedures, discovery, an adversary hearing before an Administrative Law Judge, and an administrative appeal. The FAA (D) argued that the Penalty Rules were exempt as "rules of organization, procedure, or practice" because they established "procedures" for adjudicating civil penalty actions.

ISSUE: Is the promulgation of regulations governing the adjudication of administrative civil penalty actions exempt from the requirements of notice and comment?

HOLDING AND DECISION: (Edwards, J.) No. The promulgation of regulations governing the adjudication of administrative civil penalty actions is not exempt from the requirements of notice and comment. Cases interpreting § 553(b)(A) of the Administrative Procedure Act have long emphasized that a rule does not fall within the scope of the exception merely because it is capable of bearing the label "procedural." Where nominally procedural rules contain a substantial value judgment, or substantially alter the rights or interest of regulated parties, the rules must be preceded by notice and comment. The Penalty Rules fall outside the scope of § 553(b)(A) because they substantially affect a civil penalty defendant's right to an administrative adjudication. Therefore, members of the aviation community had a legitimate interest in participating in the rulemaking process.

DISSENT: (Silberman, J.) The Penalty Rules deal with enforcement or adjudication of claims of violations of the substantive norm, but do not purport to affect the substantive norm. These kinds of rules are, therefore, clearly procedural. Of course, procedure impacts on outcomes and thus can virtually always be described as affecting substance, but to pursue this line of analysis results in the obliteration of the distinction that Congress demanded.

▶ ANALYSIS

Courts will consider the label an agency puts on its own rules, but, as in this case, such labels are not determinative as to the ruling of the court. Rather, courts will also consider whether rules go "beyond formality and substantially affect the rights of those over whom the agency exercises authority." *Pickus v. United States Board of Parole*, 507 F.2d 1107 (D.C. Cir. 1974). Thus, a rule will not be considered procedural if it has a substantive effect on the regulated parties to whom it applies.

■=■

Quicknotes

PROCEDURAL RULE Rule relating to the process of carrying out a lawsuit and not to the substantive rights asserted by the parties.

RULEMAKING The promulgation of a rule by an administrative agency, acting within the scope of its power pursuant to statute, enacting a rule governing a particular activity.

■=■

JEM Broadcasting Company, Inc. v. Federal Communications Commission

Radio station (P) v. Government agency (D)

22 F.3d 320 (D.C. Cir. 1994).

NATURE OF CASE: Appeal from denial of license application.

FACT SUMMARY: JEM Broadcasting Company, Inc. (JEM) (P) submitted a radio license application containing inconsistent information to the Federal Communications Commission (FCC) (D) which refused to allow correction of the error.

🏛 RULE OF LAW

Rules of agency organization, procedure and practice are exempt from the general notice and comment rulemaking requirements.

FACTS: In July 1988, JEM (P) submitted a license application for a radio station in Arkansas. When the FCC (D) reviewed the application, it determined that JEM (P) had provided inconsistent information that could not be resolved from the application documents. Therefore, the FCC (D) used its 1985 "hard look" regulations, which established a fixed filing window for substantially complete applications. Those applications that did not include the requisite information were returned without any opportunity to fix the errors under the hard look rules. JEM (P) contended that the hard look rules should not be applied because they were not promulgated with notice and comment in violation of the Administrative Procedure Act (APA).

ISSUE: Are rules of agency organization, procedure and practice exempt from the general notice and comment rulemaking requirements?

HOLDING AND DECISION: (Edwards, J.) Yes. Rules of agency organization, procedure and practice are exempt from the general notice and comment rulemaking requirements. The APA generally requires notice and comment before new regulations are promulgated. However, there is an exception to this general rule for procedural regulations, as opposed to substantive rules that alter the rights and interests of parties affected by the regulations. In the present case, it is unquestioned that the FCC (D) can set a deadline for applications. Although the hard look rules are significant, they do not change the substantive standards by which the FCC (D) evaluates applications. Thus, they are mostly procedural and are not required to go through notice and comment before being adopted.

▶ ANALYSIS

The court considered JEM's (P) argument that the hard look regulations were substantive because they sacrificed applications with minor errors for the sake of efficiency. However, they held that this view would swallow up the procedural exception. A previous decision that seemed to support this argument is no longer good law.

■▬■

Quicknotes

ADMINISTRATIVE PROCEDURE ACT Provides the standard for judicial review of agency rules.

RULEMAKING The promulgation of a rule by an administrative agency, acting within the scope of its power pursuant to statute, enacting a rule governing a particular activity.

■▬■

United States v. Allegheny-Ludlum Steel Corp.

Federal government (D) v. Shipper (P)

406 U.S. 742 (1972).

NATURE OF CASE: Challenge to agency regulation.

FACT SUMMARY: Allegheny-Ludlum Steel Corp. (Allegheny-Ludlum) (P) complained that the Interstate Commerce Commission (ICC) (D) should have held hearings before promulgating rules regarding railroad rates.

🏛 RULE OF LAW
Informal rulemaking is permitted where the governing statute does not require that rules be made on the record.

FACTS: The ICC (D) regulated railroad rates. Congress passed the Esch Car Service Act, which allowed the ICC (D) to establish reasonable rules and regulations on its own initiative without requiring that they be inside "on the record." The ICC (D) used informal rulemaking to set some rates and Allegheny-Ludlum (P), a shipper, sought judicial review, complaining that a hearing should have been held.

ISSUE: Is informal rulemaking permitted where the governing statute does not require that rules be made on the record?

HOLDING AND DECISION: (Rehnquist, J.) Yes. Informal rulemaking is permitted where the governing statute does not require that rules be made on the record. According to 5 U.S.C. §§ 556 and 557, rulemaking procedure includes a hearing before the promulgation of the new regulation. However, these sections apply only when the statute requires rules be made "on the record." In the present case, the Esch Act does not absolutely require that the rules be made on the record. While the precise words "on the record" are not the only factor to be considered, the language of the Esch Act does not indicate that formal rulemaking was to be involved.

▶ *ANALYSIS*

The formal rulemaking procedures of §§ 556 and 557 include a trial-type proceeding. A hybrid type of rulemaking has also arisen where Congress has expressly required it. Hybrid rulemaking is more burdensome than informal rulemaking, but less burdensome than the formal type.

■■■

Quicknotes

5 U.S.C. §§ 556, 557 Provides for certain procedures in agency rulemaking.

RULEMAKING The promulgation of a rule by an administrative agency, acting within the scope of its power pursuant to statute, enacting a rule governing a particular activity.

■■■

United States v. Florida East Coast Railway Co.

Federal government (D) v. Railroad company (P)

410 U.S. 224 (1973).

NATURE OF CASE: Appeal of nullification of certain boxcar compensation rules.

FACT SUMMARY: The Interstate Commerce Commission (ICC) (D) adopted rules regarding per diem charges on boxcars following an informal conference.

🏛 RULE OF LAW
The ICC need not hold a formal hearing prior to establishing rules with respect to car service by common carriers.

FACTS: Amendments to the Interstate Commerce Act empowered the ICC (D) to adopt rules with respect to car service by common carriers and particularly to the compensation to be paid car owners for borrowed boxcars. The ICC (D) obtained data on freight-car demand from various carriers. In response to concerns expressed by various carriers, the ICC (D) held an informal conference. The ICC (D) subsequently published rule proposals inviting criticism. The proposals were then adopted. The ICC's (D) actions were challenged for failure to hold a formal hearing. The lower court invalidated the ICC's (D) actions.

ISSUE: Must the ICC (D) hold a formal hearing prior to establishing rules with respect to car service by common carriers?

HOLDING AND DECISION: (Rehnquist, J.) No. The ICC (D) need not hold a formal hearing prior to establishing rules with respect to car service by common carriers. The Administrative Procedure Act states the evidentiary requirements for formal hearings but does not mandate that formal hearings always be held. When a statute does not expressly require a formal hearing, the agency in question may, when conducting rulemaking, take evidence by written submission if the agency believes a formal hearing unnecessary. Here, the ICC (D) took extensive steps to obtain evidence through written submission. Since this Court has already held that the Interstate Commerce Act does not require hearings, the ICC's (D) actions were proper. Reversed.

▌ ANALYSIS

The Court's opinion here took a very narrow view of the necessity for formal hearings. The Interstate Commerce Act amendment in question did contain language suggesting a hearing would be necessary, but the Court found the language insufficient to trigger the requirement of a hearing. It would seem that only statutes clearly spelling out the requirement of a hearing will bring the Administrative Procedure Act's rules for formal hearings into play.

Quicknotes

APA § 553 Establishes the minimum requirements of public rulemaking procedure.

INTERSTATE COMMERCE ACT § 1(14) Allows the Commission to prescribe per diem charges for the use of railroad cars owned by another.

PRETERMINATION HEARING A hearing held prior to the termination of a property interest.

RULEMAKING The promulgation of a rule by an administrative agency, acting within the scope of its power pursuant to statute, enacting a rule governing a particular activity.

Vermont Yankee Nuclear Power Corp. v. Natural Resources Defense Council, Inc.

Nuclear power plant (D) v. Environmental group (P)

435 U.S. 519 (1978).

NATURE OF CASE: Appeal in connection with review of agency rulemaking procedure.

FACT SUMMARY: The Natural Resources Defense Council, Inc. (NRDC) (P) challenged a rule promulgated by the Atomic Energy Commission (AEC) (D) because of alleged procedural defects in the rulemaking process.

🏛 RULE OF LAW
The adequacy of the record in a rulemaking proceeding does not depend on the type of procedural devices employed, but turns on whether the agency has followed the statutory mandate of the Administrative Procedure Act.

FACTS: The NRDC (P) challenged a rule promulgated by the AEC (D) on the basis it was denied the opportunity for discovery and cross-examination and thus a meaningful opportunity to participate in the rulemaking proceedings. The reviewing court agreed that the procedures followed by the AEC (D) during promulgation of the rule were inadequate and remanded the rule to the AEC (D). The Supreme Court, however, found the reviewing court to be in error in requiring the AEC (D) to grant additional procedural rights in the exercise of its rulemaking functions.

ISSUE: Does the adequacy of the record in an agency rulemaking proceeding depend on the type of procedural devices, "or does it turn" on whether the agency has followed the statutory mandate of the Administrative Procedure Act?

HOLDING AND DECISION: (Rehnquist, J.) Yes. The adequacy of the record in an agency rulemaking proceeding is not correlated directly to the type of procedural devices employed, but turns on whether the agency has followed the statutory mandate of the Administrative Procedure Act. Vermont Yankee's (D) contention fails because the AEC (D) was well within its authority on the waste disposal and fuel reprocessing issues as they applied in individual license proceedings. However, the court of appeals was incorrect in its invalidation of the AEC's (D) rulemaking proceeding. Absent constitutional restraints or extremely compelling circumstances, the administrative agencies should be free to fashion their own rules of procedure and to pursue methods of inquiry capable of permitting them to discharge their duties. There are three compelling reasons why the agencies' discretion should be determinative. First, if courts continually review agency proceedings to determine whether the agency employed procedures that were what the court perceived to be the best or correct results, judicial review would be totally unpredictable. Second, the fact that

the court looked only at the record and not at information available to the AEC (D) when it decided to structure the proceedings in a certain way is an example of Monday morning quarterbacking that would compel the agency to conduct all rulemaking proceedings with the full panoply of procedural devices normally associated only with adjudicatory hearings. Finally, and perhaps most importantly, this type of review misconceives the standard for judicial review of an agency rule; rulemaking need not be based solely on the transcript of a hearing. In fact, in a case like this there need not be a formal hearing. Reversed and remanded.

▶ ANALYSIS

Executive Order 12044 concerned President Carter's directive to the agencies to "adopt procedures to improve existing and future regulations." 43 Fed. Reg. 12661. The order called for greater involvement by the public. This consisted, in part, of suggestions concerning published notice, conferences, hearings, and direct mailing. Gellhorn, W., Admin. Law, 203-204.

■■■

Quicknotes

5 U.S.C. § 553 Establishes minimum requirements of public rulemaking procedure.

ADJUDICATORY PROCEEDING A hearing conducted by an administrative agency resulting in a final judgment regarding the rights of the parties involved.

JUDICIAL REVIEW The authority of the courts to review decisions, actions or omissions committed by another agency or branch of government.

■■■

Chocolate Manufacturers Association v. Block

Trade group (P) v. Government agency (D)

755 F.2d 1098 (4th Cir. 1985).

NATURE OF CASE: Appeal from decision denying relief from an administrative rule.

FACT SUMMARY: The Chocolate Manufacturers Association (CMA) (P) challenged, on inadequate-notice grounds, a United States Department of Agriculture (USDA) (D) rule that prohibited the use of chocolate-flavored milk in the federally funded Special Supplemental Food Program for Women, Infants, and Children (WIC).

RULE OF LAW

The notice in the Federal Register that an agency must give of a proposed rulemaking must contain either the terms or substance of the proposed rule or a description of the subjects and issues involved.

FACTS: WIC was established by Congress in 1972 to assist pregnant, postpartum, and breastfeeding women, infants, and children from families with inadequate income whose physical and mental health was in danger because of inadequate nutrition or health care. In 1979, Congress extended the WIC Program and redefined the term "supplemental foods" that the program was established to provide. This redefinition stated that the USDA (D) must assure that the fat, sugar, and salt content of foods prescribed by the WIC were appropriate. The USDA (D) then published for comment the proposed rule at issue here, which proposed a maximum sugar content for authorized cereals but did not discuss sugar in relation to flavoring in milk. The USDA (D) notice allowed 60 days for comment and specifically invited comment on the entire scope of the proposed rule. Of the over 1,000 comments received, 78 recommended that flavored milk be deleted from the WIC list of approved foods. The USDA (D) did delete flavored milk from the list, and the CMA (P) challenged the rule on the grounds that it did not provide that the disallowance of flavored milk would be considered. The lower court denied the CMA (P) any relief and it appealed.

ISSUE: Must the notice in the Federal Register that an agency must give of a proposed rulemaking contain either the terms or substance of the proposed rule or a description of the subjects and issues involved?

HOLDING AND DECISION: (Sprouse, J.) Yes. Section 4 of the Administrative Procedure Act requires that the notice in the Federal Register that an agency must give of a proposed rulemaking contain either the terms or substance of the proposed rule or a description of the subjects and issues involved. The purpose of the notice-and-comment procedure is both to allow the agency to benefit from the experience and input of the parties who file comments and to see to it that the agency maintains a flexible and open-minded attitude toward its own rules. There is no question that an agency may promulgate a final rule that differs in some particulars from its proposal, but it does not have carte blanche to establish a rule contrary to its original proposal simply because it receives suggestions to alter it during the comment period. If the final rule materially alters the issues involved in the rulemaking or if it substantially departs from the terms or substance of the proposed rule, the notice is inadequate. Here, the final rule was an outgrowth of the original rule proposed, but perhaps not a logical outgrowth. In all of the activities setting out and discussing food packaging, including the proposed rule and its preamble, the USDA (D) never suggested that flavored milk be removed from the WIC Program. At the time of the proposed rulemaking, neither the CMA (P) nor the general public could have any indication that flavored milk was not part of the WIC Program acceptable diet. Reversed and remanded.

ANALYSIS

Section 553 of the Administrative Procedure Act has been and remains the foremost example of federal rulemaking. Section 553's provisions detail the procedure an agency must follow in promulgating a rule. These provisions state that the general public must be given a chance to comment in writing or orally about the rule to be promulgated, and that the agency promulgating the rule must incorporate in the final rule a statement of its basis and purpose.

■=■

Quicknotes

APA § 4 Requires notice in the Federal Register about proposed rules.

■=■

Home Box Office v. Federal Communications Commission

Television network (P) v. Government agency (D)

567 F.2d 9 (D.C. Cir. 1977).

NATURE OF CASE: Review of an informal rule-making procedure.

FACT SUMMARY: Ex parte comments were received in connection with an informal rulemaking procedure.

RULE OF LAW
The public record must reflect the representations made to an agency so that relevant information supporting or refuting those representations may be brought to the attention of the reviewing courts by persons participating in agency proceedings.

FACTS: Ex parte comments were received in connection with an informal rulemaking proceeding dealing with subscription television. A participant in the proceeding, and an amicus before the court, Geller (P), filed a petition with the Federal Communications Commission (FCC) (D) to disclose ex parte communications during the proceedings. The FCC (D) took no action and Geller (P) sought judicial review of the FCC's (D) order promulgating four amendments regulating subscription television. The court of appeals sua sponte ordered the FCC (D) to disclose the ex parte contacts. The FCC (D) did so and showed that the competing industry representatives had a great voice in the outcome of the proceedings.

ISSUE: Must the public record reflect what representations were made to an agency so that relevant information supporting or refuting those representations may be brought to the attention of the reviewing courts by persons participating in agency proceedings?

HOLDING AND DECISION: (Per curiam) Yes. The public record must reflect the representations made to an agency so that relevant information supporting or refuting those representations may be brought to the attention of the reviewing courts by persons participating in agency proceedings. Here, the evidence is consistent with the claim of undue industry influence over the FCC (D) proceedings. The presence of secrecy makes it difficult to judge the truth even when later disclosed by the FCC (D). Secrecy is inconsistent with fundamental notions of fairness implicit in due process. Therefore, once a notice of proposed rulemaking has been issued, discussion with interested parties should be prohibited, and if made, a written document or a summary of any oral communications must be placed in the public file immediately after the communication so that interested parties may comment. Remanded to FCC (D).

ANALYSIS

The courts encouraged agencies to use an informal rulemaking procedure. However, they became afraid that this informal procedure would fall victim to too much political pressure. Therefore, the courts are demanding that these procedures become more judicial in nature. Gellhorn, quoting Robinson, 64 Va. L. Rev. 227-230.

Quicknotes

AMICUS BRIEF A brief submitted by a third party, not a party to the action, that contains information for the court's consideration in conformity with its position.

DUE PROCESS The constitutional mandate requiring the courts to protect and enforce individuals' rights and liberties consistent with prevailing principles of fairness and justice and prohibiting the federal and state governments from such activities that deprive its citizens of a life, liberty or property interest.

EX PARTE A proceeding commenced by one party without providing any opposing parties with notice or which is uncontested by an adverse party.

SUA SPONTE An action taken by the court by its own motion and without the suggestion of one of the parties.

Sierra Club v. Costle

Environmental protection group (P) v. Government agency (D)

657 F.2d 298 (D.C. Cir. 1981).

NATURE OF CASE: Appeal from decision denying relief in a challenge to an agency rule.

FACT SUMMARY: The Sierra Club (P) and the Environmental Defense Fund (EDF) (P) challenged the Environmental Protection Agency's (EPA's) (D) adoption of the 1.2 lbs./MBtu standard for power plants using coal fuel to generate power.

🏛 **RULE OF LAW**
The Clean Air Act Amendments of 1977 provide that all relevant documents that become available after a proposed rule has been published shall be placed in the docket as soon as possible after their availability.

FACTS: The EDF (P) and the Sierra Club (P) challenged a rule promulgated by Costle (D) and the EPA (D) that adopted a 1.2 lbs/MBtu standard for power plants using coal fuel to generate power. The EDF (P) objected that comments regarding the adopted standard were filed after the close of the official comment period and that meetings between EPA (D) officials and various government and private parties interested in the outcome of the final rule took place after the close of the comment period. The EDF (P) alleged that such "late" comments, mostly from representatives of the coal or utility industries, and the meetings persuaded the EPA (D) to back away from adopting a .55 lb./MBtu limit and instead to adopt the more lenient 1.2 lbs./MBtu standard. The EDF (P) also alleged that some post-comment communications were not docketed by the EPA (D) in violation of the Clean Air Amendments of 1977 (Act) and that, therefore, the EDF (P) was not able to adequately respond to those documents before the 1.2 lbs./MBtu standard was adopted. The lower court ruled in favor of the EPA (D), and the EDF (P) appealed.

ISSUE: Do the Clean Air Act Amendments of 1977 provide that all documents that become available after a proposed rule has been published and which the Administrator determines are of central relevance to the rulemaking shall be placed in the docket as soon as possible after their availability?

HOLDING AND DECISION: (Wald, J.) Yes. The Clean Air Act Amendments of 1977 provide that all relevant documents that become available after a proposed rule has been published shall be placed in the docket as soon as possible after their availability. This provision is not limited to the comment period, and it apparently allows the EPA (D) not only to put documents in the record after the comment period is over, but also to define which documents are "of central relevance" so as to require that they be placed in the

docket. EPA (D) thus has the authority to place post-comment documents into the docket, but it need not do so in all instances. The Act does not expressly treat the issue of post-comment period meetings with individuals outside the EPA (D). Oral face-to-face discussions are not prohibited anywhere, anytime, in the Act. But at least some adequate summary of them must be made in order to preserve the integrity of the rulemaking docket. Docketing of such summaries may be needed to give practical effect to the provisions of the Act that demand that all documents of central relevance to the rulemaking shall be placed in the docket post haste. It was not unlawful in this case for EPA (D) not to docket a meeting since EPA (D) makes no effort to base the rule on any information arising from that meeting. In sum, EPA's (D) adoption of the 1.2 lbs/MBtu emissions ceiling was free from procedural error. Affirmed.

📍 **ANALYSIS**

In the above case, the comment period regarding the proposed emissions ceiling ran from September 19, 1978 to January 15, 1979. After January 15, the EPA (D) received almost 300 written submissions on the proposed rule that were accepted by the EPA (D) and entered on its administration docket. EPA (D) did not officially reopen the comment period, and it did not notify the public through the Federal Register that it had received and was entering "late" comments. Of the late comments, the EDF (P) claimed that at least 30 were from representatives of the coal or utility industries and 22 were submitted by Congressmen as advocates of those interests. The EDF (P) characterized such comments and meetings that took place after the comment period closed as an "ex parte blitz" by the coal industry to force the EPA to adapt a higher emissions ceiling.

■══■

Quicknotes

CLEAN AIR ACT § 307 Requires that documents relevant to rulemaking under the Act be docketed.

■══■

Chevron v. Natural Resources Defense Council, Inc.

Civil company (D) v. Environmental group (P)

467 U.S. 837 (1984).

NATURE OF CASE: Appeal from review of an Environmental Protection Agency (EPA) (D) regulation.

FACT SUMMARY: The EPA (D) passed a regulation incorporating a broader definition of an air pollution "source" than it had used previously.

🏛 RULE OF LAW
Where Congress has left an open question in its legislation, judicial review of an agency's interpretation of that question must be limited to whether the agency's construction is legitimate.

FACTS: In the Clean Air Act Amendments of 1977, Congress limited the issuance of permits to stationary sources of air pollution to those meeting strict requirements. The legislation was unclear as to what the term "stationary source" meant. The EPA (D) passed a regulation applying the strict standard to each individual emitting source. The EPA (D) later revised the regulation to allow all emitting sources in a single plant to be treated as a single source for the purposes of the legislation. The Natural Resources Defense Council, Inc. (P) filed a petition for review of this regulation. The court of appeals found the EPA's (D) interpretation inconsistent with the policy of the legislation. The EPA (D) appealed, and the United States Supreme Court granted certiorari.

ISSUE: Must judicial review of an agency's interpretation of a question left open in legislation by Congress be limited to whether the agency's construction is legitimate?

HOLDING AND DECISION: (Stevens, J.) Yes. Where Congress has left an open question in legislation, judicial review of the agency's interpretation of that question must be limited to whether the agency's construction is legitimate. In this case Congress did not clearly define "stationary source." The legislative history is not clear as to whether "stationary source" should have a plantwide definition. The EPA's (D) construction is reasonable in light of the plain English of the statute as well as the competing interests involved. The judiciary may not review an agency's authority in light of the policy of the statute but only based on the reasonableness of the language. Reversed.

▌ ANALYSIS

In a 1989 law review article, Justice Scalia delineated two categories of congressional ambiguity, each requiring a different standard of review by the judiciary. Where Congress clearly intended a certain result, but was unclear about it, the court must resolve the issue as a question of law. On the other hand, where congressional vagueness was intentionally

meant to delegate authority to an agency, the standard of *Chevron* must apply. *Chevron, U.S.A., Inc. v. Natural Resources Defense Council, Inc.,* 467 U.S. 837 (1984). See Scalia, Judicial Deference to Administrative Interpretations of Law, 1989 Duke L.J. 511, 516.

∎▬∎

Quicknotes

JUDICIAL REVIEW The authority of the courts to review decisions, actions or omissions committed by another agency or branch of government.

∎▬∎

Motor Vehicle Manufacturers Assoc. v. State Farm Mutual Automobile Ins. Co.

Parties not identified.

463 U.S. 29 (1983).

NATURE OF CASE: Appeal from decision finding agency action arbitrary and capricious.

FACT SUMMARY: The National Highway Traffic Safety Administration (NHTSA) (D) appealed from a decision of the court of appeals, finding that the revocation of the requirement that new motor vehicles produced after September 1982 be equipped with passive restraints to protect occupants in the event of a collision was arbitrary and capricious.

RULE OF LAW
When an agency modifies or rescinds a previously promulgated rule, it is required to supply a satisfactory, rational analysis supporting its decision.

FACTS: Standard 208 is a rule promulgated by the Department of Transportation dealing with motor vehicle occupant safety. From the time that it was originally issued in 1967, the standard has been subject to constant rescission, modification, and amendment. In 1969, the standard first included a requirement that cars come equipped with a passive restraint system. Between 1976 and 1980, a mandatory passive restraint requirement was issued. The two systems that would satisfy the standard would be an air bag system or a passive seat belt system, with the choice of system being left up to the manufacturer. It was assumed that manufacturers would install approximately 60 percent air bags and 40 percent passive belts. By 1981, the manufacturers planned to produce 99 percent of their cars equipped with passive belts. In 1981, even though studies, surveys, and other empirical evidence indicated that the use rate associated with the passive belts was more than double that associated with manual belts, the NHTSA (D) concluded that the safety benefits associated with the standard's implementation did not justify the costs of implementing the standard. In that same year, the NHTSA (D), without considering the possible use of air bags, rescinded the passive restraint requirement. The court of appeals found that the NHTSA's (D) revocation of the passive restraint requirement was arbitrary and capricious, and the NHTSA (D) appealed.

ISSUE: agency rescinds or modifies a previously promulgated rule, is it required to supply a satisfactory, rational analysis supporting its decision?

HOLDING AND DECISION: (White, J.) Yes. When an agency rescinds or modifies a previously promulgated rule, it is required to supply a satisfactory, rational analysis supporting its decision. A change or rescission is akin to the promulgation of the rule itself and is subject to

the same arbitrary and capricious standard. The agency may be required to more fully justify its decision than if the agency had not acted in the first instance. The agency must show a rational connection between the facts found and the decision rendered. If an agency relies on improper facts or fails to consider important aspects of the problem or renders a decision that runs contrary to the evidence, its decision may be considered arbitrary and capricious. The National Traffic and Motor Vehicle Safety Act of 1966 (Act) mandates the achievement of traffic safety. Given the conceded effectiveness of air bags, the logical response to the manufacturers' actions would have been to require air bags. Not only was this not done, it appears that the NHTSA (D) did not even consider it. A rational rescission decision cannot be made without the consideration of technologically feasible alternatives of proven value. Further, the empirical evidence runs counter to the agency's determination that the safety aspects associated with the use of passive belts could not be determined. The empirical evidence indicates that there is a doubling of use of passive belts over the use of manual belts, and the safety benefits associated with the increased use of safety belts is unquestioned. Finally, the NHTSA (D) has failed to articulate a basis for not requiring nondetachable passive belts. By failing to consider feasible, logical alternatives and dismissing the safety benefits associated with passive restraints in light of the evidence, the NHTSA (D) has failed to present an adequate basis or explanation for rescinding the mandatory passive restraint requirement. Vacated and remanded.

CONCURRENCE AND DISSENT: (Rehnquist, J.) The majority correctly concludes that the NHTSA must provide a rational explanation for changing course and rescinding Standard 208, and that the NHTSA arbitrarily failed to consider the benefits of air bags. Contrary to the majority's holding, however, the NHTSA met that requirement here with respect to automatic seatbelts. The Agency's changed view seems to result from the election of a president from a different political party, but that fact alone is a reasonable basis for an agency to reevaluate its priorities and change course to match the views of a new administration, so long as the agency's change stays within congressionally defined boundaries.

ANALYSIS

Standard setting by the NHTSA (D) has proved most troublesome. Initial promulgation of standards were in large part

Continued on next page.

mere adoptions of already existing standards. The promulgation of new standards is associated with a whole host of problems, including the problem of obtaining accurate information and the problem of enforcement and the problems that may be encountered in negotiating such standards with industry and other interest groups.

■■■■

Quicknotes

5 U.S.C. § 706 Authorizes judicial review of all orders establishing Federal motor vehicle safety standards.

ARBITRARY AND CAPRICIOUS STANDARD Standard imposed in reviewing the decision of an agency or court that the decision was made in disregard of the facts or law.

■■■■

Adjudication

Quick Reference Rules of Law

National Labor Relations Board v. Local Union No. 25, International Brotherhood of Electrical Workers

Government agency (P) v. Labor union (D)

586 F.2d 959 (2d Cir. 1978).

NATURE OF CASE: Petition for enforcement of order invalidating a collective bargaining agreement.

FACT SUMMARY: An administrative law judge ruled that the union (D) had engaged in unfair labor practices and that a provision of the collective bargaining agreement was illegal.

RULE OF LAW
The Administrative Procedure Act (APA) requires that there be adequate notice, argument and evidence before an administrative law judge makes a decision.

FACTS: Flores filed a complaint with the National Labor Relations Board (NLRB) (P) that the union (D) failed to provide him with job referrals because he was not a union member. The administrative law judge hearing the case agreed and found that the union (D) had engaged in unfair labor practices. The judge then went beyond the NLRB (P) complaint and found that a provision of the collective bargaining agreement at issue was illegal and invalidated it. The union (D) claimed that they were denied a fair hearing on this issue because there was no notice, argument or evidence presented on the legality of the agreement's clause.

ISSUE: Does the APA require that there be adequate notice, argument and evidence before an administrative law judge makes a decision?

HOLDING AND DECISION: (Lumbard, J.) Yes. The APA requires that there be adequate notice, argument and evidence before an administrative law judge makes a decision. APA § 554 requires that there be notice to the parties before an administrative law judge rules on an issue. In the present case, the judge hearing the NLRB's (P) complaint on behalf of Flores went ahead and ruled on the validity of the collective bargaining agreement even though the issue was not raised in the complaint or in oral argument, nor was there any evidence presented. Accordingly, the union (D) did not receive the requisite notice and the decision cannot be enforced.

▶ ANALYSIS

Different states handle administrative law judges in various manners. In some, the judges are hired by the agencies themselves. In others, there are central panels of judges not controlled by the agency.

■═■

Southwest Sunsites, Inc. v. Federal Trade Commission

Land developer (P) v. Government agency (D)

785 F.2d 1431 (9th Cir. 1986).

NATURE OF CASE: Appeal from agency cease and desist order.

FACT SUMMARY: Southwest Sunsites, Inc. (Southwest) (P) complained that the Federal Trade Commission (FTC) (D) had applied a new standard with regard to deceptive practices without advance notice.

🏛 RULE OF LAW
The notice requirement of the Administrative Procedure Act (APA) is satisfied where parties understood the relevant issues and were afforded a full opportunity to justify their conduct.

FACTS: Southwest (P) sold undeveloped land in rural west Texas to out-of-state purchasers. The FTC (D) filed a complaint against Southwest (P) contending that they were engaged in unfair and deceptive practices with regard to the sales. The complaint argued that Southwest (P) misrepresented the investment potential of the land and its suitability for use and value. An administrative law judge (ALJ) dismissed the complaint, finding that the representations did not have the tendency and capacity to mislead. The FTC (D), applying a different standard, found that the representations were likely to mislead reasonable consumers, and reversed and issued a cease and desist order. Southwest (P) appealed.

ISSUE: Is the notice requirement of the APA satisfied where parties understood the relevant issues and were afforded a full opportunity to justify their conduct?

HOLDING AND DECISION: (Beezer, J.) Yes. The notice requirement of the APA is satisfied where parties understood the relevant issues and were afforded a full opportunity to justify their conduct. The APA requires that parties involved in agency complaints be "timely informed of the matters of fact and law asserted." In the present case, the standard used by the FTC (D) was different than that used by the judge, but it imposed a greater burden on the agency since probable deception and detriment to the consumer had to be expressly proved. Thus, the ALJ's finding was based on a standard that was more narrow, and completely subsumed by the FTC's (D) new standard. Accordingly, Southwest (P) had a more than adequate opportunity to respond to the complaint. The FTC's (D) cease and desist order is affirmed.

▶ ANALYSIS

This case involves an unusual situation. The court correctly ruled that the "likely" standard applied by the FTC (D) was harder to reach than the "tendency" standard used by the

ALJ. Thus, the ALJ and the agency must have had wildly different views of the facts involved to come to opposite conclusions.

■■■

Quicknotes

ADMINISTRATIVE PROCEDURE ACT Provides the standard for judicial review of agency rules.

CEASE AND DESIST ORDER An order from a court or administrative agency prohibiting a person or business from continuing a particular course of conduct.

NOTICE AND COMMENT RULEMAKING Informal rulemaking.

■■■

John D. Copanos and Sons, Inc. v. Food and Drug Administration

Drug manufacturer (P) v. Government agency (D)

854 F.2d 510 (D.C. Cir. 1988).

NATURE OF CASE: Petition for review of agency's rejection of application.

FACT SUMMARY: The Food and Drug Administration (FDA) (D) withdrew its approval of Kanasco's (P) drug applications due to a record of manufacturing violations.

RULE OF LAW
Agencies may summarily withdraw approval for applications after providing the party with due notice.

FACTS: John D. Copanos & Sons and Kanasco (P) manufactured and distributed human and veterinary drugs. In March 1987, the FDA (D) published a Notice of Opportunity for a Hearing proposing to withdraw Kanasco's (P) applications for new drugs on the grounds that Kanasco's (P) manufacturing was substandard. Over a three-year period, periodic inspections of Kanasco's (P) facilities had resulted in numerous violations and evidence that false records were submitted to cover up other violations. Kanasco (P) requested a hearing, but in August 1987, the FDA (D) summarily withdrew the applications. Kanasco (P) petitioned for review on the ground that it had not received adequate notice of the basis for the action.

ISSUE: May agencies summarily withdraw approval for applications after providing the party with due notice?

HOLDING AND DECISION: (Ginsburg, J.) Yes. Agencies may summarily withdraw approval for applications after providing the party with due notice. The Federal Food, Drug, and Cosmetic Act (the Act) prohibits the introduction of new drugs without prior FDA (D) approval. The Act also established procedures whereby the FDA (D) can withdraw approval after due notice to the applicant. One of the grounds for withdrawal is substandard manufacturing by the applicant. This provision does not guarantee an applicant a hearing in all circumstances since the agency may summarily withdraw approval where there is no "genuine and substantial issue of fact that requires a hearing." Thus, notice being critical, it must contain enough information to provide the applicant with a genuine opportunity to identify the material issues of fact in the context of the action. In the present case, Kanasco (P) was not confronted with any significant ambiguity regarding the type of information that would warrant an agency hearing. Considering the context of the prior proceedings and violations, the hearing notice certainly advised Kanasco (P) of the type of information it would need to submit to command a hearing. Even without specific instructions telling Kanasco (P) what to produce, they have failed to identify any evidence that might have been presented but for lack of notice. Accordingly, the petition for review is denied.

ANALYSIS

The narrow grounds for Kanasco's (P) petition for review should be noted. In this case, they were not challenging the FDA's (D) finding directly, but arguing only that the lack of proper notice had invalidated the subsequent summary decision. The court did take the FDA (D) to task for not making it easier to more clearly identify the exact violations that formed the basis for the approval withdrawal.

Quicknotes

FEDERAL FOOD, DRUG, AND COSMETIC ACT Prohibits the sale of new drugs without approval from the FDA.

Wallace v. Bowen

Social Security applicant (P) v. Government agency (D)

869 F.2d 187 (3d Cir. 1989).

NATURE OF CASE: Petition for review of agency denial of benefits.

FACT SUMMARY: Wallace (P) appealed his denial of social security disability benefits, which was based on reports that were not available for cross-examination at the hearing, claiming violations of his statutory and constitutional due process rights and that one ALJ's decision was not supported by substantial evidence.

RULE OF LAW

Agencies may not make adjudications based on post-hearing reports that are not subject to cross-examination.

FACTS: In February 1985, Wallace (P) suffered a heart attack while working and a stroke a month later. The stroke may have resulted in the loss of vision in one eye. Wallace (P) applied for disability benefits and supplemental security income based on his condition. After his claims were denied, Wallace (P) was granted a hearing before an administrative law judge (ALJ) in which he introduced doctors' reports about his ailments. After the hearing, the ALJ sent Wallace (P) to two doctors, both of whom reported back that his impairments did not meet the required criteria. Thus, the ALJ ruled that Wallace (P) was not disabled under the terms of the Social Security Act. Wallace (P) sought review, arguing that he did not have an opportunity to cross-examine the two post-hearing reports.

ISSUE: May agencies make adjudications based on post-hearing reports that are not subject to cross-examination?

HOLDING AND DECISION: (Sloviter, J.) No. Agencies may not make adjudications based on post-hearing reports that are not subject to cross-examination. Section 205 of the Social Security Act provides that upon denial of a claim, applicants are entitled to a hearing where a decision will be based on evidence adduced at the hearing. A full disclosure of the facts at a hearing requires the opportunity for cross-examination, which is an element of fundamental fairness to the applicant. Even where an opinion is wholly medical, cross-examination could reveal what evidence a doctor considered or failed to consider in formulating a conclusion. Accordingly, an applicant must have the opportunity to cross-examine any post-hearing reports that are relied upon by the ALJ when such cross-examination may be required for a full and accurate disclosure of the facts. Therefore, Wallace's petition for review is upheld; the judgment is vacated and the case is remanded.

ANALYSIS

The court found that the two post-hearing reports by the doctors in this case were substantially relied upon by the ALJ. The judge even had remarked in the opinion that he had relied "in particular" on the report of the doctor who ruled that Wallace's visual impairment was not sufficient to qualify. Thus, there was little question that cross-examination could have affected the result here.

Quicknotes

SOCIAL SECURITY ACT § 205 Reasonable notice and an opportunity for a hearing must be given to an applicant who requests it after an unfavorable determination of claim.

Professional Air Traffic Controllers Organization v. Federal Labor Relations Authority

Union (D) v. Government agency (P)

685 F.2d 547 (D.C. Cir. 1982).

NATURE OF CASE: Evidentiary hearing to determine nature, extent and effect of ex parte communications in unfair labor practice case.

FACT SUMMARY: While the Federal Labor Relations Authority (FLRA) (P) was deciding a case involving Professional Air Traffic Controllers Organization (PATCO) (D), board members had ex parte contacts with some interested parties.

🏛 RULE OF LAW
Undisclosed improper ex parte communications during agency proceedings do not necessarily void an agency decision.

FACTS: PATCO (D) was the exclusive bargaining representative for air traffic controllers when negotiations over a new contract stalled in 1981. PATCO (D) struck the Federal Aviation Administration (FAA) on August 3, 1981. The government obtained a restraining order against the strike and then fired 11,000 controllers who failed to return to work two days later. The FAA also filed an unfair labor practice charge against PATCO (D) with the FLRA (P) alleging that the strike was unfair and seeking revocation of PATCO's (D) certification as the bargaining representative for the controllers. While the FLRA (P) was hearing the case, Board members who were deciding the case had brief encounters with interested parties to the case and did not disclose them. After PATCO's (D) certification was revoked, it sought to invalidate the decision based on the ex parte communications. The court ordered an evidentiary hearing.

ISSUE: Do undisclosed improper ex parte communications during agency proceedings necessarily void an agency decision?

HOLDING AND DECISION: (Edwards, J.) No. Undisclosed improper ex parte communications during agency proceedings do not necessarily void an agency decision. The Civil Service Reform Act requires that FLRA (D) hearings be conducted in accordance with the Administrative Procedure Act. As such, ex parte communications with interested parties during agency adjudications are prohibited if they are not made public and are relevant to the merits of the proceeding. Disclosure of ex parte communications can usually solve any problems that may arise since it prevents the appearance of any impropriety. Thus, it is often the first remedy. If it isn't sufficient, the violating party may have to show cause why the proceeding should not be dismissed or denied on account of the violation.

Thus, agency proceedings that have been blemished by ex parte communications are voidable based on whether the process was irrevocably tainted so as to make the ultimate judgment unfair. There are no mechanical rules to apply; rather, each case must be looked at given the surrounding circumstances. In the present case, there is insufficient reason to vacate the FLRA decision. While the ex parte communications at issue should have been disclosed, there does not appear to be any evidence that the proceedings were prejudiced against PATCO (D). Authority's decision affirmed.

▶ ANALYSIS

The court looked closely at three contacts with the FLRA (P) board members. As it turned out, the court had the most problem with a dinner between a different union's leader and a board member, where the union leader tried to convince the board member not to severely punish the union. The court found this totally unacceptable behavior but obviously found that no party had benefitted from this contact.

■═■

Quicknotes

ADMINISTRATIVE PROCEDURE ACT §§ 557(D) Governs ex parte communications in agency proceedings.

CIVIL SERVICE REFORM ACT Requires that the FRLA conduct hearings in accordance with the APA.

EX PARTE A proceeding commenced by one party without providing any opposing parties with notice or which is uncontested by an adverse party.

■═■

Stone v. Federal Deposit Insurance Corporation

Federal employee (P) v. Employer (D)

179 F.3d 1368 (Fed. Cir. 1999).

NATURE OF CASE: Appeal from final decision of the Merit Systems Protection Board.

FACT SUMMARY: The Merit Systems Protection Board sustained a decision by an administrative law judge (ALJ) that Stone's (P) removal from his position as a federal bank examiner had not violated due process.

RULE OF LAW
The introduction of new and material information by means of ex parte communications to the deciding official undermines a public employee's due process right to notice and the opportunity to respond.

FACTS: Stone (P) allegedly falsified forms for approved leave from his position as a GS-12 bank examiner in the Federal Deposit Insurance Corporations's (FDIC's) (D) Division of Supervision. The FDIC (D) began removal proceedings, and a deciding official recommended that Stone (P) be terminated. When Stone (P) appealed his dismissal to the Merit Systems Protection Board, Stone's (P) attorney requested relevant documents from the FDIC (D). Stone (P) then discovered that an ex parte memorandum urging his removal had been received by the deciding official. Stone (P) alleged that the ex parte communication was a violation of his right to due process and should automatically void his dismissal. The ALJ found there was nothing wrong with the ex parte communications and the Board sustained Stone's (P) dismissal. On appeal, Stone (P) alleged that a violation of his due process rights had occurred.

ISSUE: Does the introduction of new and material information by means of ex parte communications to the deciding official undermine a public employee's due process right to notice and the opportunity to respond?

HOLDING AND DECISION: (Gajarsa, J.) Yes. The introduction of new and material information by means of ex parte communications to the deciding official undermines a public employee's due process right to notice and the opportunity to respond. A public employee is entitled to notice and an opportunity to respond prior to removal from office. In determining whether new and material information was introduced, the Board must determine whether the ex parte communication was so substantial and likely to cause prejudice that no employee can fairly be required to be subjected to a deprivation of property under such circumstances. Where a procedural due process violation has occurred because of ex parte communications, such a violation is not subject to the harmless error test. Here Stone (P) had a property interest in continued employment with the FDIC (D); thus, he was entitled to meaningful notice of the reasons for his removal and a meaningful opportunity to respond. Vacated and remanded.

▶ ANALYSIS

The facts and circumstances of each individual case must be considered. The court listed several factors for the Board to consider. Whether the information was cumulative; whether the ex parte communications were of the type likely to result in undue pressure on the deciding official to rule in a particular manner; and whether the employee knew of the error and had a chance to respond are among the factors to consider.

Quicknotes

DUE PROCESS CLAUSE Clauses found in the Fifth and Fourteenth Amendments to the United States Constitution providing that no person shall be deprived of "life, liberty, or property, without due process of law."

EX PARTE A proceeding commenced by one party without providing any opposing parties with notice or which is uncontested by an adverse party.

MATERIALITY Importance; the degree of relevance or necessity to the particular matter.

NOTICE Communication of information to a person by an authorized person or an otherwise proper source.

Londoner v. Denver

Property owner (P) v. City council (D)

210 U.S. 373 (1908).

NATURE OF CASE: Appeal of a tax assessment.

FACT SUMMARY: Londoner (P) contended the Denver City Council (Council) (D) denied him due process by imposing an assessment of paving costs without notice and an evidentiary hearing.

🏛 RULE OF LAW
Due process requires that the taxpayers be afforded notice and an evidentiary hearing before a tax is set by an agency.

FACTS: The Council (D), under statutory authority, approved an assessment on Londoner's (P) property for the costs of paving a public street. Before approving the assessment the Council (D) gave notice to Londoner and afforded an opportunity to file written objections to the assessment. Londoner's (P) objections consisted of allegations that the hearing procedures, precluding the presentation of evidence, denied due process. The Colorado courts rejected Londoner's (P) contentions, and the Supreme Court took jurisdiction.

ISSUE: Does due process require that the taxpayers be afforded notice and an evidentiary hearing before a tax is set by an agency?

HOLDING AND DECISION: (Moody, J.) Yes. Due process requires that the taxpayers be afforded notice and an evidentiary hearing before a tax is set by an agency. While there are few constitutional restrictions on a state legislature's power to tax, there are limitations imposed where this power is delegated to an administrative agency. In such a case, as here, more than an opportunity to tender written objections to the tax is required by due process. The taxpayer must be allowed to present evidence in support of his allegations, and an opportunity to participate in oral argument. The failure to afford such opportunities in this case renders the assessments invalid as adopted through a denial of due process. Reversed.

▶ ANALYSIS

This case illustrates the general requirement that agencies exercising taxation or economic regulation follow formal procedures. This requirement can have several sources including the agency's enabling statute, its own procedural requirements, the Administrative Procedure Act, federal common law, and judicial decisions.

Quicknotes

EVIDENTIARY HEARING Hearing pertaining to the evidence of the case.

NOTICE Communication of information to a person by an authorized person or an otherwise proper source.

PROCEDURAL DUE PROCESS The constitutional mandate that if the state or federal government acts so as to deny a citizen of a life, liberty or property interest the individual is first entitled to notice and the right to be heard.

Bi-Metallic Investment Company v. State Board of Equalization

Property owner (P) v. State board (D)

239 U.S. 441 (1915).

NATURE OF CASE: Suit to enjoin enforcement of administrative order.

FACT SUMMARY: Bi-Metallic Investment Company (Bi-Metallic) (P) sued Colorado (D) to enjoin enforcement of an order increasing property taxes in Denver. Bi-Metallic (P) argued that it was entitled to an opportunity to be heard in opposition to the order.

🏛 RULE OF LAW
Where an agency rule will apply to a vast number of people, the Constitution does not require that each be given an opportunity to be heard directly for the purpose of arguing in favor for or against its adoption.

FACTS: The Colorado Tax Commission (D) and the State Board of Equalization (D) ordered a 40 percent increase in the valuation of all taxable property in the city of Denver. Bi-Metallic (P), the owner of certain real estate in Denver, sought to enjoin enforcement of the order. It argued that it had been afforded no opportunity to be heard in opposition to the order, and was thus threatened with deprivation of property without due process of law. The Supreme Court of Colorado ordered dismissal of Bi-Metallic's (P) claim, and Bi-Metallic (P) appealed to the United States Supreme Court.

ISSUE: Are all property owners entitled to an opportunity to be heard prior to adoption of an administrative order which increases property taxes?

HOLDING AND DECISION: (Holmes, J.) No. Agency orders and rules which will affect vast numbers of people may be adopted without affording every interested party a direct opportunity to be heard. In cases such as the present one, it would be impractical to allow all individuals affected to offer a direct voice in support of or in opposition to an order. Thus, the Constitution is satisfied by the fact that, as voters, the taxpayers involved exercise power, remote or direct, over those responsible for the order. Accordingly, the judgment of the state supreme court dismissing this suit must be affirmed.

▶ ANALYSIS

The result of this case is opposite to that reached in *Londoner v. Denver.* However, the apparent conflict between the two cases is explained by the observation that Bi-Metallic involved so-called "legislative" facts whereas Londoner was a case which presented an issue requiring evaluation of "adjudicative" facts. "Legislative" facts are those which primarily involve determinations of broad policies or principles of general application, e.g., whether every tract of land in a large city has been under-assessed for property tax purposes. In resolving issues pertaining to "legislative" as opposed to "adjudicative" facts, administrative agencies may dispense with the practice of according every interested party an opportunity to be heard.

Quicknotes

ADMINISTRATIVE ORDER The final disposition of an administrative hearing or the interpretation or application of a statute.

RULEMAKING The promulgation of a rule governing a particular activity by an administrative agency, acting within the scope of its power pursuant to statute.

Board of Regents v. Roth

School administrator (D) v. Professor (P)

408 U.S. 564 (1972).

NATURE OF CASE: Suit to set aside an action of a state agency.

FACT SUMMARY: Roth's (P) contract as a college professor was not renewed by the Wisconsin Board of Regents of State Colleges (D).

🏛 RULE OF LAW
The state need not hold hearings or offer reasons for its employment decisions.

FACTS: Roth (P) was hired to a one-year term of employment as an assistant professor at Wisconsin State University—Oshkosh. At the conclusion of that one year, he was informed by that university's president that his contract would not be renewed. According to state law, nontenured professors such as Roth (P) could be terminated without any hearing or explanation, and it was by this summary procedure that he was dismissed. Roth (P), however, filed suit against the Board of Regents of State Colleges (D), alleging that he was entitled by the Constitution to a pretermination hearing and statement of the reasons for his dismissal. In addition, he contended that he had been terminated solely because of his exercise of his right to free speech. The district court sustained Roth's (P) contention that he was entitled to the requisites of procedural due process. The court of appeals affirmed, whereupon the United States Supreme Court granted certiorari.

ISSUE: Are state employees entitled to a hearing and a statement of the reasons for the state's employment decisions?

HOLDING AND DECISION: (Stewart, J.) No. A state employee may not insist that the state hold hearings or offer reasons for its failure to rehire him after his initial term of employment has expired. Due process must be accorded only when an individual is threatened with deprivation of either liberty or property. Failure to rehire an employee does not abridge his liberty, unless, of course, in so doing, his employer stigmatizes him in such fashion as will restrict his freedom to seek employment elsewhere. Similarly, a contract of employment for a specific term confers upon an employee no legitimate claim to subsequent employment sufficient to constitute a property right. Accordingly, Roth (P) has made no showing that either his property or his liberty was at stake when the Board (D) acted. Therefore, he has failed to establish a right to the guarantees of procedural due process.

▶ ANALYSIS

The government may fire or refuse to hire an employee, unless, in so doing, it stigmatizes him in a way which seriously forecloses future employment opportunities or deprives him of employment to which he had shown himself entitled as a matter of right, contractual or otherwise. It is doubtful, however, whether the government may dispense with the elements of due process when its basis for firing or not hiring an employee is itself unconstitutional, i.e., when it is related to the applicant's race, sex, religion, etc. In this connection, it may be noted that the Court expressly declined to consider whether the petitioner would have merited a hearing on the contention that he had been discharged for exercising his right to free speech, an issue which the Supreme Court believed itself to be foreclosed from considering.

▬▬▬

Quicknotes

DUE PROCESS The constitutional mandate requiring the courts to protect and enforce individuals' rights and liberties consistent with prevailing principles of fairness and justice and prohibiting the federal and state governments from such activities that deprive its citizens of a life, liberty or property interest.

▬▬▬

Paul v. Davis

Police chief (D) v. Alleged shoplifter (D)

424 U.S. 693 (1976).

NATURE OF CASE: Suit against two police chiefs claiming defamation that allegedly violated the Due Process Clause of the Fourteenth Amendment.

FACT SUMMARY: Davis (P) sued Paul (D), the police chief of Louisville, Kentucky, and McDaniel (D), the police chief in Jefferson County, Kentucky, seeking redress for an alleged violation of his constitutional rights.

🏛 RULE OF LAW

A government official's defamation of a person does not constitute a deprivation of the liberty interest guaranteed by the Due Process Clause of the Fourteenth Amendment.

FACTS: Police chiefs Paul (D) and McDaniel (D) alerted local merchants to possible shoplifters who might be operating in the Louisville, Kentucky, area during the 1972 Christmas season. The chiefs (D) distributed a flyer to approximately 800 area merchants; the five-page flyer presented names and photographs of persons alleged to be shoplifters. Davis's (P) picture appeared in the flyer [because he had been arrested in Louisville, though not convicted, on a shoplifting charge]. Davis (P) sued Paul (D) and McDaniel (D) in U.S. District Court, alleging that the chiefs (D) had defamed him in violation of the liberty interest secured by the Fourteenth Amendment's Due Process Clause. [The trial judge granted the police chiefs' (D) motion to dismiss. The court of appeals reversed, holding that Davis's (P) complaint stated a claim upon which relief could be granted because, the appellate court reasoned, the complaint alleged facts that constituted a denial of due process under the Fourteenth Amendment.] Paul (D) and McDaniel (D) petitioned the United States Supreme Court for further review.

ISSUE: Does a government official's defamation of a person constitute a deprivation of the liberty interest guaranteed by the Due Process Clause of the Fourteenth Amendment?

HOLDING AND DECISION: (Rehnquist, J.) No. A government official's defamation of a person does not constitute a deprivation of the liberty interest guaranteed by the Due Process Clause of the Fourteenth Amendment. Davis (P) asserts that the flyer impermissibly deprived him of some "liberty" protected by the Fourteenth Amendment; the designation of him as an "active shoplifter," he contends, would effectively prohibit him from entering business establishments for fear of being suspected of shoplifting, and, if he were apprehended, would seriously impair his future employment opportunities. Such allegations seem to state a claim for defamation—specifically, a claim for defamation per se, given the accusation of criminal misconduct against Davis (P)—that would be actionable in almost every state. A study of our decisions, however, convinces us that they do not support Davis's (P) attempt to use defamation as a violation of due process under the Fourteenth Amendment. The words "liberty" and "property," as used in the Fourteenth Amendment, do not single out reputation for special protection, and we therefore hold that the interest in reputation asserted here is neither "liberty" nor "property" that is protected from government deprivation without due process of law. Reversed.

DISSENT: (Brennan, J.) Police officials now may brand innocent persons as criminals without constitutional limitation under the Due Process Clause. All the protections of a criminal trial are meaningless because people can now be arbitrarily punished as criminals by the very officials whose duty it is to enforce the laws fairly against all persons.

▌ ANALYSIS

The ready existence of state-law remedies strongly influenced the majority's holding in *Paul v. Davis*. As excerpted in the casebook, Justice Brennan's dissent overlooks that larger context, assuming instead that reputation equates with the liberty interests indisputably implicated by criminal proceedings.

■=■

Codd v. Velger

Employer (D) v. Employee (P)

429 U.S. 624 (1977).

NATURE OF CASE: Appeal from denial of agency employment hearing.

FACT SUMMARY: Velger (P) was dismissed as a police officer and claimed he was due a hearing because of stigmatizing information placed in his file.

🏛 RULE OF LAW
Hearings mandated by the Due Process Clause are only required when there is a clear factual dispute.

FACTS: Velger (P) was a police officer in New York City in a probationary position. He was dismissed, apparently because he had put a gun to his head in a suicide attempt. Velger (P) then obtained a job with the Penn-Central Railroad Police Department, but was dismissed when a Penn-Central officer was shown his New York City file. Velger (P), who ordinarily wasn't entitled to a hearing as probationary employee, claimed that a hearing was required because of the stigmatizing information in his file that prevented him from finding similar employment. The court decided that Velger (P) did not prove that he had been stigmatized and Velger (P) appealed. The court of appeals held that the finding of no stigma was clearly erroneous. The United States Supreme Court granted certiorari.

ISSUE: Are hearings mandated by the Due Process Clause only required when there is a clear factual dispute?

HOLDING AND DECISION: (Per curiam) Yes. Hearings mandated by the Due Process Clause are only required when there is a clear factual dispute. Whether the report in Velger's (P) file was stigmatizing need not be determined in this case because Velger (P) has failed to prove another essential element. Nowhere in the pleadings is there any assertion that the report of the suicide attempt is substantially false. The absence of this allegation is fatal to any claim or request for a hearing. If there is no factual dispute at issue, the hearing usually required by the Due Process Clause would be rendered meaningless. Thus, Velger (P) is not entitled to a hearing.

DISSENT: (Stewart, J.) The purpose of a hearing is twofold. First, it is to establish the truth or falsity of the charges, and second, to also provide a basis for deciding what action is warranted. Even if the charge is clearly true, procedural safeguards still must be observed.

▶ ANALYSIS

The dissent made a valid point when it said that the government should carry the burden in these instances. Justice Stewart argued that the agency employer should at least have to show that the denial of due process was harmless error. It is unclear from the majority opinion just how much Velger (P) would have to allege regarding the facts in order to sufficiently justify the hearing.

■══■

Quicknotes

DUE PROCESS CLAUSE Clauses found in the Fifth and Fourteenth Amendments to the United States Constitution providing that no person shall be deprived of "life, liberty, or property, without due process of law."

■══■

Shands v. City of Kennett

Volunteer firemen (P) v. City government (D)

993 F.2d 1337 (8th Cir. 1993).

NATURE OF CASE: Appeal from judgment notwithstanding the verdict in action for deprivation of due process.

FACT SUMMARY: Several volunteer firemen (P) were dismissed from their positions and claimed that they were deprived of their constitutional rights without due process.

🏛 RULE OF LAW
Government employees are entitled to procedural due process in connection with employment discharges only when they have been deprived of a constitutionally protected liberty or property interest.

FACTS: The Kennett City Council (Council) (D) dismissed several volunteer firemen (P) when they undermined the authority of the Fire Chief with respect to another employment decision. At a city Council (D) meeting, the dismissed firemen told their side of the case and were allowed to question some witnesses. Still, the Council (D) voted not to reinstate them and released a statement that the men (P) had not been dismissed for any illegal or immoral activities but rather, as the result of personnel matters. The dismissed firemen (P) then filed suit alleging that there had been false and stigmatizing statements made against them to the media and that they were entitled to a fair hearing in order to clear their names. The firemen (P) earned a favorable verdict but the court granted Kennett's (D) motion for judgment notwithstanding the verdict and the firemen (P) appealed.

ISSUE: Are government employees entitled to procedural due process in connection with employment discharges only when they have been deprived of a constitutionally protected liberty or property interest?

HOLDING AND DECISION: (Wollman, J.) Yes. Government employees are entitled to procedural due process in connection with employment discharges only when they have been deprived of a constitutionally protected liberty or property interest. To establish a protected liberty interest, a dismissed government employee must show that an official publicly made untrue charges that would stigmatize him so as to seriously damage the employee's standing in the community or prevent further employment. In the present case, the only public statements on the record about the dismissed firemen (P) expressly said that the dismissals were for "personnel" reasons and for being "insubordinate." These statements did not create the level of stigma that implicates a constitutionally protected liberty interest. The requisite stigma has generally been found in cases involving accusations of dishonesty, immorality, criminality or racism. A mere charge of insubordination is insufficient. Accordingly, the dismissed firemen (P) were not entitled to a hearing regarding their dismissal. Affirmed.

▶ ANALYSIS

There are often two steps to the due process claim. If a court decides that a hearing was required, it must then be decided what that entails. Sometimes, an administrative hearing is necessary. Other times, the courts have found that a fuller trial-type proceeding with notice and evidentiary rulings is required.

■━■

Quicknotes

DUE PROCESS The constitutional mandate requiring the courts to protect and enforce individuals' rights and liberties consistent with prevailing principles of fairness and justice and prohibiting the federal and state governments from such activities that deprive its citizens of a life, liberty or property interest.

JUDGMENT NOTWITHSTANDING THE VERDICT A judgment entered by the trial judge reversing a jury verdict if the jury's determination has no basis in law or fact.

■━■

Mathews v. Eldridge

Social Security administration (D) v. Disability benefits recipient (P)

424 U.S. 319 (1976).

NATURE OF CASE: Appeal concerning constitutional validity of procedures on termination of disability benefits.

FACT SUMMARY: Eldridge (P) had his disability benefits terminated and brought suit.

🏛 RULE OF LAW

The Due Process Clause does not require a hearing prior to termination of disability benefits.

FACTS: The state agency and the Social Security Administration (D) terminated Eldridge's (P) disability benefits. The relevant administrative procedure was the provision of the opportunity for a claimant to assert his claim prior to any administrative action, a right to an evidentiary hearing, and subsequent judicial review before the claim became final. Instead of requesting reconsideration, Eldridge (P) commenced an action challenging the constitutional validity of the administrative procedures. The district court held that the administrative procedures pursuant to which Eldridge's (P) benefits had been terminated abridged his right to procedural due process. The court of appeals affirmed. The dispute centered on what kind of procedure was required when benefits were initially terminated, pending review. The courts below held that due process required an evidentiary hearing prior to termination.

ISSUE: Does the Due Process Clause require a hearing prior to termination of disability benefits?

HOLDING AND DECISION: (Powell, J.) No. The Due Process Clause does not require a hearing prior to termination of disability benefits. Only in *Goldberg v. Kelly*, 397 U.S. 254 (1970), has this Court held that due process requires an evidentiary hearing prior to a temporary deprivation because in that case it was emphasized that welfare assistance is given to persons on the very margin of subsistence. Eligibility for disability benefits, on the other hand, is not based on financial need. The probable value of additional procedural safeguards is not that great because termination of disability benefits turn on the routine medical reports of physicians. In considering the public interest, experience with the constitutionalizing of government procedures suggests that the ultimate additional cost in terms of money and administrative burden would be substantial. The judgment of the court of appeals is reversed.

▶ *ANALYSIS*

The Supreme Court took on the issue of what due process procedures apply in the case of the revocation of a driver's license according to the three factors weighed in *Mathews*

above. It held that: (1) a driver's license is not as important as welfare; (2) the possibility of a mistake where there is no hearing before revocation is small; (3) a prior hearing would not be administratively efficient and thus is probably contrary to the public interest. Held: no prior hearing required. Gellhorn, W., Admin. Law, at 508-509.

Quicknotes

DUE PROCESS The constitutional mandate requiring the courts to protect and enforce individuals' rights and liberties consistent with prevailing principals of fairness and justice and prohibiting the federal and state governments from such activities that deprive its citizens of a life, liberty or property interest.

Board of Curators of the University of Missouri v. Horowitz

State university (D) v. Medical school student (P)

435 U.S. 78 (1978).

NATURE OF CASE: Appeal from reinstatement of action protesting a student's dismissal from school.

FACT SUMMARY: When Horowitz (P) was dismissed from medical school for unsatisfactory performance, she filed suit, alleging that the Board of Curators (D) had not accorded her procedural due process.

🏛 RULE OF LAW
A formal hearing is not required to dismiss a student for unsatisfactory performance based on the academic judgment of school officials.

FACTS: As Horowitz (P) progressed through medical school, several faculty members expressed dissatisfaction with her clinical performance during her first year. Faculty dissatisfaction with her performance continued during the following year. The Council on Evaluation finally recommended that, absent radical improvement, Horowitz (P) be dropped from school. Horowitz (P) was permitted to take a set of oral and practical examinations as an "appeal" of the eventual decision not to permit her to graduate. Only two of seven practicing physicians in the area who evaluated Horowitz (P) recommended that she be graduated on schedule. Following her dismissal, Horowitz (P) filed suit, alleging she had not been accorded procedural due process prior to that dismissal. After a trial, the district court dismissed her complaint. The court of appeals reversed. The University's Board of Curators (D) appealed.

ISSUE: Is a formal hearing required to dismiss a student for unsatisfactory performance based on the academic judgment of school officials?

HOLDING AND DECISION: (Rehnquist, J.) No. A formal hearing is not required to dismiss a student for unsatisfactory performance based on the academic judgment of school officials. The ultimate decision to dismiss Horowitz (P) was careful and deliberate. These procedures were sufficient under the Due Process Clause of the Fourteenth Amendment. The determination whether to dismiss a student for academic reasons requires an expert evaluation of cumulative information and is not readily adapted to the procedural tools of judicial or administrative decision-making. There is no reason to further enlarge the judicial presence in the academic community and thereby risk deterioration of many beneficial aspects of the faculty-student relationship. Reversed.

▶ ANALYSIS

The Court referred to its prior decision in *Goss v. Lopez*, 419 U.S. 565 (1975), in making a distinction between students who are dismissed for disciplinary purposes and those who are dismissed for academic reasons. In *Goss*, the Court felt that suspensions of students for disciplinary reasons have a sufficient resemblance to traditional judicial and administrative fact-finding to call for a "hearing" before the relevant school authority. Even in the context of a school disciplinary proceeding, however, the Court stopped short of requiring a formal hearing.

Quicknotes

FOURTEENTH AMENDMENT Declares that no state shall make or enforce any law which shall abridge the privileges and immunities of citizens of the United States.

PROCEDURAL DUE PROCESS The constitutional mandate that if the state or federal government acts so as to deny a citizen of a life, liberty or property interest the individual is first entitled to notice and the right to be heard.

Osteen v. Henley

Student (P) v. University (D)

13 F.3d 221 (7th Cir. 1993).

NATURE OF CASE: Appeal from school's decision to expel student.

FACT SUMMARY: Osteen (P) was expelled for two years from Northern Illinois University (D) for fighting.

🏛 RULE OF LAW
There is no constitutional right to counsel in student disciplinary proceedings.

FACTS: Osteen (P), a football player at Northern Illinois University (University) (D), hit two students and broke their noses after an argument involving his friends. Osteen (P) admitted his guilt to the charges at a meeting with the University's (D) judicial officer, but requested a hearing regarding the proposed sanction. At the hearing, Osteen (P) was represented by a student advocate, but the appeals board approved the recommended two-year expulsion, as did the University's (D) vice-president. Osteen (P) sought judicial review of this decision.

ISSUE: Is there a constitutional right to counsel in student disciplinary hearings?

HOLDING AND DECISION: (Posner, C.J.) No. There is no constitutional right to counsel in student disciplinary proceedings. The application of the Due Process Clause to student disciplinary hearings has not been resolved definitively by the courts. However, it is at least arguable that when faced with serious charges, a student is entitled to consult with a lawyer. But there does not seem to be any right to have a lawyer perform the traditional functions of a trial lawyer at the proceeding. To recognize that right would force disciplinary hearings into the mold of adversary litigation and would severely increase their cost and complexity. Since there is no real danger that schools will engage in unwarranted expulsions without this right, there is no reason to think that students' rights will be violated. Furthermore, the consequence to a student such as Osteen (P), who may still enroll in other colleges, is not so severe as to entitle him to litigation-type procedural protections. Therefore, Osteen's (P) claim for review is denied.

▶ ANALYSIS

The court went on to note that it doubted that any student disciplinary hearing could rise to the level requiring the right of counsel. The decision also rejected Osteen's (P) claim that the interruption of himself and his advocate at the hearing by the board was a denial of due process. The court found that the interruptions only related to times

where Osteen (P) was attempting to revisit the issue of guilt.

■━■

Quicknotes

DUE PROCESS CLAUSE Clauses found in the Fifth and Fourteenth Amendments to the United States Constitution providing that no person shall be deprived of "life, liberty, or property, without due process of law."

■━■

Withrow v. Larkin

Medical board (D) v. Physician (P)

421 U.S. 35 (1975).

NATURE OF CASE: Appeal of order enjoining an administrative hearing.

FACT SUMMARY: The district court enjoined the Wisconsin Medical Examining Board (D) from holding a contested hearing to determine whether Larkin (P) had engaged in prohibited acts.

🏛 RULE OF LAW
The performance of both prosecutorial and adjudicative functions by the same agency officials is not per se a denial of due process.

FACTS: The Wisconsin Medical Examining Board (Board) (D) held an investigative hearing to determine whether Larkin (P) had committed certain proscribed acts within his medical practice. As a result of the investigation, the Board (D) notified Larkin (P) that it would hold a contested hearing to determine whether his medical license should be suspended. Larkin (P) brought suit to enjoin the contested hearing on the basis that it was improper for the Board (D) to adjudicate the same case it had investigated. The district court granted the injunction holding that the Board (D) could not properly rule on the same charges it investigates. The Board (D) appealed.

ISSUE: Is the performance of both investigatory and adjudicative functions by the same agency officials per se a denial of due process?

HOLDING AND DECISION: (White, J.) No. The performance of both investigatory and adjudicative functions by the same agency officials is not per se a denial of due process. There is a presumption of honesty and integrity in adjudications. As a result, the performance of these two functions is not a denial of due process unless this presumption is overcome by a showing of bias on the part of those performing the dual functions of investigation and adjudication. Such bias will not be implied merely by the performance of these functions by the same entity. In this case, the only evidence offered of the impropriety of the contested hearing was the performance of both functions by the same officials. This was insufficient to constitute a denial of due process. Reversed and remanded.

▶ ANALYSIS

Some commentators argue that combining adjudicatory and prosecutorial functions, even if not inherently unconstitutional, is fundamentally unfair. An empirical study conducted by Professor Richard Posner, The Behavior of Administrative Agencies, 1 J. Legal Stud. 305 (1972), found that dismissal rates did not reflect a reluctance of agencies to dismiss complaints when performing both prosecutorial and adjudicative functions. Regardless of this empirical evidence, veteran administrators continue to argue that dual functions inhibit an agency from reaching a just conclusion.

■━■

Quicknotes

LICENSE A right that is granted to a person allowing him or her to conduct an activity that without such permission he or she could not lawfully do, and which is unassignable and revocable at the will of the licensor.

PER SE An activity that is so inherently obvious that it is unnecessary to examine its underlying validity.

PROCEDURAL DUE PROCESS The constitutional mandate that if the state or federal government acts so as to deny a citizen of a life, liberty or property interest the individual is first entitled to notice and the right to be heard.

■━■

Torres v. Mukasey

Applicant for asylum (P) v. Government department (D)

551 F.3d 616 (7th Cir. 2008).

NATURE OF CASE: Appeal of denial of application for asylum.

FACT SUMMARY: Torres's (P) petition for asylum and protection under the Convention Against Torture (CAT) was denied by the Department of Justice (DOJ) (D), U.S. Attorney General Michael Mukasey, because of inconsistencies between Torres's (P) oral testimony and his application for asylum.

🏛 **RULE OF LAW**
When the credibility determination of the immigration judge (IJ) is not supported by substantial evidence that bears a legitimate nexus to the findings, and when the improper behavior of the IJ at the immigration hearing renders the IJ's credibility determination unreliable, the reviewing court will not defer to the conclusions of the IJ.

FACTS: Torres (P) petitioned the DOJ (D) for asylum and protection under CAT because of persecution he endured as a soldier in the Honduran army. The alleged persecution was a result of his membership in a social group—namely, his family. Upon denial of his petition for asylum by the IJ, Torres (P) sought review before the Board of Immigration Appeals (BIA). The BIA affirmed the decision of the IJ, and Torres (P) appealed to the instant court. Following a review of the record, the appeals court found error in the IJ's substantive analysis and in his conduct at Torres's (P) hearing. Specifically, the appeals court determined that the record supported Torres's (P) assertion that he was tortured and abused because of the military desertions of each of his three older brothers. In rejecting the IJ's conclusions, the appeals court found no inconsistencies in Torres's (P) testimony, which established that Torres's (P) commanding officer repeatedly targeted Torres (P) because of his family history. Additionally, the appeals court determined that, in his oral testimony, Torres (P) sufficiently explained omissions in his written asylum application. As such, the appeals court found that Torres's (P) family history was the nexus for his mistreatment, and that the establishment of this nexus supported Torres's (P) credibility, without which Torres (P) could not sustain his burden of proof.

ISSUE: Must the reviewing court defer to the conclusions of the IJ when the credibility determination of the IJ is not supported by substantial evidence that bears a legitimate nexus to the findings, and when the improper behavior of the IJ at the immigration hearing renders the IJ's credibility determination unreliable?

HOLDING AND DECISION: (Kanne, J.) No. When the credibility determination of the IJ is not supported by substantial evidence that bears a legitimate nexus to the findings, and when the improper behavior of the IJ at the immigration hearing renders the IJ's credibility determination unreliable, the reviewing court will not defer to the conclusions of the IJ. In fact, the IJ's improper conduct—specifically, the IJ's overactive role during the immigration hearing, his demonstrated impatience and hostility towards Torres (P), and his reliance on personal knowledge beyond the record facts, provides sufficient basis to remand the case for further proceedings. Evaluating the IJ's findings under the substantial evidence standard, it is clear that the IJ failed to base his credibility determination on specific, cogent reasons that bear a legitimate nexus to the findings. Instead, the IJ adopted an inquisitorial role in Torres's (P) hearing, focusing on purported inconsistencies in Torres's (P) testimony regarding the involvement in and motivation for the torture of Torres (P) by his commanding officer. Thus, because the IJ ignored the consistent and credible testimony of Torres (P), and his convincing explanations for discrepancies in the material facts of the asylum application, the denial of same by the IJ and the BIA are vacated and remanded for further proceedings.

▶ **ANALYSIS**

In *Torres*, the Seventh Circuit encouraged the BIA to assign a different IJ to the case on remand. In *Huang v. Gonzales*, 403 F.3d 945 (7th Cir. 2005), the Seventh Circuit took similar action, upon similar circumstances, in encouraging assignment of a different IJ on remand. See also, *Ali v. Mukasey*, 529 F.3d 478 (2d Cir. 2008); *Wang v. Attorney General of the United States*, 423 F.3d 260 (3d Cir. 2005); *Reyes-Melendez v. I.N.S.*, 342 F.3d 1001 (9th Cir. 2003). Insofar as the conduct of the IJ affects a credibility finding, specifically when the IJ relies on his own personal experience, wholly unsupported by specific and cogent reasons that bear no legitimate nexus to the finding, case law suggests a nationwide trend of biased immigration hearings.

■═■

Quicknotes

ASYLUM A place of protection or refuge.

EVIDENCE Any type of proof offered at a trial in order to prove or disprove a disputed fact or issue.

■═■

Jackson v. Veterans Administration

Employee (P) v. Employer (D)

768 F.2d 1325 (Fed. Cir. 1985).

NATURE OF CASE: Appeal of agency employment discharge.

FACT SUMMARY: Jackson (P) was discharged from the Veterans Administration (D) due to allegations of sexual harassment of a subordinate which were disputed.

🏛 RULE OF LAW
A board must articulate sound reasons, based on the record of evidence, when its evaluation of testimony is contrary to that of the presiding official.

FACTS: Jackson (P) worked as a supervisor in the Veterans Administration (D). He was accused of sexual harassment, involving five separate incidents of misconduct, and was dismissed. A presiding official conducted a hearing and reversed the removal based on a determination that none of the incidents were established by a preponderance of the evidence. The agency requested a review and the board (D) reversed, concluding that two of the incidents were supported by the evidence. In the first incident, a subordinate employee claimed that Jackson (P) had kissed her while she was on the telephone, and the second incident involved his request for a kiss so that the employee could leave early. Jackson (P) appealed the board's (D) ruling.

ISSUE: Must a board articulate sound reasons, based on the record of evidence, when its evaluation of testimony is contrary to that of the presiding official?

HOLDING AND DECISION: (Nies, J.) Yes. A board must articulate sound reasons, based on the record of evidence, when its evaluation of testimony is contrary to that of the presiding official. The issue is whether the board's evaluation of the weight of the evidence is reasonable and supported by substantial evidence, taking into consideration that the presiding official made a different evaluation after actually hearing the witnesses. In the present case, the presiding official decided that the first alleged incident was unproven because it came down to conflicting accounts that could not be corroborated by other witnesses. Given these circumstances, the board (D) should not have reversed the presiding official given that his decision was largely based on credibility determinations. However, with regard to the second alleged incident, the presiding official apparently ignored the account of a witness who corroborated the testimony and did not discredit it. Therefore, the board (D) was certainly entitled to weigh this evidence on its own and find that a preponderance of evidence showed Jackson's (P) guilt. Jackson's (P) claim for review is denied.

▶ ANALYSIS

A board must have "substantial evidence" to support its determination when there is a factual dispute. When there is a dispute as to the legal issues involved, courts may simply look to see whether the agency action at issue conforms to the applicable law. It is a more difficult matter when the dispute revolves around a matter that is not clearly legal or factual.

Quicknotes

PREPONDERANCE OF THE EVIDENCE A standard of proof requiring the trier of fact to determine whether the fact sought to be established is more probable than not.

SEXUAL HARASSMENT An employment practice subjecting persons to oppressive conduct on account of their gender.

National Labor Relations Board v. Hearst

Labor board (P) v. News publisher (D)

322 U.S. 111 (1944).

NATURE OF CASE: Appeal of a National Labor Relations Board (NLRB) bargaining order.

FACT SUMMARY: The NLRB (P) found that newsboys selling Hearst (D) newspapers were employees under the National Labor Relations Act (NLRA) and, therefore, Hearst (D) was ordered to engage in collective bargaining with their representative.

🏛 RULE OF LAW

A reviewing court must accept an agency's application of a broad statutory term if such application is supported in the record and has a reasonable basis in law.

FACTS: Several Hearst (D) newspapers were distributed in Los Angeles through vendors, called newsboys. The price at which the newsboys bought the papers from Hearst (D) and the price they could charge the public were set by Hearst (D). The location, conditions, and hours within which the papers could be sold were determined either expressly or implicitly by Hearst (D). The newsboys organized to bargain collectively, claiming they were "employees" under the NLRA. Hearst (D) refused to bargain, contending the newsboys were independent contractors and therefore not protected by the NLRA. The NLRB (P) concluded the newsboys were employees and ordered Hearst (D) to bargain. The court of appeals made an independent evaluation of the record and found the newsboys were independent contractors. The NLRB (P) appealed.

ISSUE: Must a reviewing court accept an agency's application of a broad statutory term if such application is supported in the record and has a reasonable basis in law?

HOLDING AND DECISION: (Rutledge, J.) Yes. A reviewing court must accept an agency's application of a broad statutory term if such application is supported in the record and has a reasonable basis in the law. Congress has vested the duty of administering the NLRA in the NLRB (P). The NLRB's (P) experience in dealing with labor matters makes it a logical choice to determine the application of broad statutory terms within the context of national labor policy. Therefore, the NLRB's (P) application of the term "employee" within the present context must be upheld if supported in the record and if reasonably based in law. The measure of control over the newsboy's activities exercised by Hearst (D) is sufficient evidence for the NLRB (P) to conclude the existence of an employer-employee relationship under recognized legal principles. Therefore, the court of appeals improperly substituted its own application of the term. Reversed.

▶ ANALYSIS

In *Gary v. Powell*, 314 U.S. 402 (1941), the Court laid the foundation for Hearst. It held that where a term's definition is delegated to an agency, the development of the definition will be upheld in respect of the delegation. After the Hearst decision, Congress amended the NLRA to exclude persons having a common law independent contractor status. In Hearst, the court of appeals holding of independent contractor status was based on common law interpretations, while the NLRB's determination of employee status was a modification of the common law idea of independent contractor status as equivalent to employee status under the NLRA.

Quicknotes

COLLECTIVE BARGAINING Negotiations between an employer and employee that are mediated by a specified third party.

DELEGATION The authorization of one person to act on another's behalf.

INDEPENDENT CONTRACTOR A party undertaking a particular assignment for another who retains control over the manner in which it is executed.

QUESTION OF FACT An issue relating to a factual assertion that is disputed at trial and left to the jury to resolve.

QUESTION OF LAW An issue regarding the legal significance of a particular act or event, which is usually left to the judge to ascertain.

Evening Star Newspaper Company v. Kemp

Employer (D) v. Employee (P)

533 F.2d 1224 (D.C. Cir. 1976).

NATURE OF CASE: Appeal of order awarding benefits to widow of employee.

FACT SUMMARY: Kemp (P) was killed by his own gun while on the job for Evening Star (D) but not engaged with company business.

RULE OF LAW
Decisions by administrative law judges (ALJs) should be upheld on judicial review unless they are irrational or unsupported by substantial evidence on the record.

FACTS: Kemp (P) was employed by Evening Star (D) as a truck driver who delivered newspapers. Between delivery runs there was an hour of time where Kemp (P) was "on the clock" but allowed to do whatever he wanted. On August 10, 1971, Kemp (P) was working on his own car in a garage where the Evening Star (D) mechanics worked during this hour period. A friend began playing with a gun that Kemp (P) kept in his own car and accidentally killed Kemp (P). At a hearing before an ALJ to determine whether Kemp's widow (P) was entitled to compensation under a worker's compensation law, the ALJ found for the widow (P) because Kemp's death occurred in the course of his employment. The Department of Labor's Benefits Review Board affirmed and Evening Star (D) appealed.

ISSUE: Should decisions by administrative law judges be upheld on judicial review unless they are irrational or unsupported by substantial evidence on the record?

HOLDING AND DECISION: (Van Pelt, Sr. J.) Yes. Decisions by administrative law judges should be upheld on judicial review unless they are irrational or unsupported by substantial evidence on the record. The role of judicial review of agency adjudications is not to make independent decisions based on its own evaluation, but rather only to make sure that the decision was not arbitrary and capricious. In the present case, the ALJ expressly found that Kemp (P) was killed during an enforced lull, a condition required by the employment. His presence at the garage was clearly acquiesced in by Evening Star (D) and the ALJ found that the handgun that killed Kemp (P) was sometimes carried by him for protection while delivering newspapers. Given these findings, it cannot be said the activity that Kemp (P) was engaged in was so totally unreasonable to sever the connection between the employee and the employment. Thus, the ALJ's ruling was neither unreasonable nor unsupported by the evidence. Accordingly, it must be affirmed.

DISSENT: (Danaher, Sr. J.) Kemp (P) was not engaged at the time of the injury in an activity of benefit to Evening Star (D). Thus, his death did not arise out of the employment.

ANALYSIS

The dissent pointed out the ALJ seemed to go out of its way to develop a record that would support compensation for the widow (P). The dissent noted that it felt that many of the facts puts on the record were hardly relevant. The majority, on the other hand, seemed more concerned with deferring to the factual record and findings.

Quicknotes

JUDICIAL REVIEW The authority of the courts to review decisions, actions or omissions committed by another agency or branch of government.

Durrah v. Washington Metropolitan Area Transit Authority

Employee (P) v. Employer (D)

760 F.2d 322 (D.C. Cir. 1985).

NATURE OF CASE: Petition for review of denial of benefits claim.

FACT SUMMARY: Durrah (P) was a special police officer for the Washington Metropolitan Area Transit authority (WMATA) (D) and was injured when he left his guard post to buy a soda.

🏛 RULE OF LAW
Employees need not be engaged directly in an activity to the benefit of the employer at the time of an injury to be entitled to workers' compensation.

FACTS: Durrah (P) worked as a special police officer for the WMATA (D) and was posted at a guard post during the overnight shift at a large bus depot. At 4:00 a.m., Durrah (P) left his spot to buy a soda from a vending machine in the employees' lounge on the premises. Durrah (P) was supposed to obtain a substitute to cover his post when he took such a break but failed to do so on this occasion. On returning to his post, Durrah (P) slipped on a staircase and injured his knee. His claim for benefits was denied by an administrative law judge (ALJ) because he had left his post without permission. The Benefits Review Board affirmed the ALJ. Durrah (P) petitioned for review.

ISSUE: Do employees need to be engaged directly in an activity to the benefit of the employer at the time of an injury to be entitled to workers' compensation?

HOLDING AND DECISION: (Ginsburg, J.) No. Employees need not be engaged directly in an activity to the benefit of the employer at the time of an injury to be entitled to workers' compensation. If the "obligations or conditions" of employment create a "zone of danger" out of which an injury arises, then it is covered by workers' compensation. In the present case, it is clear that even if Durrah (P) had found a replacement for his post before leaving to buy the soda, his injury still would have occurred in the same place and in the same manner. The activity of going to the employees' lounge for a break was anticipated and expected by the WMATA (D) and Durrah's (P) violation of a policy did not place him in the path of any additional risks. The injury clearly resulted from an activity that was incidental to the employment. Accordingly, the ALJ's ruling was unsupported by the law and reason behind workers' compensation. Reversed and remanded.

▶ ANALYSIS

The court noted that the violation of policy fell far short of disconnecting Durrah (P) from the service of his employer. The court noted that Durrah (P) could have been disciplined in a separate proceeding. But eliminating his right to compensation was not properly at issue.

■■■

Quicknotes

JUDICIAL REVIEW The authority of the courts to review decisions, actions or omissions committed by another agency or branch of government.

WORKERS' COMPENSATION Fixed awards provided to employees for job-related injuries.

ZONE OF DANGER For purposes of tort liability, the requirement that the plaintiff be within the area of risk of injury from the defendant's conduct in order to recover for negligence.

■■■

Citizens to Preserve Overton Park v. Volpe

Memphis citizens group (P) v. Secretary of Transportation (D)

401 U.S. 402 (1971).

NATURE OF CASE: Suit to set aside administrative action.

FACT SUMMARY: A group of concerned citizens (P) sued the Secretary of Transportation (D), challenging his decision to construct a highway through a public park.

RULE OF LAW
When reviewing administrative decisions which are not supported by formal factual findings, courts should determine the scope of the appropriate official's authority, whether that authority was abused, and whether all applicable procedural requisites have been observed.

FACTS: The Citizens to Preserve Overton Park (Citizens) (P) sued Secretary Volpe (D) of the Department of Transportation. He was accused of violating the Department of Transportation Act and the Federal Aid Highway Act by approving plans to construct a six-lane highway through Overton Park, a popular recreation site. The Citizens (P) assailed Volpe (D) for his failure to state the factual findings upon which he based his decision. The Citizens (P) also alleged Volpe (D) failed to explain why he believed, as required by statute, that no feasible alternative location was available and that all possible steps had been taken to minimize harm to the park. The Citizens (P) sought to have Volpe's (D) decision nullified, but the district court granted the Secretary's (D) motion for summary judgment, basing its ruling on the contents of affidavits which had been prepared specifically in response to the litigation. The court of appeals affirmed, but the United States Supreme Court granted a stay and agreed to review the decisions below. On appeal, the Citizens (P) sought either a de novo review of the Secretary's (D) decision or application of the substantial evidence test.

ISSUE: In reviewing administrative decisions which are unembellished by formal findings of fact, must the court confine its evaluation to the contents of affidavits submitted by the agency at trial?

HOLDING AND DECISION: (Marshall, J.) No. The reviewing court must determine the scope of the duties of the official involved in a decision, whether he abused the authority vested in him, and whether in arriving at his decision he observed all applicable procedural requisites. This case is not one in which the Court may appropriately undertake a de novo review of the Secretary's (D) decision since it presents neither a circumstance in which an adjudicatory proceeding was supported by inadequate fact-finding procedures, nor one in which new issues are raised in a proceeding to enforce nonadjudicatory agency action. Likewise, the substantial evidence test should not be applied to the Secretary's (D) action since his decision was neither the product of a public adjudicatory hearing nor an exercise of the rulemaking function. However, the applicable statutes clearly mandate that the Secretary (D) shall act only when all effective alternative sites for highway construction have been ruled out and, even then, only after taking all available steps to minimize harm to the chosen location. The Citizens (P) were entitled to a review of the Secretary's (D) deliberative processes, which took account of more evidence than that upon which the lower courts based their decisions. Therefore, it is necessary that this case be remanded for reconsideration, based on broader evidence of whether the Secretary (D) observed the required procedure of investigating alternative routes and insuring only minimal harm to Overton Park. In reviewing the Secretary's (D) decision, the district court may undertake the unusual procedure of requiring the administrative officials to reveal the thought processes used to arrive at their conclusions. Although the district court need not adopt this drastic course, it may resort to this procedure as a means of compensating for the lack of any factual findings upon which to predicate its decision. Reversed and remanded.

ANALYSIS

The principal significance of *Citizens to Preserve Overton Park v. Volpe* rests in its concern with insuring that judicial review of administrative decisions will be meaningful. To that end, the *Overton Park* Court countenanced the extraordinary procedure of probing the deliberative processes of administrative officials. It seems clear that the provisions of the Administrative Procedure Act calling for judicial review of administrative determinations cannot be implemented in the absence of a record sufficient to accommodate review, and that when such a record is absent the courts must choose between ordering its compilation or undertaking their own review de novo.

Quicknotes

DE NOVO The review of a lower court decision by an appellate court, which is hearing the case as if it had not been previously heard and as if no judgment had been rendered.

JUDICIAL REVIEW The authority of the courts to review decisions, actions or omissions committed by another agency or branch of government.

U.S.C. § 701 Administrative actions are subject to judicial review.

Yepes-Prado v. U.S. Immigration and Naturalization Service

Immigrant (P) v. Government agency (D)

10 F.3d 1363 (9th Cir. 1993).

NATURE OF CASE: Petition for review of deportation order.

FACT SUMMARY: Yepes-Prado (P) was ordered deported based on a drug conviction, but the Board of Immigration Appeals (BIA) (D) failed to explain why it ignored or discounted factors in Yepes-Prado's (P) favor.

🏛 RULE OF LAW
Agencies must offer reasoned explanations for their rulings, even if the ruling appears reasonable and plausible.

FACTS: Yepes-Prado (P) was admitted to the United States in 1974 as a lawful permanent resident. Over ten years later, he was convicted of possession of heroin with intent to distribute and sentenced to one year in jail. On the basis of this conviction, the INS (D) ordered Yepes-Prado (P) to show cause why he should not be deported. Yepes-Prado (P) conceded that he was eligible for deportation, but sought a discretionary waiver. An immigration judge found several equities weighed in his favor, but denied the waiver. The BIA (D) found that he had "outstanding equities" but nonetheless affirmed the immigration judge's decision. Yepes-Prado (P) petitioned for review.

ISSUE: Must agencies offer reasoned explanations for their rulings, even if the ruling appears reasonable and plausible?

HOLDING AND DECISION: (Reinhardt, J.) Yes. Agencies must offer reasoned explanations for their rulings, even if the ruling appears reasonable and plausible. Discretionary relief from deportation is available to lawful permanent residents who meet a seven-year residency requirement. The factors that are relevant to this discretionary determination include family ties, hardship to the petitioner, service in the armed forces, employment history, value and service to the community, proof of rehabilitation if a criminal record exists, and evidence of the resident's good character. These are to be weighed against the underlying circumstances of the deportation, the seriousness of any criminal record, and the bad character of the resident. The BIA (D) must indicate how it weighed the factors and arrived at its conclusion. While it has considerable flexibility to make decisions, it cannot rule capriciously. This discretion is abused if conclusions are reached arbitrarily. In the present case, the immigration judge and the BIA (D) failed to offer an explanation of why the only adverse factor, Yepes-Prado's (P) drug conviction, outweighed all the other equities in his favor. Accordingly, the decision must be vacated.

▶ ANALYSIS

Apparently, the deportation decision at issue would have been upheld if the BIA (D) had simply given any reasonable explanation. The court equated providing no reason with being arbitrary. The problem was compounded in this case because there was a clear indication that many factors did favor a deportation waiver.

Quicknotes

DISCRETION The authority conferred upon a public official to act reasonably in accordance with his own judgment under certain circumstances.

Davila-Bardales v. Immigration and Naturalization Service

Immigrant (P) v. Government agency (D)

27 F.3d 1 (1st Cir. 1994).

NATURE OF CASE: Petition to review deportation order.

FACT SUMMARY: Davila-Bardales (P), 15 years old, admitted entering the United States illegally but was unrepresented while making the admission.

🏛 RULE OF LAW
Agencies are prohibited from adopting inconsistent policies that result in conflicting lines of precedent governing identical situations.

FACTS: In July 1989, Davila-Bardales (P), then 15 years old, entered the United States illegally. Deportation hearings were instituted by the Immigration and Naturalization Service (INS) (D) before an immigration judge (IJ). INS (D) presented a form on which Davila-Bardales (P) admitted illegal entry into the country. The IJ ordered that Davila-Bardales (P) be deported, but he appealed on the ground that INS (D) regulations prohibit the use of admissions by a person under sixteen who is not represented or accompanied by a parent or guardian.

ISSUE: Are agencies prohibited from adopting inconsistent policies that result in conflicting lines of precedent governing identical situations?

HOLDING AND DECISION: (Selya, J.) Yes. Agencies are prohibited from adopting inconsistent policies that result in conflicting lines of precedent governing identical situations. The purpose of this doctrine is to prevent agencies from "significantly changing [its] policies without conscious awareness of, and consideration of the need for, change." In the present case, there is a long record of cases from the BIA showing that if the INS (D) seeks to use an admission form against a juvenile, the circumstances surrounding the form must be carefully examined. In Davila-Bardales's (P) case, the INS (D) is now insisting that the form is enough since it memorializes an interview that took place with a Border Patrol officer. While it is too much to expect that all decisions made by an agency will be identical, the position taken by the INS (D) and BIA here, that the admission form alone is enough to justify deportation, is completely at odds with its interpretation in other cases, that the circumstances behind an interview with an unrepresented juvenile are relevant. Therefore, the petition for review is granted and the case is remanded for proceedings consistent with this opinion.

▶ ANALYSIS

The INS (D) was distinguishing between admissions by juveniles regarding deportability during proceedings and admissions made at other times. That was their basis for introducing the alleged admission to the officer. But as the court noted, the BIA normally found such use suspect without more context.

■==■

Quicknotes

JUDICIAL REVIEW The authority of the courts to review decisions, actions or omissions committed by another agency or branch of government.

■==■

Choice of Procedures and Nonlegislative Rules

Quick Reference Rules of Law

National Labor Relations Board v. Bell Aerospace Company Division of Textron Inc.

Government agency (D) v. Aerospace products manufacturer (P)

416 U.S. 267 (1974).

NATURE OF CASE: Appeal from denial of enforcement of an agency order.

FACT SUMMARY: Bell (P) opposed a representation election on the grounds that its buyers were "managerial employees" and were thus not covered by the National Labor Relations Act or entitled to elect union representation.

> ## 🏛 RULE OF LAW
> The National Labor Relations Board (NLRB) is not precluded from announcing new principles in an adjudicative proceeding.

FACTS: Bell Aerospace (P), which operated a plant engaging in research and development in the design and fabrication of aerospace products, opposed the petition of its employee buyers in the purchasing and procurement department for an election to decide whether a union would be certified as the buyers' bargaining representative. Bell (P) contended that the buyers were "managerial employees" and were not covered by the National Labor Relations Act (NLRA), and therefore, were not entitled to the NLRA's protections. The NLRB (D), after a representation hearing, issued an order holding that the buyers did constitute an appropriate unit for the purpose of collective bargaining and directed an election. An election was held and the union was certified by the NLRB (D) as the exclusive bargaining representative for Bell's (P) buyers. Bell (P), encouraged by an Eighth Circuit decision holding that "managerial employees" were not covered by the NLRA, moved the NLRB (D) for reconsideration of its order. The NLRB (D) denied the motion. Bell (P) then petitioned for review of the NLRB's (D) order, and the NLRB (D) cross-petitioned for enforcement. The Second Circuit Court of Appeals denied enforcement and the NLRB (D) appealed.

ISSUE: Is the NLRB precluded from announcing new principles in an adjudicative proceeding?

HOLDING AND DECISION: (Powell, J.) No. The NLRB (D) is not precluded from announcing new principles in an adjudicative proceeding; the choice between rulemaking and adjudication lies within the NLRB's (D) discretion in the first instance. In this case, there is ample indication that adjudication is especially appropriate. The duties of buyers vary widely depending on the company or industry. It is doubtful whether any generalized standard could be framed that would have more than marginal utility. The NLRB (D) thus has reason to proceed with caution, developing its standards in a case-by-case manner with attention to the specific character of the buyer's authority and duties in each company. The NLRB's (D) decision that adjudication best serves this purpose is entitled to great weight, and the agency has discretion to decide that the adjudicative procedures in this case may also produce the relevant information necessary for a mature and fair consideration of the issues. Affirmed in part, reversed in part, and remanded.

▶ ANALYSIS

When the Taft-Hartley Act of 1947 was passed, both the U.S. Senate and the House of Representatives voiced concern over the NLRB's (D) broad reading of the term "employee" which then included those clearly within the managerial hierarchy. The Senate noted that unionization of supervisors had hurt productivity, increased the accident rate, upset the balance of power in collective bargaining, and tended to blur the lines between management and labor. The House echoed the concern for reduction of industrial output and noted that unionization of supervisors had deprived employers of the loyal representatives to which they were entitled.

■=■

Quicknotes

MANAGERIAL EMPLOYEE An employee whose duties involve the administration of the business's affairs or the supervising of the work of other employees.

SUPERVISORY EMPLOYEE An employee authorized to implement his independent judgment in the management, direction and discipline of other employees.

TAFT-HARTLEY ACT An amendment to the National Labor Relations Act, imposing limitations on unions and safeguarding the rights of employers.

■=■

Retail, Wholesale and Department Store Union v. National Labor Relations Board

Union (D) v. Government agency (P)

466 F.2d 380 (D.C. Cir. 1972).

NATURE OF CASE: Appeal from unfair labor practice decision.

FACT SUMMARY: Coca-Cola (D) complained that a new rule from the National Labor Relations Board (NLRB) (P) about replacing striking workers should not be applied retroactively.

▥ RULE OF LAW
The retroactive application of a new agency rule depends upon a balancing of the danger of reaching a result contrary to law against the negative effect of the retroactive application.

FACTS: Coca-Cola (D) failed to hire workers who were permanently replaced during a strike. At the time, it was a well-settled rule with the NLRB (P) that when an employer replaced a striker, there was no obligation to hire back that employee. However, the NLRB (P) overturned this rule and held that former strikers were entitled to offers of reinstatement when the replacements vacated their positions. The NLRB (P) found that Coca-Cola (D) violated this new rule and imposed backpay liability on the company, although the underlying events occurred before the new rule was adopted. Coca-Cola (D) appealed on the basis of this retroactive application of the new rule.

ISSUE: Does the retroactive application of a new agency rule depend upon a balancing of the danger of reaching a result contrary to law against the negative effect of the retroactive application?

HOLDING AND DECISION: (McGowan, J.) Yes. The retroactive application of a new agency rule depends upon a balancing of the danger of reaching a result contrary to law against the negative effect of the retroactive application. The retroactive application of a new agency rule depends on factors such as whether the case is one of first impression. The Administrative Procedure Act authorizes agencies to conduct formal rule making so as to have rules that have prospective application. But many agencies fashion new rules and standards on a case-by-case basis through adjudications. Whether a new rule should be applied retroactively depends on the equities of the particular case, and courts may review this decision without deference to the agency. Among the key considerations are whether the case is one of first impression, whether the new rule is an abrupt departure from the old practice, the extent of reliance on the old rule, and the degree of burden the new rule imposes. The present case involving Coca-Cola (D) is not one of first impression, because the

rule was changed in a prior case. Therefore, the reasons for applying it retroactively in the first impression case may not be present in the instant case. Looking at the equities in this case, it appears that Coca-Cola (D) tried to conform its conduct to the well-established and accepted old rule and the burden of imposing the new standard is considerable. Accordingly, it is highly unfair to punish Coca-Cola (D) for failing to conform to a standard subsequently adopted. Therefore, enforcement of the NLRB (P) order is denied.

▶ ANALYSIS

The court noted that Supreme Court precedent in this area did not establish any bright line guidelines. Agencies can choose not to apply a rule retroactively after it has been adopted in one case. On the other hand, reviewing courts may refuse to enforce retroactive agency orders.

■━■

Quicknotes

BALANCING TEST Court's balancing of an individual's constitutional rights against the state's right to protect its citizens.

RETROACTIVE APPLICATION Having an effect on something that occurred in the past.

■━■

General Electric Company v. U.S. Environmental Protection Agency

Alleged polluter (D) v. Government agency (P)

53 F.3d 1324 (D.C. Cir. 1995).

NATURE OF CASE: Appeal from fine for illegal polluting.

FACT SUMMARY: General Electric (D) was fined for disposing of toxic materials in a manner that the Environmental Protection Agency (EPA) (P) believed was impermissible under its interpretation of the regulations.

🏛 RULE OF LAW
Agencies may not impose liability where a regulation is not sufficiently clear to provide fair notice to the affected party.

FACTS: General Electric (D) had a service shop in Georgia that decommissioned large electric transformers. Inside the transformers were polychlorinated bipehenyls (PCB), a dangerous pollutant that had to be disposed of in compliance with EPA (P) regulations. Essentially, the regulations stated that the PCBs had to be incinerated. General Electric (D) began a process that involved an intermediary step of recycling and distillation before incineration. The EPA (P) charged the company with violating the regulations and assessed a $25,000 fine. An administrative law judge (ALJ) and the Environmental Appeals Board upheld the fine and General Electric (D) petitioned for review.

ISSUE: May agencies impose liability where a regulation is not sufficiently clear to provide fair notice to the affected party?

HOLDING AND DECISION: (Tatel, J.) No. Agencies may not impose liability where a regulation is not sufficiently clear to provide fair notice to the affected party. Ordinarily, an agency's interpretation of its regulations is entitled to a high level of deference. However, it may be overturned if it is plainly wrong. Additionally, an order to comply with an interpretation carries more weight than a decision that a violation has occurred where an interpretation has not been expressly made before. Due process requires that parties receive fair notice before being deprived of property. This fair notice rule applies to both criminal and civil liability. An agency's pre-enforcement efforts to bring about compliance often provide adequate notice. If a regulated party could have identified the standards it was expected to have conformed to through regulations and other agency statements, then that is fair notice. In the instant case, the regulations at issue provide no notice whatsoever with regard to pre-disposal processes such as distillation. It certainly cannot be said that a reasonable person would know that distillation was to be considered a means of disposal. While the EPA (P) is entitled to conclude

that it is, given the area of expertise, it does stray from a common understanding of the terms and would be unexpected without an express statement. Accordingly, General Electric (D) had no fair warning that the EPA (P) would make such an interpretation and the fine must be vacated.

▶ ANALYSIS

The court left the EPA (P) with room to apply its interpretation in future cases. But the court clearly found that the interpretation barring General Electric's (D) method to be unnatural given the language of the prior regulations. Thus, it had no difficulty in finding that there was no fair prior warning and notice.

■■■

Quicknotes

DUE PROCESS The constitutional mandate requiring the courts to protect and enforce individuals' rights and liberties consistent with prevailing principles of fairness and justice and prohibiting the federal and state governments from such activities that deprive its citizens of a life, liberty or property interest.

NOTICE Communication of information to a person by an authorized person or an otherwise proper source.

NOTICE AND COMMENT RULEMAKING Informal rulemaking.

■■■

American Hospital Association v. Bowen

Trade organization (P) v. Government agency (D)

834 F.2d 1037 (D.C. Cir. 1987).

NATURE OF CASE: Appeal from declaration that documents issued by the Department of Health and Human Services (HHS) (D) were invalid.

FACT SUMMARY: The American Hospital Association (AHA) (P) claimed that HHS (D) had improperly issued rules and regulations by not first undertaking the notice and comment rulemaking prescribed by the Administrative Procedure Act (APA) § 553.

🏛 RULE OF LAW
The requirement of notice and an opportunity for comment does not apply to general statements of policy.

FACTS: When HHS (D) implemented the system of peer review of Medicare, it issued many documents without first undertaking the notice and comment rulemaking prescribed by the APA § 553. When the AHA (P) claimed a document soliciting proposed contracts from entities seeking to become PROs contained legislative rules, the district court held those parts of the Request for Proposals (RFP) to be invalid. HHS (D) appealed, claiming the RFP was a nonbinding statement of policy and was therefore exempt from provisions of the APA.

ISSUE: Does the requirement of notice and an opportunity for comment apply to general statements of policy?

HOLDING AND DECISION: (Wald, C.J.) No. The requirement of notice and an opportunity for comment does not apply to general statements of policy. A general statement of policy does not establish a "binding norm" and leaves the agency free to exercise its discretion. Here the RFP merely established talking points and did not bind either the agency or the peer review organization to which it was sent. The RFP had no present effect and it did not prevent future exercises of agency discretion. The district court wrongly invalidated those parts of the RFP it deemed legislative in character. Reversed.

▶ ANALYSIS

The court contrasted "substantive rules" with "general statements of policy." It found that substantive rules establish standards of conduct that have the force of law. General statements of policy, on the other hand, only announce what the agency seeks to establish as policy.

■■■■

American Mining Congress v. Mine Safety & Health Administration

Industry organization (P) v. Federal agency (D)

995 F.2d 1106 (D.C. Cir. 1993).

NATURE OF CASE: Petition for review of rules promulgated by federal agency.

FACT SUMMARY: The American Mining Congress (AMC) (P) alleged that the Mine Safety and Health Administration (MSHA) (D) should have followed requirements for notice and comment prior to issuing Program Policy Letters regarding the use of x-ray results to diagnose lung disease.

RULE OF LAW
Substantive rules have the force of law if Congress delegated legislative power to the agency and the agency intended to exercise that power in promulgating the rules.

FACTS: Under relevant rules adopted via notice and comment by the MSHA (D), mine operators are required to report within ten days all accidents, occupational injuries and occupational illnesses that occur at a mine. The MSHA (D), in response to inquiries from mine operators about whether certain x-ray results had to be reported as diagnoses (P), issued three Program Policy Letters (PPLs) regarding when x-ray results constituted a "diagnosis" without following the notice and comment procedures of the Administrative Procedure Act (APA) § 553. The AMC (P) petitioned for judicial review of the MSHA's (D) decision to act without notice and comment in issuing the PPLs. The MSHA (D) claimed that the PPLs were interpretive, not substantive, rules and therefore were exempt from the notice and comment requirements under the APA § 553(b)(3)(A).

ISSUE: Do substantive rules have the force of law if Congress delegated legislative power to the agency and the agency intended to exercise that power in promulgating the rules?

HOLDING AND DECISION: (Williams, J.) Yes. Substantive rules have the force of law if Congress delegated legislative power to the agency and the agency intended to exercise that power in promulgating the rules. Only substantive rules are subject to the notice and comment requirements. In determining whether a purported interpretive rule has legal effect, the relevant inquiry is: (1) whether in the absence of the rule there would not be an adequate legislative basis for enforcement action or other agency action; (2) whether the rule has been published in the Code of Federal Regulations; (3) whether the agency expressly invoked its general legislative authority; or (4) whether the rule amends a prior legislative rule. If the answer to any of these inquiries is yes, the rule is legislative and not interpretive. Here the PPLs were interpretive rules, since the agency did not purport to act legislatively. Petitions denied.

▶ ANALYSIS

The distinction between those agency pronouncements subject to notice and comment requirements and those that are exempt is described by the court as "enshrouded in considerable smog." The court reviewed three types of agency rules. Substantive rules are pronouncements of law. Interpretative rules and general statements of policy are interpretive only and do not amend legislative rules.

Quicknotes

ADMINISTRATIVE PROCEDURE ACT Provides the standard for judicial review of agency rules.

INTERPRETIVE RULE A rule issued by an administrative agency for the purpose of explaining or interpreting a statute.

NOTICE AND COMMENT RULEMAKING Informal rulemaking.

RULEMAKING The promulgation of a rule governing a particular activity by an administrative agency, acting within the scope of its power pursuant to statute.

Metropolitan School District v. Davila

Local school district (P) v. Department of Education (D)

969 F.2d 485 (7th Cir. 1992).

NATURE OF CASE: Appeal from summary judgment in action challenging agency regulation.

FACT SUMMARY: A Michigan school district (P) claimed that a U.S. Department of Education (Department) (D) regulation should have been subject to notice and comment requirements.

🏛 RULE OF LAW
Interpretive rules are statements as to what an administrative officer thinks a statute or regulation means and are not subject to notice and comment requirements.

FACTS: Part B of the Individuals with Disabilities Act provides federal funding to states to support the education of disabled children. In order to qualify for the funds, a state must establish a policy of assuring a free education to all disabled children. The Office of Special Education and Rehabilitative Services (OSERS) administers the Act. Davila (D), an administrator for OSERS, sent a letter regarding the policy for states providing educational services to disabled children who are expelled. This position was not made subject to notice and comment requirements. The Metropolitan School District (P) sued the Department (D) on behalf of all districts, asserting that the position in Davila's (D) letter imposed a large financial burden and should have been subject to notice and public comment. Both parties moved for summary judgment. The district court granted Metropolitan's (P) motion and the Department (D) appealed.

ISSUE: Are interpretive rules statements as to what an administrative officer thinks a statute or regulation means and not subject to notice and comment requirements?

HOLDING AND DECISION: (Bauer, C.J.) Yes. Interpretive rules are statements as to what an administrative officer thinks a statute or regulation means and are not subject to notice and comment requirements. The Administrative Procedure Act does not require that administrative agencies follow notice and comment procedures in all situations. Interpretive rules and general statements of policy are exempt from this process. The starting point in determining whether a rule is interpretive is the agency's characterization of the rule. An interpretive rule simply states what the agency thinks the underlying statute means and reminds affected parties of existing duties. On the other hand, substantive or legislative rules create new duties, have the force and effect of law, and have effects independent of the statute. Interpretative rules, although entitled to deference, do not bind reviewing courts. In the

present case, the letter from Davila (D) purports to be interpretative and satisfies the general test. It relies upon the language of the statute and legislative history. Accordingly, it was not subject to notice and comment. Reversed and remanded.

▶ ANALYSIS

The distinction between interpretative and legislative rules is a very blurry one, as even many courts have remarked. For a time, some courts used a "substantial impact" test to make the distinction. But this test has fallen out of favor.

Quicknotes

INTERPRETIVE RULES A rule issued by an administrative agency for the purpose of explaining or interpreting a statute.

LEGISLATIVE RULE The promulgation of a rule by an administrative agency, acting within the scope of its power pursuant to statute, enacting a law governing a particular activity.

SUMMARY JUDGMENT Judgment rendered by a court in response to a motion by one of the parties, claiming that the lack of a question of material fact in respect to an issue warrants disposition of the issue without consideration by the jury.

Alaska Professional Hunters Association, Inc. v. Federal Aviation Administration

Professional organization (P) v. Government agency (D)

177 F.3d 1030 (D.C. Cir. 1999).

NATURE OF CASE: Petition for judicial review of agency rule.

FACT SUMMARY: When the Federal Aviation Administration (FAA) (D) published a notice to operators aimed at Alaskan hunting and fishing guides who pilot light aircraft, the Alaska Professional Hunters Association (APHA) (P) claimed the FAA (D) should have proceeded by way of notice and comment rule making instead.

🏛 RULE OF LAW
Where an agency has given its regulation a definitive interpretation, and later significantly revises that interpretation, the agency has in effect amended its rule, and must proceed by way of notice and comment rulemaking.

FACTS: The FAA (D) had, since 1963, consistently advised fishing and hunting guides who pilot light planes in Alaska that they were not governed by regulations dealing with commercial pilots. In 1998 the FAA (D) published a notice to operators in the Federal Register requiring the Alaska pilots to abide by FAA (D) regulations applicable to commercial air operations. APHA (P) claimed that § 553 of the Administrative Procedure Act required notice and comment rule making instead of official publication of the new rule. The FAA (D) claimed that the Alaska Region's earlier advice to pilots stemmed from a misreading of case precedent and did not represent the official position of the agency (D).

ISSUE: Where an agency has given its regulation a definitive interpretation, and later significantly revises that interpretation, has the agency in effect amended its rule, and must it proceed by way of notice and comment rule making?

HOLDING AND DECISION: (Randolph, J.) Yes. Where an agency has given its regulation a definitive interpretation, and later significantly revises that interpretation, the agency has in effect amended its rule, and must proceed by way of notice and comment rule making. Alaskan guide pilots and lodge operators (P) relied on the advice the FAA (D) gave them. That advice had become an authoritative departmental interpretation. If the FAA (D) wishes to apply new regulations to the Alaskan pilots (P), it must give them an opportunity to comment before doing so. The notice to operators was published without notice and comment and was therefore invalid. So ordered.

▶ ANALYSIS
Fishing and hunting are big business in Alaska. The APHA (P) had submitted a petition for rulemaking regarding licensing requirements. The FAA (D) never responded to that petition.

■=■

Quicknotes
ADMINISTRATIVE PROCEDURE ACT Provides the standard for judicial review of agency rules.

NOTICE AND COMMENT RULEMAKING Informal rulemaking.

RULEMAKING The promulgation of a rule governing a particular activity by an administrative agency, acting within the scope of its power pursuant to statute.

■=■

MetWest, Inc. v. Secretary of Labor

Employer (P) v. Secretary of Labor (D)

550 F.3d 506 (D.C. Cir. 2009).

NATURE OF CASE: Petition for judicial review of agency regulation.

FACT SUMMARY: Following development of "single-use" blood tube holders, and upon issuance of a guidance document by the Occupational Safety and Health Administration (OSHA) (D) stating that use of reusable blood tube holders violated initial OSHA (D) regulations, OSHA (D) began enforcement of its regulations applicable to the removal of contaminated needles by phlebotomists. Thereafter, OSHA (D) issued a citation to MetWest, Inc. (P), an operator of clinical testing facilities, for supplying its phlebotomists with reusable blood tube holders.

> ### 🏛 RULE OF LAW
> When an agency has never established an authoritative interpretation of its regulation on which an employer justifiably relied to its detriment, the agency is not required to engage in notice and comment rulemaking before commencing enforcement of its regulation.

FACTS: In 1991, OSHA (D) promulgated safety standards related to the needle removal methods of phlebotomists. OSHA (D) determined that the "one-handed" needle removal method developed by medical suppliers, by which the contaminated needle was released into a safe container, was less likely to result in needlesticks than the "two-handed" removal technique. The 1991 regulations provided that contaminated needles should not be removed unless there existed no feasible alternative, or the procedure was medically necessary. If an exception were met, the regulations required that the "one-handed" removal technique be used. But by 2003, and the advent of "single-use" blood tube holders, OSHA (D) issued a guidance document stating that use of "one-handed" or reusable blood tube holders likely violated its 1991 regulations. OSHA (D) began enforcement of its regulations and, ultimately, issued a citation to MetWest, Inc. (P) for supplying its phlebotomists with reusable holders. Thereafter, an administrative law judge and the OSHA Review Commission upheld the citation, and MetWest (P) filed a petition for judicial review.

ISSUE: When an agency has never established an authoritative interpretation of its regulation on which an employer justifiably relied to its detriment, must the agency engage in notice and comment rulemaking before commencing enforcement of its regulation?

HOLDING AND DECISION: (Randolph, J.) No. When an agency has never established an authoritative interpretation of its regulation on which an employer justifiably

relied to its detriment, the agency is not required to engage in notice and comment rulemaking before commencing enforcement of its regulation. The record clearly demonstrates that the 1991 OSHA (D) regulations permitted only qualified use of "one-handed" or reusable blood tube holders. MetWest (P) contention that OSHA (D) interpreted its 1991 regulations to permit the removal of needles from reusable blood tube holders in all circumstances is without merit. As such, MetWest's (P) argument that the 2003 OSHA (D) guidance document effectively amended its rule without notice and comment rulemaking required by the Administrative Procedure Act (APA) is equally unfounded. Inasmuch as MetWest (P) itself misread the 1991 OSHA (D) regulations, MetWest (P) erred in its reliance on said regulations. And because the 2003 guidance document—which reiterates OSHA's (D) long-standing policy against manual removal of needles from blood tube holders—can reasonably be interpreted as consistent with the 1991 regulations, the guidance document does not usurp the role of notice and comment rulemaking. Affirmed.

▶ ANALYSIS

The court in *MetWest* distinguished the instant circumstances from those of *Alaska Professional Hunters Association, Inc. v. Federal Aviation Administration*, 177 F.3d 1030 (D.C. Cir. 1999). Specifically, the *MetWest* court explained that, unlike the instant matter, the relevant agency in *Alaska Professional Hunters* engaged in the practice of advising affected entities over a thirty year period, thereby establishing an authoritative departmental interpretation that could not be changed without notice and comment. In *Alaska Professional Hunters*, the affected parties substantially and justifiably relied on authoritative interpretation of that agency's regulations. In *MetWest*, however, the petitioner's practices stemmed not from reliance on the authoritative interpretation of OSHA, but on its own misreading of OSHA regulations and, seemingly, on its reluctance to purchase the higher cost "single-use" blood tube holders.

Quicknotes

NOTICE AND COMMENT RULEMAKING Informal rulemaking.

Heckler v. Community Health Services

Government agency (D) v. Medicare provider (P)

467 U.S. 51 (1984).

NATURE OF CASE: Review of reversal of administrative determination.

FACT SUMMARY: Community Health Services (CHS) (P) claimed that the Department of Health and Human Services (HHS) (D) was estopped from demanding repayment of federal funds CHS (P) had improperly received.

🏛 RULE OF LAW
A party claiming an estoppel must have relied on the adversary's conduct in such a manner as to change his position for the worse, and the reliance must have been reasonable under the circumstances.

FACTS: CHS (P) had received government reimbursement for home health care services it had provided to patients under the Medicare program. In seeking reimbursement, CHS (P) had relied on oral statements made by an insurance company that had acted as a fiscal intermediary in the proceedings. HHS (D) later determined that the expenses were not reimbursable under Medicare, and notified the insurance company who made a formal demand on CHS (P) for repayment. CHS (P) obtained a temporary injunction pending the outcome of an administrative review. The district court affirmed the administrative determination that HHS (D) should not have paid CHS (P). The court of appeals reversed, holding that the government may be estopped due to the affirmative misconduct of the government employees and the insurance company's erroneous advice. HHS (D) appealed, asserting that an estoppel may not run against the government.

ISSUE: Must a party claiming an estoppel have relied on the adversary's conduct in such a manner as to change his position for the worse, and must the reliance have been reasonable under the circumstances?

HOLDING AND DECISION: (Stevens, J.) Yes. A party claiming an estoppel must have relied on the adversary's conduct in such a manner as to change his position for the worse, and the reliance must have been reasonable under the circumstances. Here CHS (P) did not lose any rights in reliance on HHS's (D) misconduct. CHS (P) was merely induced to do something that could be corrected later. It was not reasonable for CHS (P) to rely on oral advice from the insurance company when it knew that fiscal intermediaries did not resolve policy questions. Reversed and remanded.

▶ ANALYSIS

The court found that the elements of estoppel had not been established. Although stopping short of holding that the government may never be estopped, the court here found that the burden was heavier when applied to the government. The interest of the citizenry as a whole in obedience to the rule of law is undermined when the government is unable to enforce the law because the conduct of its agents gave rise to an estoppel.

Quicknotes

AGENT An individual who has the authority to act on behalf of another.

DETRIMENTAL RELIANCE Action by one party, resulting in loss, that is based on the conduct or promises of another.

EQUITABLE ESTOPPEL A doctrine that precludes a person from asserting a right to which he or she was entitled due to his or her action, conduct or failing to act, causing another party to justifiably rely on such conduct to his or her detriment.

Office of Personnel Management v. Richmond

Human resources office (D) v. Navy welder (P)

496 U.S. 414 (1990).

NATURE OF CASE: Appeal from an award of damages for loss of disability annuity.

FACT SUMMARY: Richmond (P) retired from his job as a welder after the Office of Personnel Management (OPM) (D) approved his application for a disability annuity due to his impaired eyesight.

🏛 RULE OF LAW
No money shall be drawn from the Treasury but in consequence of appropriations made by law.

FACTS: As a welder for the Navy, Richmond's (P) impaired eyesight qualified him for a disability annuity under 5 U.S.C. § 8337(d). The statute, however, provided that disability payments would end if the retiree earned an amount fairly comparable to the current rate of pay of the position occupied at the time of retirement. The original measuring period for restoration of earning capacity was two years, but after 1982, the measuring period was changed to one year. Upon retirement, Richmond (P) took a part-time job. Concerned about losing his eligibility if he made too much money, Richmond (P) twice consulted the Navy's Civilian Personnel Department and was given advice based on the former two-year eligibility rule. Richmond (P) then worked overtime in the erroneous belief his eligibility would not be affected, and OPM (D) suspended his disability annuity for six months. The court of appeals ruled that estoppel was properly applied against the federal government and ordered the suspended payments restored to Richmond (P). This appeal by OPM (D) followed.

ISSUE: Will estoppel against the government lie where payment is requested from the Treasury without appropriations made by law?

HOLDING AND DECISION: (Kennedy, J.) No. No money shall be drawn from the Treasury, but in consequence of appropriations made by law (Appropriation Clause of the Constitution, Art. I, § 9, cl. 7). Judicial use of the equitable doctrine of estoppel cannot grant a money remedy that Congress has not authorized. The general purpose of the clause is to prevent fraud and corruption. But the direct purpose relevant to this case is to assure that public funds will be spent according to the letter of the difficult judgments reached by Congress as to the common good, and not according to the individual favor of government agents or the individual pleas of litigants. Estoppel claims based on real or imagined claims of misinformation by disgruntled citizens would impose an unpredictable drain on the public. An assertion of estoppel against the government by a claimant seeking public funds has never been upheld, for courts cannot estop the Constitution. Reversed.

▶ ANALYSIS

Because of dicta in the Court's more recent cases, the courts of appeals had begun to apply equitable estoppel against the government. In *Richmond*, the Court declared it was not deciding whether an estoppel claim could ever succeed against the government. However, it also declared that it has reversed every finding of estoppel that it has reviewed.

■=■

Quicknotes

ANNUITY The payment or right to receive payment of a fixed sum periodically, for a specified time period.

APPROPRIATION The act of making something one's own or making use of something to serve one own's interest.

ESTOPPEL An equitable doctrine precluding a party from asserting a right to the detriment of another who justifiably relied on the conduct.

■=■

Appeal of Eno (New Hampshire Department of Employment Security)

Applicant for benefits (P) v. State agency (D)

N.H. Sup. Ct., 126 N.H. 650, 495 A.2d 1277 (1985).

NATURE OF CASE: Appeal from denial of unemployment benefits.

FACT SUMMARY: Eno (P) was denied unemployment benefits because the New Hampshire Department of Employment Security (Department) (D) claimed that she had made insufficient efforts to find a job.

🏛 RULE OF LAW
Agencies deny due process when they apply different standards after causing persons to rely on lesser standards.

FACTS: Eno (P) was laid off from her job in February. In March, she applied for unemployment benefits from the Department (D). She was given a pamphlet that stated the conditions of eligibility including a provision for seeking employment. When she appeared to make weekly applications, Eno (P) was asked if she was seeking employment and answered affirmatively. There was no further explanation or inquiry. Eno (P) had been answering want ads by telephone and sending out resumes, but she did not make personal visits to possible employers. The Department (D) later determined that she was ineligible for benefits since she had made insufficient efforts to obtain other employment. Eno (P) appealed.

ISSUE: Do agencies deny due process when they apply different standards after causing persons to rely on lesser standards?

HOLDING AND DECISION: (Souter, J.) Yes. Agencies deny due process when they apply different standards after causing persons to rely on lesser standards. A claim of entitlement to unemployment compensation is a claim to a property interest that is subject to due process guarantees. Thus, the Department (D) may not deny a claim by a procedure that is fundamentally unfair. In the present case, it appears that Eno (P) did not comply with the statutory standard for eligibility because she did not make personal visits to potential employers. However, the Department's (D) contacts with Eno (P) indicated that different standards were applicable. When asked whether she was seeking employment, she answered truthfully that she had. Since these answers were accepted without further inquiry, it left Eno (P) with the natural impression that she had satisfied the eligibility conditions. It also signaled to Eno (P) that she should continue on that course. If she had been told that it was insufficient, she could have made a greater effort the following week. Since Eno (P) acted in reliance on the Department's (D) apparent standards, it was unfair to deny her benefits based on more exacting conditions. Reversed.

▌ ANALYSIS

The court also noted that the Department (D) revised its pamphlets after this case. The pamphlet now states that personal visits to employers are expected. The court sympathized with the Department's (D) indication that it was understaffed at the time Eno (P) was seeking benefits, but found that it didn't justify the denial of benefits.

■═■

Quicknotes

DUE PROCESS The constitutional mandate requiring the courts to protect and enforce individuals' rights and liberties consistent with prevailing principles of fairness and justice and prohibiting the federal and state governments from such activities that deprive its citizens of a life, liberty or property interest.

■═■

United States v. Mead Corporation

Federal government (P) v. Corporation (D)

533 U.S. 218 (2001).

NATURE OF CASE: Appeal in a tariff assessment action.

FACT SUMMARY: Mead Corporation (Mead) (D) was assessed a tariff on its day planners, and it protested to the United States Custom Service (Customs Service). The Customs Service issued a ruling letter explaining why Mead (D) was assessed a tariff.

🏛 RULE OF LAW
There is a presumption that agency discretion does not exist unless the statute, expressly or impliedly, says so. Classification rulings, therefore, are best treated as interpretations contained in policy statements, agency manuals, and enforcement guidelines and do not require a *Chevron*-type deference; under *Skidmore*, however, the ruling is eligible to claim respect according to its persuasiveness.

FACTS: Mead (D) imports "day planners." [The tariff schedule in regard to day planners is regulated by the Harmonized Tariff Schedule of the United States (the Schedule), which subjects day planners to a tariff of 4.0 percent.] Until 1993, when the Customs Service Headquarters issued a "ruling letter" classifying Mead's day planners as "Diaries . . . bound," day planners had been duty-free. In response to Mead's protest of the reclassification, Customs Service Headquarters issued a new letter, never published, and discussed the two definitions of diary from the dictionary; it concluded that the definition reflects commercial usage. As for the definition of "bound," Customs Service Headquarters concluded that "bound" meant "reinforcements or fittings of metal, plastics, etc." In the Schedule, Congress had conferred upon the Customs Service the power to issue regulations to establish procedures for the issuance of binding ruling prior to the entry of the merchandise concerned and to disseminate information necessary to secure uniformity. A ruling letter represents the official position of the Customs Service with respect to a particular transaction or issue described therein. Since ruling letters respond to transactions of the moment, they are not subject to notice and comment before being issued, and although they may be published, they need only be made available for public inspection. In addition, the ruling letter has no bearing on nonparties to the transaction at issue. Forty-six different Customs Service offices issue 10,000-15,000 ruling letters per year. The court of appeals ruled that the Customs Service ruling letters do not fall within *Chevron*, 467 U.S. 837 (1984).

ISSUE: Does a tariff classification ruling by the United States Customs Service deserve judicial deference?

HOLDING AND DECISION: (Souter, J.) No. A tariff classification has no claim to judicial deference under *Chevron* because there is no indication that Congress intended such a ruling to carry the force of law; under *Skidmore*, 323 U.S. 134 (1944), however, the ruling is eligible to claim respect according to its persuasiveness. On the face of the statute, there is no congressional intent to give the Custom Service's classification rulings the force of law. In addition, there is in the agency's practice no indication that the Custom Service ever set out with a lawmaking pretense in mind when it undertook to make such classifications. Moreover, the amendments to the statute don't reveal any new congres-sional objective of treating classification decisions generally as rulemaking with force of law. Furthermore, the authorization for classification rulings, and the Custom Service's practice in making them, present a case far removed not only from the notice-and-comment process but from any other circumstances reasonably suggesting that Congress ever thought of classification rulings as deserving the deference claimed for them here. The Custom Service's ruling at issue here fails to qualify for deference under *Chevron*, although the possibility that it deserves some deference under *Skidmore* means the case is to be vacated and remanded. Remanded.

▌ ANALYSIS

This case demonstrates that the majority of the Court did not want to take an all-or-nothing approach in deferring to administrative agencies but preferred to support a variety of forms for such deference.

■=■

Barnhart v. Walton

Social Security Administration (D) v. Social Security applicant (P)

535 U.S. 212 (2002).

NATURE OF CASE: Suit challenging the denial of Social Security disability benefits.

FACT SUMMARY: A depressed, schizophrenic teacher lost his job because of his mental illness. The Social Security Administration denied his request for disability benefits because he was unable to engage in significant work for only eleven months instead of what the agency considered to be the statutorily required period of twelve months.

🏛 RULE OF LAW
The Social Security Act requires that applicants for disability benefits be unable to engage in substantial gainful activity for at least twelve months.

FACTS: Walton (P) developed a mental illness involving both schizophrenia and depression. He lost his teaching job because of his mental impairment, and the impairment then prevented him from engaging in "substantial gainful activity" for eleven months after he lost his teaching job. The plaintiff applied to the Social Security Administration (Agency) (D) for disability benefits, but the Agency (D) denied his request. The Agency (D) reasoned that the statutory definition of disability required the plaintiff's inability to engage in substantial gainful activity to last at least twelve months. The plaintiff sued, and the trial court upheld the Agency's (D) denial of the plaintiff's request for benefits. The court of appeals reversed, concluding that the twelve-month duration requirement applied to the underlying medical impairment itself, not to the period of inability to engage in substantial work that resulted from the impairment. The Agency (D) petitioned the United States Supreme Court for further review.

ISSUE: Does the Social Security Act require that applicants for disability benefits be unable to engage in substantial gainful activity for at least twelve months?

HOLDING AND DECISION: (Breyer, J.) Yes. The Social Security Act requires that applicants for disability benefits be unable to engage in substantial gainful activity for at least twelve months. The Social Security Act defines disability to require both an inability to perform substantial work and a medical impairment that causes the inability to work and lasts at least twelve months. The Agency (D) has promulgated a formal rule that extends the twelve-month duration requirement to the "inability to engage in substantial gainful activity." The statute itself does not unambiguously foreclose the Agency's (D) interpretive regulation, and the Agency's (D) interpretation is permissible. Also worth noting is that the Agency's (D)

interpretation is long-standing and has remained unaffected by several congressional amendments to the pertinent statutory provisions. Reversed.

▶ ANALYSIS

Significant here is the Court's rejection of the "linguistic" reading of the statute used by the court of appeals. According to the strict letter of the statute, the twelve-month duration requirement clearly modifies the word "impairment." Whether it also modifies the word "inability," however, is an ambiguous question. Under *Chevron,* 467 U.S. 837 (1984), that ambiguity justifies a permis-sible interpretation of whether the twelve-month requirement also modifies "inability."

■▬■

Quick Reference Rules of Law

Lujan v. Defenders of Wildlife

Secretary of Interior (D) v. Environmental group (P)

504 U.S. 555 (1992).

NATURE OF CASE: Appeal from denial of defense motion for summary judgment in action for injunctive relief.

FACT SUMMARY: In Defenders' (P) action against Lujan (D), the appellate court, agreeing with the district court, denied Lujan's (D) motion for summary judgment that challenged, on specificity grounds, the standing of this action.

🏛 RULE OF LAW

Standing is established when a plaintiff shows that he has suffered an actual and redressable injury that is fairly traceable to the challenged action of the defendant.

FACTS: Section 7 (a)(2) of the Endangered Species Act (ESA) of 1973 requires federal agencies to consult with the Secretary of the Interior to "insure that any action authorized, funded, or carried out by such agency . . . is not likely to jeopardize the continued existence of an endangered" or threatened species or to adversely modify its habitat. In lieu of the ESA requirement, the Secretary, Lujan (D), issued a regulation which limited the consultation requirement to agency action "in the United States or upon the high seas." As a result, Defenders of Wildlife (Defenders) (P) challenged this regulation in federal district court, averring that the regulation threatened the habitat of various endangered species abroad and caused injury to its cognizable interests. In rebuttal, Lujan (D) moved for summary judgment based on standing, on the grounds that Defenders' (P) complaint failed to adequately specify the connection between the regulation and its alleged injuries. The district court and the appellate court on appeal, however, denied this motion. Lujan (D) appealed.

ISSUE: Is standing established when a plaintiff shows that he has suffered an actual and redressable injury that is fairly traceable to the challenged action of the defendant?

HOLDING AND DECISION: (Scalia, J.) Yes. Standing is established when a plaintiff shows that he has suffered an actual and redressable injury that is fairly traceable to the challenged action of the defendant. This rule represents the end result of common law principles requiring, at a bare minimum, that a plaintiff establish the actuality, redressability, and traceability of an injury in order to have standing. In this vein, various stages of the litigative process require varying degrees of specificity for a plaintiff to establish standing; however, at the summary judgment stage, he must set forth, by his evidence, specific facts which for the purposes of the summary judgment motion will be taken as

true. Even still, when this plaintiff asserts an injury arising from the government's allegedly unlawful action or inaction as affecting someone else, he must cross an even larger threshold to satisfy the necessary standing elements since, in this instance, causality and redressability issues become somewhat strained. In the instant case, since Defenders (P) failed to adequately demonstrate that any of its members suffered injury to a cognizable interest or, assuming injury, that relief would satisfactorily cushion this interest, Lucan's (D) motion to summarily dismiss Defenders' (P) injunctive action was wrongly denied. Reversed.

CONCURRENCE: (Kennedy, J.) Although the Court reached the correct result, the possibility that in different circumstances an ecosystem, animal, or vocational nexus theory might support a finding of standing should not be foreclosed. Also, the majority correctly notes that Congress may define injuries and specify chains of causation; Congress may exercise that power, though, only if it identifies the protected injury and relates it to the persons permitted to file suit. The citizen-suit provision at issue here fails these minimal conditions by failing to establish any injury in any person that results from any violation. Consistent with the case-or-controversy requirement of Article III, the person filing suit must have been injured in a concrete and personal way. Such a requirement is necessary to preserve the judiciary's limited role in our constitutional order.

CONCURRENCE: (Stevens, J.) Section 7(a)(2) of the ESA does not apply to occurrences in foreign countries, and the judgment of reversal is therefore correct on that basis. The plaintiffs here, however, do have standing because they have visited the affected habitat, have a professional interest in that habitat, and plan to visit that habitat again. Congress has recognized the very interests that the plaintiffs allege have been invaded by the interpretation of the ESA, and courts therefore have no power to ignore those interests. Accordingly, since the "imminence" of the injury here should depend on when the threatened harm is likely to occur, these plaintiffs do have standing to sue.

DISSENT: (Blackmun, J.) Under proper summary-judgment standards, the respondents (i.e., the original plaintiffs) have shown genuine issues of fact sufficient to survive summary judgment on the issues of injury and redressability. As the majority itself notes, the respondents' affidavits do make it "questionable" whether the agency-funded projects threaten protected species. On the personal-injury element of standing, the Court today creates a pointless formality: the respondents still can simply buy

Continued on next page.

airline tickets for their expected return trips. Likewise, the majority mistakenly rejects the theories of ecosystem nexus, vocational or professional injury, and procedural injury. Contrary to today's ruling, ecosystem nexus does not always depend on close proximity, and the distance of the site is irrelevant to a professional-injury analysis. Moreover, procedural injuries, as a class, are not automatically beyond judicial review. Frequently, procedural rights are so intertwined with substantive rights that courts cannot properly override the legislative decisions that link procedure with substance. The Court's broad language in denying procedural injury as a basis for standing is accordingly misplaced.

▶ *ANALYSIS*

In *Japan Whaling Association v. American Cetacean Society,* 478 U.S. 221 (1986), the Society brought suit against the Secretary of Commerce to compel him to certify that Japan's whaling practices "diminish the effectiveness" of the International Convention for the Regulation of Whaling because Japan's annual harvest exceeded quotas established under the Convention. Such a certification would have required the President to impose economic sanctions against the offending nation. The Court raised the standing issue only in a footnote in the Solicitor General's Supreme Court brief, whereby it noted, in effect, that since the Society's right of action was expressly created by the Administrative Procedure Act (APA), which states that "final agency action for which there is no other adequate remedy in court [is] subject to judicial review" (§ 704) at the behest of "[a] person . . . adversely affected or aggrieved by agency action," (§ 702) no separate indication of congressional intent to make agency action reviewable under the APA is necessary.

■══■

Quicknotes

ENDANGERED SPECIES ACT § 7 Provides that federal agencies insure that their actions do not threaten endangered species.

■══■

Massachusetts v. EPA

Coalition (P) v. Government agency (D)

549 U.S. 497 (2007).

NATURE OF CASE: Review of denial of rulemaking petition by agency.

FACT SUMMARY: A coalition of state and local governments and private organizations (collectively "coalition") (P) petitioned the Environmental Protection Agency (EPA) (D) to regulate greenhouse gas emissions pursuant to the Clean Air Act (CAA). In response, the EPA contended that to reach the merits of the coalition's petition, at least one of the petitioning coalition members must have Article III standing to invoke federal court jurisdiction.

RULE OF LAW
A state is entitled to special treatment in asserting standing to challenge agency action in federal court even if traditional standing requirements are relaxed.

FACTS: In response to the coalition's (P) petition for certiorari to the United States Supreme Court, the EPA (D) argued that the Court could not address the merits of the case without determining whether at least one member of the coalition (P) had standing to invoke jurisdiction under Article III of the Constitution. Thereupon, the Court recognized that States are not normal litigants for the purposes of invoking federal jurisdiction, but determined that inasmuch as the parties' dispute turned on the proper construction of a congressional statute, the underlying matter was properly addressed before the federal court. To make applicable to the coalition (P) the federal statute authorizing challenge to EPA (D) action, the Court considered the special position and interest of petitioner Massachusetts (P).

ISSUE: Is a state entitled to special solicitude in asserting standing to challenge agency action in federal court such that traditional standing requirements are relaxed?

HOLDING AND DECISION: (Stevens, J.) Yes. A state is entitled to special treatment in asserting standing to challenge agency action in federal court even if traditional standing requirements are relaxed. Congress authorized challenge of the EPA (D) action in 42 U.S.C. § 7607(b)(1). Moreover, the law of *Lujan v. Defenders of Wildlife*, 504 U.S. 555 (1992), prescribes special status to the litigant with a vested procedural right—in particular, status to assert standing without meeting all the normal standing requirements. As such, and because of the quasi-sovereign interests of Massachusetts (P) in preserving its coastal land, the sovereign prerogatives of Massachusetts (P) must be protected pursuant to federal statute. The fact that climate-change risks caused by global warming, to which the underlying emissions contribute, are widely shared does not diminish the threat of harm to Massachusetts (P) in particular. The rising seas, as caused by global warming, have begun to swallow Massachusetts's (P) coastal land, thus creating a particularized injury to same. Over time, the rising sea levels will continue to harm Massachusetts (P) and, accordingly, despite the increasing emissions from developing nations such as China and India, the EPA (D) must take the incremental steps to slow or reduce the effects of global warming. And although the risk of catastrophic consequences associated with man-made global warming are remote, EPA (D) action here would redress injury to Massachusetts (P). Thus, it is manifest that the coalition (P) has standing to challenge the EPA's (D) denial of their rulemaking petition. Remanded for further proceedings.

DISSENT: (Roberts, C.J.) The problem of global climate change is properly addressed to the Executive and Legislative branches of government. The case and controversy requirement of Article III of the Constitution in fact precludes the Court from deciding the instant matter. Specifically, the party asserting standing to sue must allege concrete and particularized injury that is actual or imminent; the injury must be fairly traceable to the defendant's allegedly unlawful conduct; and the relief sought must likely redress the petitioner's injury. Here, by definition, the injury associated with global warming is not particularized to Massachusetts (P). But if the loss of coastal land may be considered particularized, the loss must be actual or imminent. Thus, because the record does not support the conclusion that sea levels rose between 10 and 20 centimeters in the 20th century as a result of global warming and because the prediction that global warming will cause sea levels to rise by 20 to 70 centimeters by the year 2100 nullifies the immediacy factor, it is clear that the coalition's (P) injury argument fails. Moreover, it is wholly unclear how new EPA (D) regulations will likely prevent the loss of Massachusetts (P) coastal land. The coalition (P) cannot establish a causal connection between loss of coastal land in Massachusetts and the EPA's (D) lack of regulation of greenhouse gas emissions. Indeed, the majority uses "the dire nature of global warming itself as a bootstrap for finding causation and redressability." Nonetheless, neither statute—specifically, 42 U.S.C. § 7607(b)(1)—nor case law (see, *Georgia v. Tennessee Copper Co.*, 206 U.S. 230 (1907)) provides a basis for the relaxing of Article III standing requirements because the interests of a State are asserted. And to claim otherwise underscores the coalition's (P) fatal inability to establish standing on traditional terms.

Continued on next page.

▶ *ANALYSIS*

In a speech following the decision in *Massachusetts v. EPA*, EPA Administrator Lisa Jackson related that only a small percentage of greenhouse gas emitting facilities—the largest 10,000 of tens of millions of American businesses—will be required to report their emissions. Administrator Jackson observed that the EPA does not seek to place an undue burden on American business and does not seek to regulate everything from "cows to the local Dunkin' Donuts." See, Speech: Administrator Lisa P. Jackson, Remarks to the 2nd Annual Governors' Global Climate Summit at http://yosemite. epa.gov/opa/admpress.nsf/. However, it is the position of the Small Business Administration, Office of Advocacy, that numerous small business entities will be subject to the EPA permitting requirements for greenhouse gas emissions, thereby causing said small businesses significant additional expense. See, Small Business Administration: Letter dated 12/23/09 at http://www.sba.gov/advo/laws/comments/ epa09_1223.html. As such, it may be that resulting litigation will affect both public and private sectors of the American economy for years to come.

■≡■

Quicknotes

ARTICLE III, U.S. CONSTITUTION Limits federal judicial power to cases and controversies.

STANDING The right to commence suit against another party because of a personal stake in the resolution of the controversy.

■≡■

Summers v. Earth Island Institute

Government agency (D) v. Environmental groups (P)

_____ U.S. _____, 129 S.Ct. 1142 (2009).

NATURE OF CASE: Review of question as to whether environmental groups (P) had standing to challenge government agency (D) regulations.

FACT SUMMARY: Environmental groups—among others, Earth Island Institute (collectively "Earth Island") (P)—sought to prevent the U.S. Forest Service (Forest Service), namely, District Ranger Priscilla Summers (D), from enforcing regulations that exempt certain projects from the notice, comment, and appeal process. Following settlement of the parties' dispute, the Government (D) argued that Earth Island (P) lacked standing to continue its challenge of the underlying regulations issues. The district court disagreed and proceeded to adjudicate the merits of Earth Island's (P) challenge.

> 🏛 **RULE OF LAW**
> An organization does not retain standing to challenge the lawfulness of government regulations following settlement of the underlying issues of the sole aggrieved member identified by the organization.

FACTS: Upon approval by the Forest Service of a salvage sale of burned timber located in the Sequoia National Forest, Earth Island (P) filed a complaint challenging the Forest Service's failure to establish a notice, comment, and appeal process relevant to the sale. The Government (D) responded that its regulations provide that certain procedures would not be applied to environmentally insignificant projects—of which the underlying salvage sale qualified. Shortly after the district court granted a preliminary injunction against the salvage sale project, the parties settled their dispute and the court concluded that the timber sale was no longer at issue. Notwithstanding same, the court proceeded to adjudicate the merits of Earth Island's (P) challenge to the timber sale. Thereafter, because Earth Island's (P) named member no longer suffered concrete or particularized threat of imminent harm to his interests, the Government (D) sought review of the question whether Earth Island had standing to challenge Government (D) regulations.

ISSUE: Does an organization retain standing to challenge the lawfulness of government regulations following settlement of the underlying issues of the sole aggrieved member identified by the organization?

HOLDING AND DECISION: (Scalia, J.) No. An organization does not retain standing to challenge the lawfulness of government regulations following settlement of the underlying issues of the sole aggrieved member

identified by the organization proceedings. The doctrine of standing requires that the petitioner allege a personal stake in the outcome of the controversy; actual or imminent injury in fact that is concrete and particularized; injury that is fairly traceable to the challenged action; and likelihood of redressability. Moreover, the regulations at issue here neither require nor forbid any action on the part of Earth Island (P). As such, and because Earth Island's (P) named member's threatened injury was remedied prior to adjudication of the merits, it cannot be that Earth Island (P) retained standing to challenge the lawfulness of Government (D) conduct in project planning. Significantly, to create Article III standing, Earth Island's (P) alleged deprivation of a procedural right must be accompanied by a concrete interest that is affected by the deprivation. To proceed otherwise—to adjudicate the merits of the public's nonconcrete interest in the proper administration of the laws—would go beyond the limited role of the courts in a democratic society. And contrary to the dissent's proposed test for organizational standing, it is insufficient to speculate that some unidentified members of a large environmental group have suffered concrete harm as a result of the Government's (D) procedures. Reversed.

CONCURRENCE: (Kennedy, J.) Deprivation of a procedural right absent an accompanying concrete interest affected by the deprivation is insufficient to create Article III standing.

DISSENT: (Breyer, J.) It is counterintuitive that the members of environmental organizations do not suffer concrete injury when the Forest Service sells timber for logging on thousands of parcels, which by the Service's own implementing regulations it exempts from management procedures. Such procedures, if followed, may result in the cancellation or modification of said sales.

❱ **ANALYSIS**

Environmental law professor Richard Lazarus, of Georgetown University Law Center, expects the United States Supreme Court to continue to visit the issue of Article III standing of environmentalists in federal court inasmuch as the Justices are so sharply divided on the topic. See, http://www.law.harvard.edu/news/spotlight/environmental-law/lazarus.html. Mirroring the division of the Justices, the Court's growing environmental docket reflects, in part, says Professor Lazarus, the political parties' efforts, in the absence of federal environmental legislation, "to achieve their desired ends in the

Continued on next page.

absence of clear statutory authority, and therefore through regulatory action that teeters on the border of legality."

■■■■

Quicknotes

ARTICLE III, U.S. CONSTITUTION Limits federal judicial power to cases and controversies.

STANDING The right to commence suit against another party because of a personal stake in the resolution of the controversy.

■■■■

Abbott Laboratories v. Gardner

Pharmaceutical manufacturers and trade association (P) v. Commissioner of Food and Drugs (D)

387 U.S. 136 (1967).

NATURE OF CASE: Suit challenging regulations promulgated by the Commissioner of Food and Drugs (D).

FACT SUMMARY: Manufacturers of prescription drugs (P) brought suit against the Commissioner of Food and Drugs (D), challenging regulations requiring the manufacturers to include both their "established name" and the proprietary name of the drugs on all labels and in all advertisements.

> ## 🏛 RULE OF LAW
> Only upon a showing of clear and convincing evidence of a contrary legislative intent should the courts restrict access to judicial review of final agency actions.

FACTS: In 1962 Congress amended the federal Food, Drug, and Cosmetic Act to require manufacturers of prescription drugs to print the "established name" corresponding to any proprietary name of the drug prominently on its labels. A similar rule was passed with respect to advertisements for such drugs. Thirty-seven (37) individual drug manufacturers (P) and the Pharmaceutical Manufacturers Association (P) to which they belonged brought suit challenging the regulations on the basis that the Commissioner (D) exceeded his authority in promulgating the rule.

ISSUE: Should the courts restrict access to judicial review of final agency actions only upon a showing of clear and convincing evidence of a contrary legislative intent?

HOLDING AND DECISION: (Harlan, J.) Yes. Only upon a showing of clear and convincing evidence of a contrary legislative intent should the courts restrict access to judicial review of final agency actions. The issue here is whether Congress intended to forbid pre-enforcement review of this type of regulation promulgated by the Commissioner (D). Cases have held that judicial review of a final agency action by an aggrieved person will not be cut off unless it appears that that was Congress's intent. The Administrative Procedure Act (Act) also provides for review of agency actions for which review is provided by statute or for which there is no other adequate legal remedy. The statutory scheme of the Act does not preclude judicial review of such actions as those taken in the present case, nor has the government demonstrated such an intent.

▶ ANALYSIS

The Court notes that the intent to preclude judicial review must be gleaned from the statutory scheme as a whole. Furthermore, where a statute expressly provides that certain actions are reviewable, it should not be presumed that all other actions are not reviewable by the courts.

■≡■

Quicknotes

CLEAR AND CONVINCING EVIDENCE An evidentiary standard requiring a demonstration that the fact sought to be proven is reasonably certain.

JUDICIAL REVIEW The authority of the courts to review decisions, actions or omissions committed by another agency or branch of government.

■≡■

Block v. Community Nutrition Institute

Government agency (D) v. Consumer Group (P)

467 U.S. 340 (1984).

NATURE OF CASE: Appeal of a reversal of a dismissal of an action challenging certain milk pricing regulations.

FACT SUMMARY: The Community Nutrition Institute (P) challenged the Department of Agriculture (D) minimum milk price regulations.

RULE OF LAW

Consumers do not have standing to challenge regulations promulgated under the Agricultural Marketing Agreement Act of 1937.

FACTS: In 1937 Congress enacted the Agricultural Marketing Agreement Act, which provided, among other things, for extensive rulemaking authority in the Department of Agriculture (D) to prevent dairy price collapses. Pursuant to this authority, the Department (D) promulgated rules fixing minimum prices on various classes of milk products. These rules were challenged by individual consumers, several milk handlers, and a consumer organization, the Community Nutrition Institute (P). The district court dismissed for lack of standing and failure to exhaust administrative remedies. The court of appeals reversed as to the consumers, holding that the statutory scheme did not expressly prohibit consumer challenges.

ISSUE: Do consumers have standing to challenge regulations promulgated under the Agricultural Marketing Agreement Act of 1937?

HOLDING AND DECISION: (O'Connor, J.) No. Consumers do not have standing to challenge regulations promulgated under the Agricultural Marketing Agreement Act of 1937. The Administrative Procedure Act gives rise to a presumption of such standing, but it is only a presumption. Where such standing is contrary to the legislative scheme or expressly prohibited, it will not be found. Contrary to the holding of the court of appeals, an explicit prohibition on such standing need not be found. Here, Congress envisioned a complex administrative procedure, and to allow consumer suits would bypass this procedure. Reversed.

ANALYSIS

Prior to this decision some courts tended to hold, as the court of appeals did here, that congressional desire to prevent citizen standing in challenges to regulations had to be explicit. This was described as "clear and convincing evidence." The Supreme Court, in this opinion, quite clearly rejected this standard.

Quicknotes

ADMINISTRATIVE REMEDIES Relief that is sought before an administrative body as opposed to a court.

STANDING Whether a party possesses the right to commence suit against another party by having a personal stake in the resolution of the controversy.

Heckler v. Chaney

FDA director (D) v. Prison inmate (P)

470 U.S. 821 (1985).

NATURE OF CASE: Appeal of reversal of dismissal of action to compel Food and Drug Administration (FDA) (D) enforcement proceedings.

FACT SUMMARY: Chaney (P) brought an action to compel the FDA (D) to stop the use of lethal drugs in executions.

🏛 RULE OF LAW
A decision by the FDA (D) to refrain from enforcement proceedings is not subject to judicial review.

FACTS: The Food, Drug, and Cosmetic Act mandated that the FDA (D) take steps to prevent unauthorized or dangerous uses of approved drugs. Chaney (P), contending that use of approved drugs for execution by injection constituted an unauthorized and dangerous use of drugs, petitioned the FDA (D) to take steps to prevent such use. The FDA (D) declined. Chaney (P) brought an action to compel the FDA (D) to take such steps. The district court granted the FDA (D) summary judgment and dismissed, holding that such agency actions were unreviewable. The appellate court reversed, holding that such actions were reviewable, and further held the decision by the FDA (D) to be improper.

ISSUE: Is a decision by the FDA (D) to refrain from enforcement proceedings subject to judicial review?

HOLDING AND DECISION: (Rehnquist, J.) No. A decision by the FDA (D) to refrain from enforcement proceedings is not subject to judicial review. Traditionally, agency decisions to decline enforcement proceedings have been unreviewable. This is largely due to a respect for the greater knowledgeability that an agency will be presumed to have over a court. Another reason is that agency lack of enforcement generally does not involve coercive intrusion upon personal liberty, the protection of which is the main concern of the courts. As the Act in question gives no hint of an exception of this rule, the decision of the court of appeals must be reversed.

CONCURRENCE: (Brennan, J.) While Congress intended to afford administrative agencies broad discretion in making enforcement decisions, Congress did not intend administrative agencies to ignore clear jurisdictional, regulatory, statutory or constitutional requirements.

CONCURRENCE: (Marshall, J.) Refusals to enforce should be reviewable in the absence of clear and convincing legislative intent to the contrary.

▶ **ANALYSIS**

Judicial unreviewability of agency inaction is often likened to prosecutorial discretion. In both instances, societal, not individual, interests are at stake. Justice Marshall takes issue with the analogy, contending that societal interests in criminal prosecutions are much more intangible than agency decisions.

■▬■

Quicknotes

5 U.S.C. § 701 Judicial review does not apply where statistics preclude it.

5 U.S.C. § 706 Authorizes judicial review of all orders establishing federal motor vehicle safety standards.

FICA § 306 Provides that FDA is not required to report minor violation if public warning is adequate.

■▬■

Webster v. Doe

CIA director (D) v. CIA employee (P)

486 U.S. 592 (1988).

NATURE OF CASE: Appeal from vacation of denial of claim for reinstatement.

FACT SUMMARY: When the Central Intelligence Agency (CIA) (D) terminated Doe's (P) employment upon learning that he was homosexual, Doe (P) filed an action alleging statutory and constitutional violations by Webster (D), the CIA (D) director.

> 🏛 **RULE OF LAW**
> Under § 102(c) of the National Security Act (NSA), employee termination decisions made by the Director of the CIA are not judicially reviewable.

FACTS: After working for the CIA (D) for nine years, being promoted to a position as a covert electronics technician, and being consistently rated as an excellent or outstanding employee, John Doe's (P) employment was terminated after he revealed to the CIA (D) that he was a homosexual. Webster (D), director of the CIA (D), concluded that Doe's (P) homosexuality presented a security threat. Doe (P) submitted to a polygraph test concerning his homosexuality and possible security violations, denied having sexual relations with any foreign nationals, and maintained that he had not disclosed classified information to any of his sexual partners. The test results indicated he had answered all questions truthfully. When Doe (P) refused the CIA's (D) request that he resign, Webster (D) "deemed it necessary and advisable in the interests of the United States to terminate his employment." Doe (P) then filed an action, asserting a variety of statutory and constitutional claims against Webster (D), who moved for dismissal on the ground that § 102(c) of the NSA precluded judicial review of his termination decisions under § § 701, 702, and 706 of the Administrative Procedure Act (APA). The district court granted Doe's (P) motion for partial summary judgment, and found that Doe (P) had been unlawfully discharged. The court of appeals vacated the district court's judgment and remanded the case for further proceedings, deciding first that judicial review of the CIA's (D) decision was not precluded under APA § 701(a)(1) or (a)(2) and, second, that the CIA (D) regulations cited by Doe (P) did not limit Webster's (D) discretion in making termination decisions.

ISSUE: Under § 102(c) of the NSA, are employee termination decisions made by the Director of the CIA judicially reviewable?

HOLDING AND DECISION: (Rehnquist, C.J.) No. Under § 102(c) of the NSA, employee termination decisions made by the Director of the CIA are not judicially reviewable. Section 701(a) of the APA limits application of

the entire APA to situations in which judicial review is not precluded by statute; subsection (a)(1) is concerned with whether Congress expressed an intent to prohibit judicial review, while subsection (a)(2) applies "in those rare instances where 'statutes are drawn in such broad terms that in a given case there is no law to apply.'" The standard set forth in § 102(c) of the NSA defers to the director and appears to foreclose the application of any meaningful judicial standard of review. Thus, the language and structure of § 102(c) indicate that Congress meant to commit individual employee discharges to the director's discretion and that § 701(a)(2) accordingly precludes judicial review of these decisions under the APA. However, nothing in § 102(c) demonstrates that Congress meant to preclude consideration of colorable constitutional claims arising out of the actions of the director pursuant to that section. Reversed [as to judicial review of terminations under § 102(c)]; remanded [for consideration of Doe's (P) constitutional claims].

DISSENT: (Scalia, J.) Congress can prescribe, at least within broad limits, that for certain jobs the dismissal decision will be unreviewable—that is, will be "committed to agency discretion by law." Further, it is entirely beyond doubt that if Congress intended to exclude judicial review of the President's decision (through the Director of Central Intelligence) to dismiss an officer of the CIA (D), that disposition would be constitutionally permissible. Not the Constitution, our laws, or common sense gives an individual a right to come into court to litigate the reasons for his dismissal as an intelligence agent.

> ▶ **ANALYSIS**
>
> On remand, *Doe v. Webster*, 769 F. Supp. 1 (D.D.C. 1991), the district court concluded that CIA (D) regulations gave Doe (P) a postprobation property interest in his position and that his discharge without a statement of reasons why his homosexuality posed a security threat and an opportunity to respond to those reasons violated due process. Contrary to the opinion expressed by both Justices O'Connor and Scalia that judicial review of constitutional claims is also precluded in this context, the majority's rejection of all arguments made on this point by Webster (D) sends a clear message that a legislative attempt to preclude review of constitutional claims would be unacceptable. Further, even where national security is concerned, methods exist to balance the need of the individual asserting constitutional claims against the extraordinary needs of the CIA (D) for confidentiality.

Continued on next page.

Quicknotes

5 U.S.C. § 701 Judicial review does not apply where statistics preclude it.

NATIONAL SECURITY ACT § 102 Precludes judicial review of CIA director's employment decisions.

■▬■

Lujan v. National Wildlife Federation

Government official (D) v. Environmental group (P)

497 U.S. 871 (1990).

NATURE OF CASE: Appeal of preliminary injunction against federal reclassification of wildlife lands.

FACT SUMMARY: Two members of the National Wildlife Federation (NWF) (P) claimed an injury due to the reclassification of wildlife lands by Lujan (D), the Secretary of the Interior, because the two members had visited "in the vicinity" of the reclassified lands.

> ## 🏛 RULE OF LAW
> A general allegation of visits "in the vicinity" of reclassified land is not sufficient to show "injury in fact" as a result of the reclassification.

FACTS: Lujan (D), the Secretary of the Interior, reclassified vast tracts of federal land in a way that the NWF (P) claimed opened those lands to various kinds of detrimental development, including mining. To establish standing and demonstrate an "injury in fact," the NWF (P) relied primarily upon affidavits from two members who asserted that they visited places "in the vicinity" of areas that two of Lujan's (D) land decisions had affected. The NWF (P) claimed that Lujan's (D) reclassification of the wildlife lands violated the National Environmental Policy Act (NEPA) and the Administrative Procedure Act (APA), along with certain other land management statutes, by failing to follow various procedures and failing to pay proper attention to the environment. The NWF (P) appeared to be seeking improvement overall of the programs established by the Department of the Interior and the Bureau of Land Management. Lujan (D) filed a motion for summary judgment challenging NWF's (P) standing. The district court found for Lujan (D) and dismissed the action. The D.C. Circuit reversed, with the result that for two years a preliminary injunction prohibited Lujan (D) from making changes in the use classifications of millions of acres of public lands. The United States Supreme Court then reviewed the matter.

ISSUE: Is a general allegation of visits "in the vicinity" of reclassified land sufficient to show "injury in fact" as a result of the reclassification?

HOLDING AND DECISION: (Scalia, J.) No. A general allegation of visits "in the vicinity" of reclassified land is not sufficient to show "injury in fact" as a result of the reclassification. While there is some room for debate as to how "specific" the "specific facts" required for summary judgment under Rule 56(e) must be in a particular case, the Rule is not satisfied by averments which state only that some NWF (P) members use unspecified portions of an immense tract of territory, on some portions of which

mining activity has occurred or probably will occur by virtue of the governmental action. Further, the overall programmatic improvements sought by NWF (P) are normally made by actions of the Interior Department or Congress, not through court decree. The NWF (P) cannot demand a general judicial review of the Department of the Interior's and the Bureau of Land Management's day-to-day operations. (Disposition not stated in the casebook excerpt).

DISSENT: (Blackmun, J.) The Court's hypothetical inquiry into the reviewability of the entire "land withdrawal review program" seems superfluous, given the ruling that the NWF (P) lacks standing. Even so, the Court's analysis of that issue is generally correct. Under 5 U.S.C § 702, a broad rule may be invalidated by one plaintiff who is injured by the rule; at the same time, a generally lawful rule may not be invalidated by one injured plaintiff if the injury arose only in one unlawful application of the rule. Thus, what matters in this case is whether the challenged actions are required by the agency plan or policy. If they are not, they may not be invalidated as to all applications of the agency action.

▷ **ANALYSIS**

The Court distinguished its decision in *United States v. Students Challenging Regulatory Agency Procedures (SCRAP)*, 412 U.S. 669 (1973), on the ground that *SCRAP* involved a Rule 12(b) motion to dismiss on the pleadings, not a Rule 56 motion for summary judgment. The Court stated that a Rule 12(b) motion presumes that general allegations embrace those specific facts that are necessary to support the claim, unlike a Rule 56 motion for summary judgment. However, the Court's decision in *SCRAP* represented a very expansive interpretation of what constitutes standing. Since *SCRAP*, the Court's decisions as to standing and the "injury in fact" requirement have been much less expansive, as demonstrated in the instant case.

■■■

Quicknotes

INJURY-IN-FACT Harm that is sufficiently certain to give a plaintiff standing to sue, and which is redressable by court-ordered relief.

JUDICIAL REVIEW The authority of the courts to review decisions, actions or omissions committed by another agency or branch of government.

Continued on next page.

PRELIMINARY INJUNCTION A judicial mandate issued to require or restrain a party from certain conduct; used to preserve a trial's subject matter or to prevent threatened injury.

STANDING Whether a party possesses the right to commence suit against another party by having a personal stake in the resolution of the controversy.

■■■■

Norton v. Southern Utah Wilderness Alliance

Secretary of Interior (D) v. Environmental group (P)

542 U.S. 55 (2004).

NATURE OF CASE: Suit for declaratory and injunctive relief challenging federal management of potential wilderness areas.

FACT SUMMARY: The Bureau of Land Management (BLM) (D) permitted the use of off-road vehicles (ORVs) on federal lands in Utah. The Southern Utah Wilderness Alliance (SUWA) (P) sued the BLM (D) and others for an alleged failure to satisfy the BLM's (D) statutory mandate to manage such lands in a way that did not impair their suitability as wilderness.

RULE OF LAW
The Administrative Procedure Act, 5 U.S.C. § 706(1), does not provide a right of action for an agency's failure to take a general action that it is not required to take.

FACTS: The BLM (D) permitted users of potential wilderness areas on federal lands in Utah to operate ORVs for recreational purposes on those lands. ORVs cause significant damage to the lands themselves, to wildlife, and to wilderness enthusiasts. To try to stop such detrimental impacts, the SUWA (P) filed suit against the BLM (D) and others, requesting declaratory and injunctive relief requiring the BLM (D) to take action, by changing its management of the use of ORVs, in order to manage its Wilderness Study Areas in Utah "in a manner so as not to impair the suitability of such areas for preservation as wilderness." 43 U.S.C. § 1782(c). [The district court ordered dismissal on the claim challenging the BLM's (D) alleged failure to act, and the court of appeals reversed.] The BLM (D) petitioned the United States Supreme Court for further review.

ISSUE: Does the Administrative Procedure Act, 5 U.S.C. § 706(1), provide a right of action for an agency's failure to take a general action that it is not required to take?

HOLDING AND DECISION: (Scalia, J.) No. The Administrative Procedure Act (APA) 5 U.S.C. § 706(1), does not provide a right of action for an agency's failure to take a general action that it is not required to take. Sections 702, 704, and 706(1) of the APA all require an "agency action" as the basis for suit, and the APA defines these litigable "agency actions" as discrete actions, not as general, amorphous goals or directives. Even where the APA permits suit for failures to act, the failures must be failures to take "agency actions," which are, by statute, necessarily discrete actions. Moreover, § 706(1) permits suit to compel agency action only when the action is required. Accordingly, there is no right of action even as

against discrete agency action if the agency action is not required by law. The basis of the SUWA's (P) claim against the BLM (D), 42 U.S.C. § 1782(c), does mandate a goal for the BLM (D), but it also grants a broad discretion to the BLM (D) for deciding how to achieve the mandated goal. The total exclusion of ORVs, for example, certainly is not mandated by the non-impairment statute—at any rate, not with the clarity required by § 706(1). These limitations imposed by the APA serve the legislative purpose, as they do in this case, of prohibiting the courts from interfering with the discretion vested in administrative agencies. Reversed and remanded.

ANALYSIS

Principles of separation of powers and judicial restraint pervade administrative law. Here the Court defers to congressional requirements for reviewability, as established by 5 U.S.C. § 706(1), and the Administrative Procedure Act itself in turn exists largely to protect executive-branch agencies from what Justice Scalia calls "undue judicial interference with their lawful discretion." The Court was unanimous in *Southern Utah Wilderness Alliance,* which demonstrates how clearly those fundamental principles apply in this case.

■■■

Quicknotes

INJUNCTIVE RELIEF A court order issued as a remedy, requiring a person to do, or prohibiting that person from doing, a specific act.

■■■

Air Courier Conference of America v. American Postal Workers Union, AFL-CIO

Agency (D) v. Union (P)

498 U.S. 517 (1991).

NATURE OF CASE: Appeal from refusal to dismiss action to reinstate suspended statutes.

FACT SUMMARY: In the American Postal Workers Union's (APWU's) (P) suit against Air Courier (D), challenging the Postal Service's suspension of the Private Express Statutes, the court of appeals, agreeing with the district court, found that the APWU (P) had standing to bring the suit.

🏛 RULE OF LAW
Plaintiffs have no standing to challenge the suspension of a statute unless they are within that statute's zone of interest.

FACTS: The APWU (P) challenged the Postal Service's suspension of the Private Express Statutes, which prohibited private express carriers from competing with the Postal Service, by arguing that the suspension jeopardized postal worker job security. The court of appeals, agreeing with the district court, found that the APWU (P) had standing to bring the challenge since the revenue-protective purposes of the statutes plausibly related to the APWU's (P) interest in preventing the reduction of employment opportunities. Air Courier (D), a private express carrier, appealed.

ISSUE: Do plaintiffs have standing to challenge the suspension of a statute if they are outside that statute's zone of interest?

HOLDING AND DECISION: (Rehnquist, C.J.) No. Plaintiffs have no standing to challenge the suspension of a statute, unless they are within that statute's zone of interest. In respect to examining the legitimacy of the APWU's (P) standing to challenge the suspension of the Private Express Statutes, the express language and legislative purpose of these statutes shed light. First, their express language appears to be concerned not with opportunities for postal workers but with the receipt of necessary revenues for the Postal Service. Second, the legislative purpose behind the statutes is not to ensure employment for postal workers but to ensure that postal service is provided to the citizenry at large. Hence, postal unions are not within the Private Express Statutes' zone of interest. In the instant case, since APWU (P) is not within the Private Express Statutes' zone of interest, it lacks standing to challenge the Statutes' suspension by the Postal Service. Reversed.

▶ ANALYSIS

Justice White was one of the justices to join the majority above. He also authored *Clarke v. Securities Industry Assn.* 479 U.S. 388 (1987), where he expansively read the zone-of-interests test. However, the remaining majority justices above did not join his reading of this test in *Clarke*. This raises the possibility that the Court may be retooling the doctrine, perhaps because of a changed understanding of the purposes to be served by deploying the injury-in-fact and zone-of-interests tests.

■■■

Quicknotes

STANDING TO SUE Plaintiff must allege that he has a legally predictable interest at stake in the litigation.

ZONE OF INTERESTS The range or category of interests that a constitutional guarantee or statute is intended to protect.

■■■

National Credit Union Admin. v. First National Bank & Trust Co.

Government agency (D) v. Banks (P)

522 U.S. 479 (1998).

NATURE OF CASE: Appeal from petition for federal court review of agency interpretation of a statute.

FACT SUMMARY: First National Bank (First National) (P) and others alleged that the National Credit Union Association (NCUA) (D), the agency which administers the Federal Credit Union Act (FCUA), had erred in permitting multiple unrelated employer groups to participate in the same federal credit union.

🏛 RULE OF LAW
The limitation of the markets that federal credit unions can serve is within the "zone of interests" of banks that compete with credit unions and is sufficient to confer standing.

FACTS: Since 1982 the NCUA (D) has interpreted provisions of the FCUA to allow groups of unrelated employers having a common bond of the same occupation to belong to the same credit union. First National (P) and other banks alleged that they had standing to seek federal court review of this interpretation. The challenged interpretation was found impermissible and the appellate court affirmed. The United States Supreme Court granted certiorari.

ISSUE: Is the limitation of the markets that federal credit unions can serve within the "zone of interests" of banks that complete with credit unions and is it sufficient to confer standing?

HOLDING AND DECISION: (Thomas, J.) Yes. The limitation of the markets that federal credit unions can serve is within the "zone of interests" of banks that compete with credit unions and is sufficient to confer standing. Since the interest sought to be protected by the complainant is arguably within the zone of interests to be protected by the statute, First National (P) had standing under the Administrative Procedure Act to challenge the NCUA's (D) interpretation. Affirmed.

DISSENT: (O'Connor, J.) Competitive injury to commercial interests does not arguably fall within the zone of interests sought to be protected by the common bond provision of the FCUA. First National (P) failed to establish standing. The judgment of the court of appeals should be vacated and the case should be remanded with instructions that it be dismissed.

▌ ANALYSIS

The Court here found that the banks had standing to challenge the NCUA's interpretation of federal law. It also concluded that the NCUA's interpretation was erroneous.

By applying the canons of construction of statutes, the agency's interpretation was found lacking.

▪━▪

Quicknotes

CERTIORARI A discretionary writ issued by a superior court to an inferior court in order to review the lower court's decisions; the Supreme Court's writ ordering such review.

JUDICIAL REVIEW The authority of the courts to review decisions, actions or omissions committed by another agency or branch of government.

ZONE OF INTERESTS The range or category of interests that a constitutional guarantee or statute is intended to protect.

▪━▪

Taylor-Callahan-Coleman Counties District Adult Probation Department v. Dole

Employer (P) v. Government agency (D)

948 F.2d 953 (5th Cir. 1991).

NATURE OF CASE: Appeal of challenge of opinion letters dismissed for lack of subject matter jurisdiction.

FACT SUMMARY: Taylor-Callahan-Coleman Counties District Adult Probation Department employees (Taylor-Callahan) (P) challenged opinion letters issued by the Department of Labor (DOL) (D) because they had not gone through notice and comment.

🏛 RULE OF LAW
Where the action complained of was not final agency action, it is not subject to judicial review.

FACTS: Under the Fair Labor Standards Act of 1938 (FLSA), administrative and professional employees are exempt from overtime requirements. Taylor-Callahan (P) were advised that, under Department of Labor regulations, they were exempt as administrative employees. When the DOL (D) later issued two opinion letters stating that probation officers were not exempt, based on the fact circumstances provided by the requesting parties, Taylor-Callahan (P) claimed that the opinion letters were legislative rules which were inconsistent with prior regulations and the statute and therefore should have gone through notice and comment. The district court dismissed the case for lack of subject matter jurisdiction. Taylor-Callahan (P) appealed.

ISSUE: Where the action complained of was not final agency action, is it subject to judicial review?

HOLDING AND DECISION: (Clark, C.J.) No. Where the action complained of was not final agency action, it is not subject to judicial review. Advisory opinions issued to guide the DOL (D) in its operations are neither final nor binding. The letters at issue here did not constitute agency action that was broad or definitive. Rather, the letters were expressly limited to the factual situations provided by the requesting parties. They did not have the status of law and had no direct or immediate impact on the DOL (D). They were more in the nature of threshold determinations and did not constitute final agency action. Affirmed.

▶ ANALYSIS

This was an action for declaratory judgment. The court found that an FLSA enforcement action could be brought instead. Informal advisory letters are necessary for the proper administration of FLSA.

Quicknotes

FAIR LABOR STANDARDS ACT Enacted in 1938, the statute establishes a minimum wage applicable to all employees of covered employers and provides for mandatory overtime payment for covered employees who work more than 40 hours a week. Executive, administrative, and professional employees paid on a salary basis are exempt from the statute.

NOTICE AND COMMENT RULEMAKING Informal rulemaking.

OPINION LETTER A letter that is drafted by an attorney for the benefit of his client, stating his knowledge of the law as applied to a particular set of facts.

SUBJECT MATTER JURISDICTION A court's ability to adjudicate a specific category of cases based on the subject matter of the dispute.

■=■

Appalachian Power Company v. Environmental Protection Agency

Trade associations (P) v. Government agency (D)

208 F.3d 1015 (D.C. Cir. 2000).

NATURE OF CASE: Petitions for judicial review.

FACT SUMMARY: Appalachian Power Company (Appalachian) (P) and other electric power companies and trade associations (P) claimed that the Environmental Protection Agency (EPA) (D) improperly published a regulatory document without notice and comment.

🏛 RULE OF LAW
Where a publication reflects a settled policy position with legal consequences, it is final agency action subject to judicial review.

FACTS: The EPA (D) issued a publication interpreting regulations for periodic monitoring of compliance with air pollution standards. Appalachian (P) claimed that the periodic monitoring required in the new publication would raise the cost of compliance and that the document was unlawfully promulgated without public participation. The EPA (D) claimed that the Periodic Monitoring Guidance publication was not subject to judicial review because it was not final or binding.

ISSUE: Where a publication reflects a settled policy position with legal consequences, is it final agency action subject to judicial review?

HOLDING AND DECISION: (Randolph, J.) Yes. Where a publication reflects a settled policy position with legal consequences, it is final agency action subject to judicial review. Agency action is "final" if the action marks the consummation of the agency's decision-making process and determines legal rights or consequences. Here the agency treated the document in the same manner as it would treat a legislative rule, and it based enforcement actions on the policies in the document. The document was therefore binding on private parties and states. Appalachian (P) would not be able to continue operating if it did not comply with the new permit program. Petition granted.

▶ ANALYSIS

The court later held that the document in question was unlawful. The court set aside the Guidance on the basis that it impermissibly went beyond the regulation.

■▬■

Quicknotes

FINAL AGENCY ORDER The final disposition of a hearing before a public agency or the agency's interpretation or application of a statute.

NOTICE AND COMMENT RULEMAKING Informal rulemaking.

RULEMAKING The promulgation of a rule governing a particular activity by an administrative agency, acting within the scope of its power pursuant to statute.

■▬■

McCarthy v. Madigan

Inmate (P) v. Prison employees (D)

503 U.S. 140 (1992).

NATURE OF CASE: Appeal from dismissal of action for damages for constitutional rights violations.

FACT SUMMARY: McCarthy (P), an inmate, contended that he should not have to resort to an internal grievance procedure before initiating suit against prison employees (D) for money damages.

> ### 🏛 RULE OF LAW
> Exhaustion of administrative remedies is not required when the litigant's interests in immediate judicial review outweigh the government's interests in efficiency or administrative autonomy.

FACTS: McCarthy (P), an inmate in a federal prison, filed a complaint against four prison employees (D) for violating his constitutional rights under the Eighth Amendment. He sought money damages only. He chose not to pursue the grievance procedure set up by the Federal Bureau of Prisons, which requires an inmate to first seek informal resolution of his claim. If this fails, the inmate must file a written complaint within fifteen days, then appeal within thirty days to the Regional Director, and file a final appeal within an additional thirty days. The district court dismissed the complaint on the ground that McCarthy (P) had failed to exhaust prison administrative remedies, and McCarthy (P) appealed.

ISSUE: Is exhaustion of administrative remedies required when the litigant's interests in immediate judicial review outweigh the government's interests in efficiency or administrative autonomy?

HOLDING AND DECISION: (Blackmun, J.) No. Exhaustion of administrative remedies is not required when the litigant's interests in immediate judicial review outweigh the government's interests in efficiency or administrative autonomy. The general rule is that exhaustion is required because it protects administrative agency authority and promotes judicial efficiency. However, the Court has recognized three sets of circumstances in which individual interests weigh against requiring exhaustion: (1) when exhaustion principles would unduly prejudice subsequent court action; (2) when an administrative agency is unable to grant effective relief; and (3) when an agency is shown to be biased. In this case, the prison grievance procedure imposes rapid filing deadlines that could penalize an inmate who is unable to comply with them. Furthermore, it does not authorize an award of monetary damages—the only relief requested by McCarthy (P). Therefore, given the type of claim raised by McCarthy (P) and the particular characteristics of the Bureau's grievance procedure, McCarthy's (P) individual interests outweigh institutional interests favoring exhaustion. McCarthy (P) is not required to exhaust the grievance procedure. Reversed.

CONCURRENCE: (Rehnquist, C.J.) Rehnquist agreed that a federal prisoner did not need to exhaust the Federal Bureau of Prisons' procedures, because the grievance procedure at issue here did not provide for any award of monetary damages. Where prisoners seek monetary relief, the remedy is not effective, and it is, therefore, improper to impose such a requirement.

▶ ANALYSIS

In addition to those articulated in this case, courts have fashioned a number of exceptions to the doctrine of exhaustion. For example, exhaustion is not required when the administrative agency's decision is a forgone conclusion, according to *Orion Corp. v. State,* 693 P.2d 1369 (Wash. 1985). Nor is it required in instances where the agency's action would have a chilling effect on the plaintiff's First Amendment rights. See *Wolff v. Selective Serv. Local Bd.,* 372 F.2d 817 (2d Cir. 1967).

∎▬∎

Quicknotes

ADMINISTRATIVE REMEDIES Relief that is sought before an administrative body as opposed to a court.

FIFTH AMENDMENT Provides that no person shall be compelled to serve as a witness against himself, or be subject to trial for the same offense twice, or be deprived of life, liberty, or property without due process of law.

∎▬∎

Darby v. Cisneros

Real estate developer (P) v. HUD (D)

509 U.S. 137 (1993).

NATURE OF CASE: Appeal from dismissal of action to enjoin administrative sanctions.

FACT SUMMARY: Darby (P) and Garvin (P) argued that they should not be required to exhaust available administrative remedies prior to seeking judicial review after being barred from participating in Department of Housing and Urban Development (HUD) (D) programs.

> ## 🏛 RULE OF LAW
> A litigant seeking judicial review of a final agency action under the Administrative Procedure Act need not exhaust available administrative remedies, unless such exhaustion is expressly required by statute or agency rule.

FACTS: Darby (P), a South Carolina real estate developer, and Garvin (P), a mortgage banker, developed a plan to obtain single-family mortgage insurance from HUD for multi-unit projects. The plan circumvented HUD (D) rules that prevented rental properties from receiving single-family mortgage insurance if the mortgagor had financial interests in seven or more similar rental properties in the same project. Darby (P) ultimately obtained financing for three separate multi-unit projects using this plan, but defaulted in 1988, making HUD (D) responsible for $6.6 million in insurance claims. Although HUD (D) had previously audited Garvin's (P) financing plan and concluded there was no wrongdoing, upon default, HUD (D) prohibited Darby (P) and Garvin (P) from participating in any South Carolina HUD (D) program for one year. Darby (P) and Garvin (P) sought administrative review of the decision. The administrative law judge (ALJ) conducted hearings and found that good cause existed to bar petitioners for 18 months. Instead of seeking further administrative review of the ALJ's decision, as permitted under HUD (D) regulations, Darby (P) and Garvin (P) filed suit in district court seeking injunctive relief. HUD (D) moved to dismiss the complaint for failure to seek review. The district court denied the motion and HUD (D) appealed. The court of appeals reversed, and the United States Supreme Court granted certiorari.

ISSUE: Must a litigant seeking judicial review of a final agency action under the APA exhaust all available administrative remedies?

HOLDING AND DECISION: (Blackmun, J.) No. A litigant seeking judicial review of a final agency action under the Administrative Procedure Act (APA) need not exhaust available administrative remedies, unless such exhaustion is expressly required by statute or agency rule.

APA § 10(a) grants individuals who are adversely affected by an administrative agency's action the general right to seek judicial review. However, APA § 10 establishes that such review is available only when the aggrieved party has exhausted all administrative remedies expressly prescribed by statute or agency rule. When both §§ 10(a) and (c) are satisfied, the agency action is final and therefore subject to review. As such, courts are not free to impose an additional exhaustion requirement where agency action has become final under APA § 10(c). Reversed and remanded.

▶ ANALYSIS

Notice that the APA provides a two-prong test. The agency decision must be final and the aggrieved party must have exhausted all administrative remedies if mandated to do so by statute or regulation. While finality is concerned with whether the decisionmaker has reached a definitive position that inflicts an actual, concrete injury, exhaustion refers to the procedures by which an injured party may seek review of an adverse decision.

■=■

Quicknotes

APA § 10(a) Provides for a general right of judicial review.

APA § 10(c) Judicial review is available for final agency actions.

INJUNCTION A remedy imposed by the court ordering a party to cease the conduct of a specific activity.

■=■

Abbott Laboratories v. Gardner

Pharmaceuticals manufacturers and trade association (P) v. Government agency (D)

387 U.S. 136 (1967).

NATURE OF CASE: Review of suit seeking judicial review of agency rule.

FACT SUMMARY: Abbott Laboratories (Abbott) (P) claimed the Commissioner of Food and Drugs (D) had exceeded his authority in promulgating an order requiring all printed matter relating to prescription drugs to designate the name of the particular drug involved every time its trade name was used.

🏛 RULE OF LAW
Where the legal issue presented is fit for judicial resolution, and a regulation requires an immediate and significant change in plaintiffs' conduct, with serious penalties attached to noncompliance, a controversy is ripe for review.

FACTS: When the Commissioner of Food and Drugs (D) promulgated rules requiring the manufacturers of prescription drugs to print the established name of the drug prominently on its labels, Abbott (P) and almost all prescription drug manufacturers (P) challenged the regulations in court. The Commissioner (D) claimed pre-enforcement review was not possible since there were no issues ripe for judicial resolution. Both parties sought summary judgment. The United States Supreme Court granted certiorari.

ISSUE: Where the legal issue presented is fit for judicial resolution, and a regulation requires an immediate and significant change in plaintiffs' conduct, with serious penalties attached to noncompliance, is a controversy ripe for review?

HOLDING AND DECISION: (Harlan, J.) Yes. Where the legal issue presented is fit for judicial resolution, and a regulation requires an immediate and significant change in plaintiffs' conduct, with serious penalties attached to noncompliance, a controversy is ripe for review. The regulations in issue constitute final agency action. The impact of the regulations upon Abbott (P) in its day-to-day operations is significant and costly. Serious criminal and civil penalties could result from the unlawful distribution of misbranded drugs. Access to the courts should be denied only if there is a statutory bar or other unusual circumstance, neither of which appears here. Such a pre-enforcement challenge by nearly all prescription drug manufacturers is calculated to speed enforcement and is in the public interest.

DISSENT: (Fortas, J.) The public interest in avoiding delay far outweighs the private interest here. A much stronger showing is necessary than the expense and trouble of compliance. Enforcement actions would be appropriate to test the regulations only in specific, concrete situations.

▶ ANALYSIS

This case involved a petition for pre-enforcement review of an agency rule. In general, the test for ripeness involves two prongs. First, the issue must be fit for judicial decision. Second, the hardship to the parties is considered.

■══■

Quicknotes

JUDICIAL REVIEW The authority of the courts to review decisions, actions or omissions committed by another agency or branch of government.

RIPENESS A doctrine precluding a federal court from hearing or determining a matter, unless it constitutes an actual and present controversy warranting a determination by the court.

■══■

Ohio Forestry Association, Inc. v. Sierra Club

Government and wood processors (D) v. Environmental organization (P)

523 U.S. 726 (1998).

NATURE OF CASE: Review of denial of judicial review.

FACT SUMMARY: The Sierra Club (P) alleged that Ohio Forestry (D) and the National Forest Service (D) violated various laws when they approved a plan permitting logging in the Wayne National Forest.

 RULE OF LAW
Where a dispute is not ripe for judicial review, the dispute is not justiciable.

FACTS: When the Forest Service (D) developed a land and resource management plan for Ohio's Wayne National Forest, the Sierra Club (P) claimed that the plan violated various laws by permitting logging, and that various regulations were unlawful, arbitrary and capricious. Ohio (D) claimed that the suit was nonjusticiable because the Sierra Club (P) did not have standing and because the issues were not yet ripe for adjudication.

ISSUE: Where a dispute is not ripe for judicial review, is the dispute justiciable?

HOLDING AND DECISION: (Breyer, J.) No. Where a dispute is not ripe for judicial review, the dispute is not justiciable. In determining ripeness, the Court must consider the fitness of the issues for judicial decision and the hardship to the parties of withholding court consideration. Courts cannot get involved in abstract disagreements over administrative policies. Withholding court consideration now will not cause the parties significant hardship. The Sierra Club (P) can bring its legal challenge at a time when harm is more imminent and more certain. Affirmed.

▶ *ANALYSIS*

The Court found that agencies should be protected from judicial interference until an administrative decision has been formalized and its effects felt in a concrete way by the parties. Congress had not provided for pre-implementation review of forest plans. Congress has specifically instructed the courts to review certain agency rules pre-enforcement.

■■■■

Quicknotes

JUDICIAL REVIEW The authority of the courts to review decisions, actions or omissions committed by another agency or branch of government.

JUSTICIABILITY An actual controversy that is capable of determination by the court.

RIPENESS A doctrine precluding a federal court from hearing or determining a matter, unless it constitutes an actual and present controversy warranting a determination by the court.

■■■■

Agency Structure

Quick Reference Rules of Law

Whitman v. American Trucking Associations, Inc.

Trucking associations (P) v. Government agency (D)

531 U.S. 457 (2001).

NATURE OF CASE: Appeal from a finding upholding a delegation of legislative power to the Environmental Protection Agency (EPA).

FACT SUMMARY: The American Trucking Associations (P) brought suit against the EPA (D), arguing that § 109(b)(1) of the Clean Air Act unconstitutionally delegated legislative power to the EPA (D).

🏛 RULE OF LAW
Section 109(b)(1) of the Clean Air Act constitutionally delegates legislative power to the EPA.

FACTS: Acting under § 109(b)(1) of the Clean Air Act, the administrator of the EPA (D) revised the national air quality control standards for particulate matter and ozone. The American Trucking Associations (Associations) (P) challenged the new standards. Although the federal court of appeals agreed with the Associations (P) that the delegation of legislative power to the EPA (D) was overly broad, the court held it would avoid the unconstitutional delegation by adopting a restrictive construction of § 109(b)(1). The Associations (P) appealed.

ISSUE: Does § 109(b)(1) of the Clean Air Act constitutionally delegate legislative power to the EPA?

HOLDING AND DECISION: (Scalia, J.) Yes. Section § 109(b)(1) of the Clean Air Act constitutionally delegates legislative power to the EPA (D). The text of § 109(b)(1) at a minimum requires that for a discrete set of pollutants and based on published air quality criteria that reflect the latest scientific knowledge, the EPA (D) must establish uniform national standards at a level that is requisite to protect the public health from the adverse effects of the pollutant in the ambient air. Requisite, in turn, means sufficient, but not more than necessary. These limits on the EPA's (D) discretion closely resemble the Occupational Safety and Health Act provision, which the United States Supreme Court has upheld, requiring the agency to set the standard that most adequately assures, to the extent feasible, on the basis of the best available evidence, that no employee will suffer any impairment of health. Section 109(b)(1) also closely resembles agency limits in a case in which the United States Supreme Court permitted the Attorney General to designate a drug as a controlled substance for purposes of criminal drug enforcement if doing so was necessary to avoid an imminent hazard to the public safety. The scope of discretion § 109(b)(1) allows is in fact well within the outer limits of constitutionally permissible nondelegation precedents. Reversed as to this issue.

CONCURRENCE: (Stevens, J.) It would be wiser to admit that agency rulemaking authority actually is "legislative power"; hence as long as the delegation provides a sufficiently intelligible principle, there is nothing inherently unconstitutional about it.

▶ ANALYSIS

In the *Whitman* decision, the United States Supreme Court noted that the Court has never suggested that an administrative agency can cure an unlawful delegation of legislative power by adopting in its discretion a limiting construction of the statute.

■=■

Quicknotes

CLEAN AIR ACT Required certain states to establish a permit program for stationary sources of air pollution.

■=■

International Union, United Automobile, Aerospace & Agricultural Implement Workers of America, UAW v. Occupational Safety & Health Administration

Labor and industry groups (P) v. Government agency (D)

938 F.2d 1310 (D.C. Cir. 1991).

NATURE OF CASE: Challenge of agency rules as unconstitutional.

FACT SUMMARY: International Union (International) (P) claimed that the Occupational Safety & Health Administration's (OSHA's) (D) regulations dealing with industrial injuries were invalid as an improper delegation of legislative authority.

⬛ RULE OF LAW
Where at least one interpretation that is reasonable and consistent with the nondelegation doctrine exists, a statute should be given a narrow construction.

FACTS: International (P) claimed that an OSHA (D) regulation requiring lockout and tagout of dangerous equipment applied to virtually all equipment in almost all industries. International (P) therefore alleged the OSHA (D) regulation was an unconstitutional delegation of legislative power, or, in the alternative, that OSHA should adopt a safety standard only after a cost-benefit analysis. OSHA (D) claimed that it could impose any restriction so long as it was feasible.

ISSUE: Where at least one interpretation that is reasonable and consistent with the nondelegation doctrine exists, should a statute be given a narrow construction?

HOLDING AND DECISION: (Williams, J.) Yes. Where at least one interpretation that is reasonable and consistent with the nondelegation doctrine exists, a statute should be given a narrow construction. Here, a cost-benefit analysis requirement is a reasonable interpretation of the statute. International's (P) nondelegation claim fails because the statute may be read as providing for cost-benefit analysis. Remanded.

CONCURRENCE: (Henderson, J.) I concur, with the exception of the majority's statement that if reasonable alternative readings can be found, OSHA's (D) must be rejected as unreasonable.

▌ *ANALYSIS*

The nondelegation doctrine is based on Article I, § 1, of the U.S. Constitution. Only two statutes have ever been struck down on this basis. The nondelegation doctrine has been used to give narrow constructions to statutes that otherwise would violate it.

Quicknotes

OSHA, § 3(8) Defines occupational safety and health standards.

Commodity Futures Trading Commission v. Schor

Government agency (D) v. Investor (P)

478 U.S. 833 (1986).

NATURE OF CASE: Review of dismissal of counterclaims appended to a complaint seeking reparations filed with the Commodity Futures Trading Commission (CFTC).

FACT SUMMARY: Schor (P), seeking reparations from a commodities broker before the CFTC (D), contended that the CFTC (D) had no jurisdiction to entertain common law counterclaims.

RULE OF LAW
The adjudication of common law counterclaims by the CFTC is not unconstitutional.

FACTS: Schor (P), dissatisfied with the performance of certain commodity futures investments he had made, filed an action seeking reparations with the CFTC (D) against Conti (D), a commodities broker. Conti (D) counterclaimed for payment of certain fees. The CFTC (D) administrative law judge (ALJ), ruled in Conti's (D) favor in both the complaint and the counterclaim. Schor (P) then appealed, contending that the CFTC (D) had no jurisdiction to entertain common law counterclaims. The court of appeals dismissed the counterclaim, holding that the CFTC (D) lacked jurisdiction to entertain it. Conti (D) obtained review in the United States Supreme Court.

ISSUE: Is the adjudication of common law counterclaims by the CFTC (D) unconstitutional?

HOLDING AND DECISION: (O'Connor, J.) No. The adjudication of common law counterclaims by the CFTC (D) is not unconstitutional. First, the CFTC (D) itself considers such jurisdiction to be valid, and the views of an administrative agency toward matters germane to it are given no small weight. More importantly, CFTC (D) jurisdiction over counterclaims in actions before it does not violate the purposes underlying Article III. Article III is meant to ensure a free and independent judiciary. It was not meant to, nor does it, confer plenary jurisdiction over all matters in Article III courts. In deciding whether the delegation of quasi-judicial power to a non-Article III court is constitutional, the main question must be whether the delegation tends to encroach on the essential attributes of judicial power. Here, this does not appear to be the case. For one, only a particularized area of law is implicated here; the CFTC (D) has not been given broad power to adjudicate common law cases. Further, decisions of the CFTC (D) ALJs are subject to de novo review. Finally, the level of review, "weight of the evidence," is not excessively deferential. In short, the enabling statute has not expanded the power of the legislature or executive at the expense of the judiciary and, therefore, was valid. Reversed.

ANALYSIS

Four years prior to the present action, the Court had invalidated the statutory bankruptcy system based on the same considerations discussed here. Congress had entrusted the bankruptcy system to non-Article III judges and had given them very broad powers. The Court in this action distinguished that case, *Northern Pipeline Construction Co. v. Marathon Pipe Line Co.*, 458 U.S. 50 (1982), by noting that the jurisdiction of the CFTC here was much narrower.

Quicknotes

DE NOVO The review of a lower court decision by an appellate court, which is hearing the case as if it had not been previously heard and as if no judgment had been rendered.

U.S. CONSTITUTION, ARTICLE III Guarantees an independent an impartial adjudication by federal judiciary.

Immigration and Naturalization Service v. Chadha

Government agency (P) v. Deported immigrant (D)

462 U.S. 919 (1983).

NATURE OF CASE: Challenge to constitutionality of resolution procedure for overturning deportation suspension.

FACT SUMMARY: Chadha (D) challenged the constitutionality of an Immigration Act provision allowing either the House of Representatives (P) or the Senate, acting individually, to overturn the Attorney General's suspension of deportation proceedings by passing a resolution stating in substance that the deportation suspension is not favored.

🏛 RULE OF LAW
Where the action of either house of Congress is legislative in nature, such action is subject to the presentment and bicameral requirements of Article I of the Constitution.

FACTS: Chadha (D), who was born in Kenya, remained in the United States after his visa expired. He was ordered deported, but the Attorney General suspended the deportation. Pursuant to an Immigration Act provision allowing either House of Congress to overturn a deportation suspension by adopting a resolution to that effect, the House of Representatives (P) adopted a resolution overturning Chadha's (D) suspension, and he was ordered deported. There was no public hearing, report, or meaningful statement of reasons on the committee's recommendation favoring the resolution. Chadha (D) challenged the constitutionality of the House of Representatives' (P) action under the Immigration Act provision.

ISSUE: Where the action of either house of Congress is legislative in nature, is such action subject to the presentment and bicameral requirements of Article I of the Constitution?

HOLDING AND DECISION: (Burger, C.J.) Yes. Where the action of either house of Congress is legislative in nature, such action is subject to the presentment and bicameral requirements of Article I of the Constitution. The clear and unambiguous dictates of Article I of the Constitution require that, before any legislation is to take effect, it must have been passed with the concurrence of the prescribed majority of both houses of Congress, and must be presented to the President for approval. Presentment of legislation to the President establishes a salutary check on the legislature, and assures that a "national" perspective is grafted on the legislative process. The bicameral requirement assures that the legislative power will be exercised only after full study and debate in separate settings. The powers delegated to each branch of government are identifiable, and when any branch acts, it presumptively exercises the power delegated to it. The legislative character of the House's (P) action in the present case is apparent, since it is conceded that, absent the Immigration Act provision, Chadha's (D) deportation could only have been accomplished by legislation requiring deportation. The House's (P) action does not fall into one of the constitutionally prescribed exceptions to the bicameral requirement, and involves determinations of policy which should only be implemented by adhering to the presentment and bicameral requirements of Article I. The action taken by the House (P) pursuant to the IMA provision was in violation of Article I of the Constitution.

DISSENT: (White, J.) If possible, this decision should have been decided on the narrower grounds of separation of powers, and sounds a death knell for nearly 200 other statutes where Congress has reserved a legislative veto. The decision is inconsistent with the accepted practice of delegating lawmaking power to independent executive agencies and private persons and ignores the fact that the operation of the Immigration Act provision at question satisfies the bicameral and presentment requirements of Article I.

▶ ANALYSIS

It is not clear to what extent the "legislative veto" is dead. It is clear, however, that Congress can accomplish many of the legislative veto's objectives through the use of traditional weapons in its legislative and political arsenal. Among others, Congress can tailor statutes more carefully, can provide that an agency's legislative power will expire after a given period of time, and perhaps most importantly, can control an agency's budget. Each of these alternatives has obvious drawbacks and can serve to greatly undermine an agency's effectiveness.

■=■

Quicknotes

BICAMERALISM The necessity of approval by a majority of both houses of Congress in ratifying legislation or approving other legislative action.

LEGISLATIVE VETO A resolution passed by one or both legislature houses that is intended to block an administrative regulation or action.

PRESENTMENT The act of bringing a congressional decision before the President for his approval or veto.

SEPARATION OF POWERS The system of checks and balances preventing one branch of government from infringing upon exercising the powers of another branch of government.

■=■

Buckley v. Valeo

Member of Federal Election Commission (P) v. Opposing member (D)

424 U.S. 1 (1976).

NATURE OF CASE: Appeal of challenge to portions of the Federal Election Campaign Act of 1971.

FACT SUMMARY: Members of the Federal Election Commission were to be appointed by a method deviating from Article II, § 2 of the Constitution.

🏛 RULE OF LAW
Officers of the United States must be appointed in a manner consistent with Article II, § 2 of the Constitution.

FACTS: The Federal Election Campaign Act of 1971 (Act) created the Federal Election Campaign Commission (Commission), which was given broad sanctioning and investigative power with respect to elections. The Commission consisted of six voting members appointed by the President Pro Tem of the Senate, the Speaker of the House, and the President, who each selected two members of the Commission. The Secretary of the Senate and the Clerk of the House were nonvoting members. The Act was challenged on constitutional grounds. The court of appeals upheld the section dealing with the Commission.

ISSUE: Must officers of the United States be appointed in a manner consistent with Article II, § 2 of the Constitution?

HOLDING AND DECISION: (Per curiam) Yes. Officers of the United States must be appointed in a manner consistent with Article II, § 2 of the Constitution. The Constitution provides that no member of Congress will be appointed an officer of the United States during his term. This demonstrates that the Framers intended that strict separation be maintained between executive officers and legislative officials. Further, the Constitution mandates that all such executive officials shall be nominated by the President and confirmed by the Senate. The Commission in question exercises important executive functions, and, therefore, its members are officers of the United States. This being the case, they must be appointed per the constitutional requirements of Article II. Reversed.

▶ ANALYSIS

In theory, the Court created a fairly simple standard to follow in this area. Congress may appoint officials who perform purely legislative acts but not officers who perform executive or judicial acts. Of course, the principle is much easier in theory than in practice, and uncertainty will always exist as to which sort of officials do not have to be appointed pursuant to Article II.

Quicknotes

FEDERAL ELECTION CAMPAIGN ACT Created a commission to investigate and administrate federal elections.

U.S. CONSTITUTION, ARTICLE II, § 2 Provides that the President shall nominate, with the Senate's advice and consent, executive officials.

Morrison v. Olson

Independent prosecutor (P) v. Assistant attorney general (D)

487 U.S. 654 (1988).

NATURE OF CASE: Appeal from order quashing subpoenas issued at behest of a special prosecutor.

FACT SUMMARY: The independent counsel provisions of the Ethics in Government Act were challenged as unconstitutional.

🏛 RULE OF LAW
The independent counsel provision of the Ethics in Government Act is not unconstitutional.

FACTS: In passing the Ethics in Government Act (Act), Congress created the office of Special Prosecutor to investigate misdeeds by government officials. The Act provided that the Attorney General must investigate allegations and report to a special judicial division, which was enabled to appoint an independent counsel which in turn would have full prosecutorial authority. The counsel could be removed only by impeachment or by the Attorney General for good cause. The Act also provided for congressional oversight. Olson (P), under investigation by Prosecutor Morrison (D), filed an action seeking to quash certain grand jury subpoenas issued at the behest of Morrison (D). The district court denied such relief, but the court of appeals reversed, holding the independent counsel portions of the Act unconstitutional. The United States Supreme Court accepted review.

ISSUE: Are the independent counsel provisions of the Ethics in Government Act unconstitutional?

HOLDING AND DECISION: (Rehnquist, C.J.) No. The independent counsel provisions of the Ethics in Government Act are not unconstitutional. Due to the limited scope of the counsel's office, the counsel is an inferior officer, not a principal officer that must be appointed by the President. Also, there is no constitutional prohibition on interbranch appointments, so a judicial body appointing an executive officer does not in itself violate the Constitution. This Court is of the opinion that the supervisory powers of the special division are of a ministerial nature and do not trespass on the authority of the Executive. Apart from impeachment, it is only the Attorney General who can remove the Special Prosecutor. Finally, this Court is of the opinion that the office of the Special Prosecutor does not violate the principle of separation of powers. While the Prosecutor does report to Congress, he is much more answerable to the Attorney General, who, significantly, retains the power to remove the Prosecutor. The Court believes that this does not unduly interfere with the powers of the President in enforcing the laws. For these reasons, the Court considers the office of the Special Prosecutor to be constitutional. Reversed.

DISSENT: (Scalia, J.) The function of the independent counsel is clearly an executive function. However, in the light of the position's broad powers and the fact that the independent counsel cannot be removed at the will of the executive branch, it cannot be considered an inferior position. Thus, the Court is incorrect in using the inferior status to uphold the appointment. The independent counsel infringes on the President's power, which the Congress cannot limit by legislation.

▶ ANALYSIS

The Appointments Clause of Article II mandates appointment of noninferior officers by the President, with consent of the Senate. The Special Prosecutor is not so appointed. The Court looked to the breadth of the Prosecutor's office and decided that although the Prosecutor has wide-ranging powers, the ad hoc nature of the office mandated a conclusion that the office was inferior.

■■■

Quicknotes

APPOINTMENT'S CLAUSE, ARTICLE II, U.S. CONSTITUTION President shall nominate principal officials with the Senator's advice and consent.

ETHICS IN GOVERNMENT ACT Allows for the appointment of a special prosecutor to investigate high-ranking government officials.

INDEPENDENT COUNSEL An officer, whose appointment is authorized by the Ethics in Government Act, who is charged with the investigation of possible criminal activity by high-level government officials.

■■■

Humphrey's Executor v. United States

Executor of estate (P) v. Federal government (D)

295 U.S. 602 (1935).

NATURE OF CASE: Action to recover back pay for wrongful discharge.

FACT SUMMARY: Humphrey (P) contended that the President could not remove him as a commissioner of the Federal Trade Commission merely because of a difference in philosophy.

🏛 RULE OF LAW
The President cannot remove officials whose agency functions are quasi-legislative and quasi-judicial in nature and not merely extensions of the Executive Branch of government.

FACTS: President Roosevelt felt that his predecessors had appointed commissioners to the Federal Trade Commission whose philosophies were contradictory to the legislative intent in creating that body. As a result he attempted to remove Humphrey (P) as a commissioner based on this conflict of philosophy and not on any wrongdoing on Humphrey's (P) part. Humphrey (P) challenged his removal as unconstitutional and beyond the President's power. The Government (D) defended, contending the President's power to remove administrators could not be constitutionally limited. The Court of Claims certified Humphrey's (P) suit for back pay to the United States Supreme Court.

ISSUE: Can the President remove administrative officials whose agencies perform quasi-legislative and quasi-judicial functions and are not merely extensions of the executive branch?

HOLDING AND DECISION: (Sutherland, J.) No. Although the President may remove administrators whose functions are merely executive in nature, those whose statutory authority and duty is to act in a legislative or judicial mode cannot be so removed unless by congressional consent. The Federal Trade Commission was created not as a department of the executive branch but as a means of carrying into effect legislative and judicial powers. Thus it is an agency of the legislative and judicial departments of government. Therefore, in order to prevent the executive department from obtaining indirect control over an agency outside its purview, the President is denied removal power except for enumerated reasons in the Federal Trade Commission Act. Therefore Humphrey's (P) removal was invalid.

▶ ANALYSIS

This case specifically clarifies and limits the holding of an earlier case, *Myers v. United States*, 272 U.S. 52 (1926), which held that the President could unilaterally remove an administrator whose function was purely executive in nature. The

rationale stated in *Myers* was that the President must be able to command loyalty and confidence from those performing executive functions. The Court in this case limits *Myers* to executive agencies, and states the President's removal power depends upon the character of the office involved.

■■■

Quicknotes

ADMINISTRATIVE OFFICIAL An official of the executive branch of the government.

EXECUTIVE BRANCH The branch of government responsible for the administration of the laws.

WRONGFUL DISCHARGE Unlawful termination of an individual's employment.

■■■

Morrison v. Olson

Independent prosecutor (P) v. Assistant attorney general (D)

487 U.S. 654 (1988).

NATURE OF CASE: Appeal from order quashing subpoenas issued at behest of a special prosecutor.

FACT SUMMARY: Olson (P) alleged that a provision of the Ethics in Government Act impermissibly interfered with the President's exercise of his constitutionally appointed functions.

🏛 RULE OF LAW
The Constitution does not require that an independent counsel be terminable at will by the President.

FACTS: Olson (P) was under investigation for allegedly giving false and misleading testimony to a House Subcommittee when he was the Assistant Attorney General for the Office of Legal Counsel. Morrison (D), acting as independent counsel pursuant to the Ethics in Government Act, caused subpoenas to be issued and served on Olson (P). Olson (P) moved to quash the subpoenas, alleging that the provisions of the Act, restricting the Attorney General's power to remove the independent counsel only when good cause could be shown, were unconstitutional because they interfered with the President's absolute discretion to discharge purely executive officials at will.

ISSUE: Does the Constitution require that an independent counsel be terminable at will by the President?

HOLDING AND DECISION: (Rehnquist, C.J.) No. The Constitution does not require that an independent counsel be terminable at will by the President. The President's need to control the independent counsel's discretion is not so central to the functioning of the Executive Branch as to require, as a matter of constitutional law, that the counsel be terminable at will. Imposition of the good cause standard for removal does not by itself unduly trammel on executive authority.

DISSENT: (Scalia, J.) The clear constitutional prescription that the executive power belongs to the President has been replaced by a balancing test. No standard has been established to govern this test, leaving it to the unfettered discretion of a majority of this Court. This is not government of laws at all.

▎ *ANALYSIS*

There was no dispute that the functions of the independent counsel were executive. The dissent argued that no standards were set to determine how the new test functioned. In the aftermath of Kenneth Starr's investigation of President Clinton, the independent counsel statute was allowed to expire.

■══■

Quicknotes

APPOINTMENTS CLAUSE Article II, section 2, clause 2 of the United States Constitution conferring power upon the president to appoint ambassadors, public ministers and consuls, judges of the United States Supreme Court and all other officers of the United States with the advice and consent of the Senate.

ETHICS IN GOVERNMENT ACT Allows for the appointment of special independent counsel to investigate high ranking government officials.

INDEPENDENT COUNSEL An officer, whose appointment is authorized by the Ethics in Government Act, who is charged with the investigation of possible criminal activity by high-level government officials.

SEPARATION OF POWERS The system of checks and balances preventing one branch of government from infringing upon exercising the powers of another branch of government.

■══■

Bowsher v. Synar

Party Unknown (P) v. Congress (D)

478 U.S. 714 (1986).

NATURE OF CASE: Appeal from order invalidating the Balanced Budget Act.

FACT SUMMARY: Synar (P) contended that the Balanced Budget Act violated separation of powers by providing strict requirements for appointment of an executive branch office.

🏛 RULE OF LAW
Congress cannot retain power to remove executive branch officers except by impeachment.

FACTS: Congress enacted the Balanced Budget Act which invested in the Comptroller General the power to make broad budgetary decisions as a member of the executive branch. The Comptroller was appointed by the President from a list provided by Congress. Removal was obtained by a joint resolution of Congress. Synar (P) sued, contending the statute unconstitutionally violated the separation of powers doctrine. The district court invalidated the statute. The court of appeals affirmed, and the United States Supreme Court granted certiorari.

ISSUE: Can Congress retain power to remove executive branch officers?

HOLDING AND DECISION: (Burger, C.J.) No. Congress cannot retain power to remove executive branch officers except by impeachment. Any other removal power over executive officers imposes undue power over that branch and is inconsistent with separation of powers. Such a power would make the executive officer subservient to Congress and, in effect, allow Congress to execute the laws. The Comptroller General's duties under the statute are not merely mechanical and ministerial, but they are indeed the very essence of executive functions. The statute requires the Comptroller General to both interpret the Act and exercise judgment in how to apply the Act—functions usually committed to executive officers. As a result, the statute was unconstitutional. Affirmed.

▶ ANALYSIS

The Comptroller General performs many functions which identify the office more closely with Congress than with the executive branch. The office settles all claims against the government and determines all accounts owed or owing. Despite this, the office was created under the executive branch.

Quicknotes

EXECUTIVE BRANCH The branch of government responsible for the administration of the laws.

IMPEACHMENT The discrediting of a witness by offering evidence to show that the witness lacks credibility.

LEGISLATIVE BRANCH The branch of government charged with the promulgation of laws.

SEPARATION OF POWERS The system of checks and balances preventing one branch of government from infringing upon exercising the powers of another branch of government.

■=■

Clinton v. City of New York

U.S. President (D) v. City (P)

524 U.S. 417 (1998).

NATURE OF CASE: Challenge to the constitutionality of new presidential powers.

FACT SUMMARY: The Line Item Veto Act of 1996 allowed the president to cancel provisions that have been signed into law. Parties affected by President Clinton's cancellation of a provision of the Balanced Budget Act of 1997 challenged the constitutionality of the Act.

🏛 RULE OF LAW
The cancellation provisions authorized by the Line Item Veto Act are not constitutional.

FACTS: President Clinton used his authority under the Line Item Veto Act of 1996 to cancel a provision of the Balanced Budget Act of 1997. This forced New York to repay certain funds to the federal government under the Medicaid program and removed a tax benefit to food processors acquired by farmers' cooperatives. New York City and several private organizations challenged the constitutionality of the Medicaid cancellation and the Snake River Potato Growers (a farmer's cooperative) challenged the food processors provision.

ISSUE: Are the cancellation provisions authorized by the Line Item Veto Act constitutional?

HOLDING AND DECISION: (Stevens, J.) No. The cancellation provisions authorized by the Line Item Veto Act are not constitutional. The Line Item Veto Act gives the President the power to "cancel in whole" three types of provisions that have already been signed into law: (1) any dollar amount of discretionary budget authority; (2) any item of new direct spending; or (3) any limited tax benefit. With respect to each cancellation, the President must determine that it will (i) reduce the federal budget deficit; (ii) not impair any essential government functions; and (iii) not harm the national interest. A cancellation takes effect upon receipt by Congress of the notification of the cancellation. However, a majority vote of both Houses is sufficient to make the cancellation null and void. Although the Constitution expressly authorizes the President to veto a bill under Article I, § 7, it is silent on the subject of unilateral Presidential action that repeals or amends parts of duly enacted statues as authorized under the Line Item Veto Act. Constitutional silence should be construed as express prohibition. If there is to be a new role for the President in the procedure to determine the final text of a law, such a change must come through the amendment procedures and not by legislation. Affirmed.

CONCURRENCE: (Kennedy, J.) Separation of powers was designed to protect liberty, because the concentration of power in any single branch is a threat to liberty.

CONCURRENCE AND DISSENT: (Scalia, J.) If the Line Item Veto Act authorized the President to "decline to spend" any item of spending rather than "cancelling" it, it would have been constitutional. Given that there is only a technical difference between the two actions and that it is no different from what Congress has permitted the President to do since the formation of the Union, the Line Item Veto does not offend Article I, § 7.

DISSENT: (Breyer, J.) Given how complex our nation has become, Congress cannot divide bills into thousands or tens of thousands of separate appropriations bills, each of which the President would have to veto or sign separately. Therefore, the Line Item Veto may help representative government work better.

▶ ANALYSIS

The majority did not comment on the wisdom of the Line Item Veto Act, because they found this step unnecessary given their finding that the Act was unconstitutional. Justice Kennedy did not let that stop him, since he felt that the Line Item Veto Act affected the separation of powers, which in turn threatened liberty.

■═■

Quicknotes

LINE ITEM VETO ACT Act authorizes a government official to veto specified items in appropriation bills.

■═■

CHAPTER 7

Inspections, Reports and Subpoenas

Quick Reference Rules of Law

Camara v. Municipal Court

Apartment owner (D) v. Court (P)

387 U.S. 523 (1967).

NATURE OF CASE: Appeal from conviction for not permitting a building inspection.

FACT SUMMARY: Camara (D) refused to let city building inspectors enter his apartment.

RULE OF LAW

Administrative searches are reasonable searches, but still require a warrant.

FACTS: San Francisco building inspectors sought to inspect Camara's (D) apartment pursuant to a general city ordinance. Camara (D) refused to allow the inspectors to enter his apartment without a warrant and was convicted of violating the municipal code. Camara (D) appealed, claiming that the proposed search violated the Fourth Amendment.

ISSUE: Are administrative searches reasonable searches requiring a warrant?

HOLDING AND DECISION: (White, J.) Yes. Administrative searches are reasonable searches, but still require a warrant. The Fourth Amendment was designed to safeguard the privacy and security of individuals against arbitrary invasions by governmental officials. Except in certain cases, a search of private property without proper consent is an unreasonable search, unless a warrant has authorized the search. Probable cause is the standard by which a decision to search is considered reasonable and constitutional. Administrative searches that cover an entire area to enforce community building standards have a long history of acceptance, are necessary to protect the public, and involve a limited invasion of privacy. Thus, an area inspection is reasonable as long as a warrant is issued prior to the inspection. A warrant does not need to consider a specific condition or knowledge about a particular dwelling. Without a warrant, a person is unable to verify the need for, or the appropriate limits of, the inspection. Accordingly, the city building inspectors should have obtained a warrant first, and Camara (D) should not have been charged with a crime for refusing to allow the inspection.

▶ ANALYSIS

The Court acknowledged that some administrative searches might be justified by emergency situations. Obviously, this case did not provide that justification, since the inspectors tried on three different occasions to inspect Camara's (D) apartment. Subsequently, the Court made an exception to the warrant requirement for administrative searches of industries that had a long history of close government regulation.

■==■

Quicknotes

FOURTH AMENDMENT Provides that persons be secure as to their person and private belongings against unreasonable searches and seizures.

WARRANT An order issued by a court directing an officer to undertake a certain act (i.e., an arrest or search).

■==■

Trinity Industries, Inc. v. OSHRC

Manufacturer (D) v. Government agency (P)

16 F.3d 1455 (6th Cir. 1994).

NATURE OF CASE: Appeal from administrative penalties for safety violations.

FACT SUMMARY: Trinity (D) complained that the Occupational Safety and Health Administration's (OSHA's) (P) inspection was broader than the scope of the complaint that prompted the inspection.

🏛 RULE OF LAW
An administrative inspection, based upon specific evidence of a violation, must bear a relation to that violation.

FACTS: Trinity (D) manufactures tanks and pressure vessels at its plant in Ohio. In 1988, an employee filed a complaint with OSHA (P) alleging multiple safety violations at the plant. Trinity (D) refused to permit an inspection, so OSHA (P) obtained an administrative inspection warrant. OSHA (P) ended up reviewing and inspecting Trinity records and sites that exceeded the allegations of the original complaint. Trinity (D) was charged with multiple violations and fined $33,000. Trinity (D) contested some of the citations based on that part of the inspection that went beyond the reach of the complaint, which enabled the warrant to be issued.

ISSUE: Must an administrative inspection, based upon specific evidence of a violation, bear a relation to that violation?

HOLDING AND DECISION: (Martin, J.) Yes. An administrative inspection, based upon specific evidence of a violation, must bear a relation to that violation. Warrants are required for administrative inspections. Probable cause justifying the issuance of a warrant for administrative purposes may be based on either specific evidence of an existing violation or on a showing that a specific business has been chosen for a search on the basis of a general administrative plan derived from neutral sources. Inspections done pursuant to a general administrative plan may properly extend to the entire workplace. However, warrants issued because of specific complaints have an increased danger of abuse of discretion and intrusiveness. Therefore, a complaint inspection must bear an appropriate relationship to the violation alleged in the complaint. In the present case, OSHA (P) used an employee complaint to trigger a full-scope inspection of Trinity (D) without the required showing of probable cause. However, OSHA (P) was entitled to review all the inspection records of Trinity (D), even if a comprehensive plant inspection was unauthorized. Reversed and remanded.

▶ ANALYSIS

The court noted that OSHA (P) should have reviewed Trinity's (D) records first. Then, if the review of the injury and illness records led to further suspicions, OSHA (P) could have applied for a second warrant. This second warrant could have included a full and comprehensive inspection of the physical facility.

■■■

Quicknotes

COMPLAINT The initial pleading commencing litigation which sets forth a claim for relief.

WARRANT An order issued by a court directing an officer to undertake a certain act (i.e., an arrest or search).

■■■

In re Trinity Industries, Inc.

Manufacturers (D) v. Government agency (P)

876 F.2d 1485 (11th Cir. 1989).

NATURE OF CASE: Appeal of order to permit inspection.

FACT SUMMARY: Two industrial manufacturers, Trinity (D) and Mosher (D), claimed that warrant applications for Occupational Safety and Health Administration (OSHA) inspections of their plants were defective.

🏛 RULE OF LAW
A warrant application for an administrative search is valid if the plan is based on specific, neutral criteria and it adequately establishes that the particular company was selected pursuant to the neutral criteria.

FACTS: OSHA regulations for safety and health inspections establish a ranking system for inspecting companies in high-hazard industries. The agency ranks employers based on lost workday injury rates, and companies that are below average are subject to placement on the inspection list. Companies that recently underwent inspections are taken off the list and higher priority is given to larger companies. Pursuant to this administrative search plan, OSHA obtained warrants for inspecting Trinity (D) and Mosher (D), two manufacturers. The companies refused to permit the inspections. Under threat of contempt, Mosher (D) permitted the inspection, but the court was forced to fine Trinity (D), who then appealed the court's order.

ISSUE: Is a warrant application for an administrative search valid if the plan is based on specific, neutral criteria and it adequately establishes that the particular company was selected pursuant to the neutral criteria?

HOLDING AND DECISION: (Cox, J.) Yes. A warrant application for an administrative search is valid if the plan is based on specific, neutral criteria and it adequately establishes that the particular company was selected pursuant to the neutral criteria. To satisfy the Fourth Amendment, a warrant for an administrative search must be obtained prior to the inspection. Probable cause for this warrant can be justified by a general administrative plan for the enforcement of the law as long as the criteria for picking the individuals who will be inspected is neutral. In making this determination, the court must apply a two-priority test: (1) whether the plan pursuant to which the warrant is to be issued is based on neutral criteria; and (2) whether the warrant application clearly and adequately established that the company was selected for inspection pursuant to the neutral criteria. In the present case, the OSHA administrative plan is rational and neutral. It is intended and designed to protect the greatest number of employees who are exposed to the greatest risks. Although the plan may result in more frequent inspections of select portions of all industries, it seems eminently reasonable that OSHA has decided to allocate its resources in this manner. The warrant at issue in the present case contained a detailed description of the procedure used in selecting companies and a sworn affidavit that Trinity (D) and Mosher (D) were selected according to the procedure. This was sufficient for the magistrate to issue the warrant. Therefore, the district court was not in error in holding the companies in contempt for failing to allow the inspections. Affirmed.

▶ ANALYSIS

The probable cause standard for an administrative warrant is obviously somewhat less than for a criminal-type search. Still, illegal searches do happen. Agencies and officials can be liable for civil penalties for violating the Fourth Amendment.

■=■

Quicknotes

FOURTH AMENDMENT Provides that persons be secure as to their person and private belongings against unreasonable searches and seizures.

PROBABLE CAUSE A reasonable basis for believing that a crime has been committed.

■=■

United States v. Janis

IRS (P) v. Alleged bookie (D)

428 U.S. 433 (1976).

NATURE OF CASE: Appeal from motion to exclude evidence from back taxes proceeding.

FACT SUMMARY: Bookmaking records were seized in an illegal search but the Internal Revenue Service (IRS) (P) sought to use the records against Janis (D) to prove that back taxes were owed.

🏛 RULE OF LAW
The exclusionary rule that bars illegally seized evidence from being used in a criminal prosecution does not apply in a civil proceeding.

FACTS: Los Angeles police officers searched an apartment, seized records of illegal bookmaking and arrested the occupants. The records were then turned over to the IRS (P), which made an assessment for back taxes against Janis (D). Subsequently, a judge determined that the search was illegal based on defects in the warrant. Janis (D) argued that the IRS (P) claim should be dismissed because of the illegal search.

ISSUE: Does the exclusionary rule that bars illegally seized evidence from being used in a criminal prosecution apply in a civil proceeding?

HOLDING AND DECISION: (Blackmun, J.) No. The exclusionary rule that bars illegally seized evidence from being used in a criminal prosecution does not apply in a civil proceeding. In 1914, the United States Supreme Court ruled that the Fourth Amendment barred use of evidence from an illegal search at a federal criminal trial. The primary purpose of this exclusionary rule is to deter future unlawful police conduct. It is a judicially created remedy designed to safeguard Fourth Amendment rights. Thus, application of the rule is limited to those circumstances where the remedial objectives are served. The additional marginal deterrence provided by also forbidding use of the evidence in a separate civil proceeding does not outweigh the cost to society of the exclusion. Therefore, this Court declines to extend application of the exclusionary rule to civil proceedings.

DISSENT: (Brennan, J.) The exclusionary rule is an intrinsic, essential protection guaranteed by the Fourth Amendment.

DISSENT: (Stewart, J.) This decision undercuts the deterrent effect by allowing police to crack down on gambling by illegally seizing evidence and turning it over to the IRS (P).

▶ ANALYSIS

It should be noted that this decision does not allow agency officials to illegally seize evidence and use it in civil proceedings. It applies only to an illegal search by a police officer for use in a criminal trial. Still, the dissent does rightly point out that there is a potential for abuse.

Quicknotes

EXCLUSIONARY RULE A rule precluding the introduction at trial of evidence unlawfully obtained in violation of the federal constitutional safeguards against unreasonable searches and seizures.

FOURTH AMENDMENT Provides that persons be secure as to their person and private belongings against unreasonable searches and seizures.

INS v. Lopez-Mendoza

Government agency (P) v. Illegal alien (D)

468 U.S. 1032 (1984).

NATURE OF CASE: Appeal from evidence ruling in a deportation hearing.

FACT SUMMARY: Lopez-Mendoza (D), an illegal alien, sought to have an admission barred from evidence because it was the product of an illegal arrest.

RULE OF LAW

The exclusionary rule for illegally seized evidence does not apply in civil deportation hearings.

FACTS: Lopez-Mendoza (D) was arrested unlawfully and admitted that he was an illegal alien. At the deportation hearing conducted by the Immigration and Naturalization Service (INS) (P), Lopez-Mendoza (D) argued that the admission should be excluded because it was the product of the illegal arrest.

ISSUE: Does the exclusionary rule for illegally seized evidence apply in civil deportation hearings?

HOLDING AND DECISION: (O'Connor, J.) No. The exclusionary rule for illegal seized evidence does not apply in civil deportation hearings. The exclusionary rule barring the use of evidence from an illegal search applies only where its deterrent effect is greater than the costs imposed on society. In a civil deportation hearing, there are several factors that reduce the likely deterrent value. The INS (P) will still be able to deport with other evidence of alienage. Given that virtually all INS (P) agent arrests lead to voluntary deportations, the arresting officers are unlikely to change their conduct to avoid exclusion in a subsequent deportation hearing. The INS (P) also has its own comprehensive scheme for deterring Fourth Amendment violations by its officers. On the other hand, the social costs of applying the exclusionary rule are unusual and significant. It would require courts to look past an ongoing violation of the law—the continued presence of an illegal alien in the country. It would also necessitate changing the nature of deportation hearings, which are already strained by the numbers of illegal aliens and time constraints. Finally, applying the rule might preclude the INS (P) from conducting mass arrests of illegal aliens, even if they are usually in full compliance with the Fourth Amendment. Accordingly, the exclusionary rule should not be applied in civil deportation hearings and Lopez-Mendoza (D) may not exclude his admission.

ANALYSIS

The court further noted that its conclusion could have been different if there was a record that INS (D) Fourth Amendment violations were widespread. It is interesting that one of the reasons for not applying the rule is that the INS (D) officers wouldn't change their conduct anyway. It seems unlikely that police officers would be allowed to make this argument against application of the exclusionary rule.

■■■

Quicknotes

EXCLUSIONARY RULE A rule precluding the introduction at trial of evidence unlawfully obtained in violation of the federal constitutional safeguards against unreasonable searches and seizures.

FOURTH AMENDMENT Provides that persons be secure as to their person and private belongings against unreasonable searches and seizures.

■■■

Board of Education of Independent School District No. 92 of Pottawatomie County v. Earls

Public school district (D) v. Student (P)

536 U.S. 822 (2002).

NATURE OF CASE: Suit by students to invalidate a public school district's drug-testing policy.

FACT SUMMARY: A public school district required all students who wanted to participate in any extracurricular activity to first pass a drug test and to consent to future drug tests.

> 🏛 **RULE OF LAW**
> A public school's drug-testing policy for students is reasonable, as required by the Fourth Amendment, if the policy requires no individualized suspicion and is mandatory for participation in all extracurricular activities.

FACTS: The School District (District) (D) implemented a drug-testing policy that conditioned student participation in any school-sponsored extracurricular activity upon a student's consent to drug testing. Despite this breadth in the policy, the District (D) applied the policy to competitive extracurricular activities, most of which were non-athletic activities. Specifically, the policy required students to consent to a drug test before they participated in an extracurricular activity, to consent to random testing while they participated in their activity, and to consent to random testing whenever reasonable suspicion justified a test. The tests revealed the presence of only illegal drugs and did not confirm the presence of any medical conditions or authorized medications. A student in the District (D), Lindsay Earls (P), participated in show choir, marching band, the Academic Team, and the National Honor Society. Another student in the District (D), Daniel James (P), wanted to participate in the Academic Team. The two students (P) sued the District (D) to invalidate the policy, and the trial court entered judgment for the District (D). The court of appeals reversed, and the District (D) petitioned the Unites States Supreme Court for further review.

ISSUE: Is a public school's drug-testing policy for students reasonable, as required by the Fourth Amendment, if the policy requires no individualized suspicion and is mandatory for participation in all extracurricular activities?

HOLDING AND DECISION: (Thomas, J.) Yes. A public school's drug-testing policy for students is reasonable, as required by the Fourth Amendment, if the policy requires no individualized suspicion and is mandatory for participation in all extracurricular activities. As the students (P) correctly agree, probable cause is not required for the tests here because these tests are not part of a criminal investigation. Contrary to the students' (P) position, however, not

even individualized suspicion is required in the administrative context when "special needs," such as those inherent in the school setting, justify the search. The Court's upholding of suspicionless drug tests for high school athletes in *Vernonia School District 47J v. Acton,* 515 U.S. 646 (1995), requires the same result on the slightly different facts presented here. Even students engaged in extracurricular activities who are not athletes have only a limited expectation of privacy, considering the requisite travel for non-athletic activities and students' consent to various other rules and regulations. Further, compared to the policy in *Vernonia,* this policy's requirement that a faculty monitor wait outside a closed bathroom stall for a student's urine sample imposes a less-than-negligible intrusion upon students' privacy. The policy itself also requires that test results remain confidential, that they not be divulged to law-enforcement officials, and that they not be used for disciplinary action. Finally, the District (D) faces immediate risks to students' health and safety because of the nationwide drug epidemic, and these risks have specifically appeared in the District (D). The policy at issue in this case, therefore, was entirely reasonable. The challenging students' (P) argument for requiring a "surpassing" safety risk is misplaced because drugs jeopardize the health and safety of all students. Similarly misplaced is the students' (P) argument for a presumption favoring individualized suspicion in such circumstances; the Fourth Amendment does not require government actors to use the least-intrusive methods. Reversed.

CONCURRENCE: (Breyer, J.) This policy discourages drug use by removing peer pressure; students can offer their peers a specific reason to decline to use drugs. Moreover, conscientious objectors still have an option, too—short of being expelled from school—though they must forego the privilege of participating in extracurricular activities if they exercise that option. Furthermore, in the school context, requiring individualized suspicion would only cause more problems than it solved because such a requirement would invite targeting students for improper reasons. The policy satisfies the Fourth Amendment.

DISSENT: (Ginsburg, J.) This policy is not only not reasonable; it is capricious and perverse, largely because the students targeted by this policy are the least likely to be at risk of using illegal drugs. *Vernonia* does not control here: the communal undress required for the activity there, as well as the risk of physical injury there, dispositively distinguish *Vernonia* from this case. The school district in *Vernonia* faced a genuinely dangerous situation. The nature

Continued on next page.

and immediacy of the District's (D) concern here, however, are lacking: the District (D) in this case has repeatedly reported to the federal government that drugs were not a major problem in the period leading up to the policy's adoption. This case is thus more like *Chandler v. Miller*, 520 U.S. 305 (1997), in which a suspicionless drug test was held to violate the Fourth Amendment. In this case, too, as in *Chandler,* the government's sole genuine benefit from using the policy is the image of itself that it wants to project. The District's (D) policy does not promote the "special needs" that exist in our schools.

▶ *ANALYSIS*

In *Earls,* the majority's focus on the "special needs" present in schools effectively determined the outcome in the case. Justice Ginsburg, in dissent, concluded that the record evidence did not justify allowing the "special needs" rationale to trump what she saw as several other mitigating considerations (such as the District's (D) repeatedly informing the federal government that drugs were not a problem in the District's (D) schools). Justice Thomas and the rest of the majority, however, placed special emphasis on the District's (D) "custodial and tutelary responsibility for children" and held for the school.

■═■

Quicknotes

FOURTH AMENDMENT Provides that persons be secure as to their person and private belongings against unreasonable searches and seizures.

■═■

Safford Unified School District #1 v. Redding

Public School District (D) v. Student (P)

_____ U.S. _____, 129 S.Ct. 2633 (2009).

NATURE OF CASE: Appeal of determination that student's Fourth Amendment rights were violated and that school district officials were not entitled to qualified immunity from liability.

FACT SUMMARY: School district officials (D) conducted a strip search of a 13-year-old female student (P) in an effort to uncover prohibited prescription and over-the-counter medications.

RULE OF LAW
First, the Fourth Amendment rights of a 13-year-old female student were violated when said student was subjected to a strip search on the basis of school district officials' reasonable suspicion that she possessed and had distributed forbidden prescription and over-the-counter drugs at school. And second, the school district officials involved in the search were protected from liability through qualified immunity.

FACTS: School district officials (D), acting on reasonable suspicion that middle school student Savana Redding (P) was involved in the prohibited distribution of prescription-strength ibuprofen and over-the-counter pain relievers at school, conducted a strip search of Savana (P). Two female employees of the school district (D) directed Savana (P) to remove her clothes to her underwear, and required Savana (P) to pull her underpants and bra away from her body. The employees (P) viewed Savana's (P) exposed breasts and pelvic area, but found nothing hidden on her person. Significantly, school district officials (D) understood prior to the search of Savana (P) that the contraband involved was of limited threat and quantity. Furthermore, the record reflects both that school district officials (D) had no reason to believe that Savana (P) was hiding the underlying medications in her underwear and that the preceding strip search of another female student suspected of receiving pills from Savana (P) yielded no contraband. It was never determined, in fact, at what time—whether the day of the strip search or in days prior—Savana (P) had distributed the prohibited pills.

ISSUE: First, were the Fourth Amendment rights of a 13-year-old female student violated when said student was subjected to a strip search on the basis of school district officials' reasonable suspicions that she possessed and had distributed forbidden prescription and over-the-counter drugs at school. And second, were the school district officials involved in the search protected from liability through qualified immunity?

HOLDING AND DECISION: (Souter, J.) Yes. The Fourth Amendment rights of a 13-year-old female student were violated when said student was subjected to a strip search on the basis of school district officials' reasonable suspicions that she possessed and had distributed forbidden prescription and over-the-counter drugs at school. And, yes. The school district officials involved in the search were protected from liability through qualified immunity. Pursuant to the Court's holding in _New Jersey v. T.L.O._, 469 U.S. 325 (1985), in a school setting, searches by school officials require a modification of the level of suspicion of illicit activity needed to justify a search. As such, and in lieu of requiring probable cause to search, school officials need only have a reasonable suspicion of illegality to justify a search of a student. Nonetheless, a search of a student by school officials must be reasonably related to the objectives of the search and not excessively intrusive considering the age and sex of the student and the nature of the infraction. In light of the instant school district's (D) strict policy prohibiting the nonmedical use and possession of prescription or over-the-counter drugs, and on the strength of the suspicion that Savana (P) was involved in prohibited pill distribution, it is manifest that the school district (D) would be justified in searching Savana's (P) backpack and outer clothing. The record demonstrates, however, that the content of the suspicion of school district officials (D) did not support a strip search of a 13-year-old female student. There was simply no indication that Savana (P) possessed the kind or quantity of drug that would endanger other students, or that she concealed them in her underwear. Notwithstanding the Fourth Amendment violation at issue, school district officials (D) were entitled to qualified immunity in the execution of their professional judgment. Particularly because the lower courts have reached divergent conclusions regarding the application of the _T.L.O._ standard to student searches, it is doubtful that this Court was sufficiently clear in its articulation of the _T.L.O._ standard to withhold immunity here. Thus, school district officials (D), motivated here to eliminate drugs from the school and protect students from harm, are entitled to qualified immunity. Affirmed in part and reversed in part.

CONCURRENCE AND DISSENT: (Stevens, J.) Because the law is clearly established, and because the conduct of the school official who authorized the underlying search was clearly outrageous, qualified immunity is not justified.

CONCURRENCE AND DISSENT: (Ginsburg, J.) Upon the Fourth Amendment violation at issue here, qualified immunity is not justified.

Continued on next page.

CONCURRENCE AND DISSENT: (Thomas, J.) Courts should not be able to second-guess the measures school district officials take to ensure the health and safety of their students. As such, and because the search of Savana Redding did not violate the Fourth Amendment, it was proper to extend immunity to school district officials.

▶ *ANALYSIS*

While the Court in *Redding* cleared the actors of liability, it remanded the case on the issue of the whether immunity extended to the School District itself, as a government entity. In support of its remand, the Court cited *Monell v. New York City Department of Social Services*, 436 U.S. 658, 694 (1978), which held that a local government cannot be sued for injury inflicted solely by an employee, but only if the employee acted in execution of the government's policy. See also, 42 U. S. C. § 1983. Accordingly, it may be that the *Redding* Court opened the door for redress of the student's Fourth Amendment violations.

■═■

Quicknotes

FOURTH AMENDMENT   Provides that persons be secure as to their person and private belongings against unreasonable searches and seizures.

IMMUNITY   Exemption from a legal obligation.

REASONABLE EXPECTATION OF PRIVACY   In order to invoke the Fourth Amendment's protection against unreasonable searches and seizures, an individual must have a reasonable expectation of privacy in respect to the location searched or thing seized.

■═■

Freese v. Federal Deposit Insurance Corp.

Former bank officer (P) v. Government agency (D)

837 F. Supp. 22 (D.N.H. 1993).

NATURE OF CASE: Motion to quash subpoena seeking personal financial records.

FACT SUMMARY: The Federal Deposit Insurance Corporation (FDIC) (D) sought to examine the personal records of former bank officers (P) to see if they had any potential claims against them.

🏛 RULE OF LAW
Government agencies may not use their subpoena powers for improper purposes.

FACTS: In 1991, the FDIC (D) was appointed receiver and liquidating agent for the New Hampshire Savings Bank. The following year, the FDIC (D) wanted to investigate whether there were any valid claims against the former officers (P) of the bank. In connection with this investigation, the FDIC (D) issued administrative subpoenas to the officers and directors seeking extensive personal financial information for the previous five years. Among the purposes for seeking the information claimed by the FDIC (D) were to see if there was enough money to satisfy any potential claims and to determine whether a suit would be cost effective. The officers (P) claimed that the subpoenas were issued in violation of the Fourth Amendment and challenged their legality.

ISSUE: May government agencies use their subpoena powers for improper purposes?

HOLDING AND DECISION: (Loughlin, Sr. J.) No. Government agencies may not use their subpoena powers for improper purposes. Agency subpoenas are enforceable if for a proper purpose and adequately determined in the subpoena, the information sought is relevant to that purpose, and the statutory procedures have been followed. A determination of whether a civil suit is cost effective against a potential defendant is not a proper purpose to issue a subpoena. It is impermissible to peruse a person's financial records to check their ability to satisfy a judgment. The potential liability of a person, however, could form the basis of a valid subpoena. However, in the present case, the FDIC (D) has not asserted any suspicion of wrongdoing on the part of the former officers (P). With no basis for potential liability, the FDIC (D) merely wants to go on a fishing expedition in the hope that some wrongdoing will surface. This is a violation of fundamental constitutional rights.

▶ ANALYSIS

The decision fell short of requiring that the agency make a showing of probable cause before a subpoena can be issued. However, the court came down hard on the FDIC (D) in this case. They acknowledged that the records in question were sealed and never given to the agency, but noted that the former officers (P) had nonetheless been forced to incur legal expenses and anxiety.

Quicknotes

SUBPOENA A mandate issued by a court to compel a witness to appear at trial.

Adams v. Federal Trade Commission

Dairy company (D) v. Government agency (P)

296 F.2d 861 (8th Cir. 1961).

NATURE OF CASE: Appeal of decision to deny enforcement of administrative subpoenas.

FACT SUMMARY: The Federal Trade Commission (FTC) (P) issued a series of subpoenas covering an extensive amount of information pursuant to an investigation into whether Adams (D) had engaged in fixing prices.

RULE OF LAW
Subpoenas are not too broad as long as the information sought is reasonably relevant.

FACTS: The FTC (P) issued a complaint against Adams Dairy Company (D) alleging that the company was involved in a conspiracy to fix prices. A hearing examiner issued several administrative subpoenas for various documents of Adams (D). Among those documents sought were product sales records from 1940 to 1959, the names of all companies that Adams did business with since its incorporation and all writings to these companies, and all types of corporate records. The FTC (P) was forced to seek judicial enforcement when Adams (D) refused to comply. The district court decided to deny enforcement of many of the aspects of the subpoenas based on the fact that they were too broad in scope. The FTC (P) appealed.

ISSUE: Can subpoenas be too broad if the information sought is reasonably relevant?

HOLDING AND DECISION: (Matthes, J.) No. Subpoenas are not too broad as long as the information sought is reasonably relevant. The critical issue in the validity of an administrative subpoena is the relevance of the requested information to the charges and allegations that the agency is making. In the present case, the FTC (P) is alleging a sweeping conspiracy involving many companies over a long period of time. Accordingly, the agency has wide latitude in seeking documents that pertain to the alleged conspiracy. Therefore, the district court's denial of enforcement of many of the subpoenas on the ground that they were too burdensome and broad is overruled. Where the district court found that the documents sought were not relevant because they dated back past 1954, denial in part of the scope of those administrative subpoenas was appropriate. Reversed in part, affirmed in part.

▶ ANALYSIS

The court had to look at each of the subpoena specifications individually to determine their relevance. This decision does indicate that claims of burden will not go far in quashing administrative subpoenas. This decision might also lead agencies to expand the scope of their allegations so that they have access to a fuller document record.

Quicknotes

CONSPIRACY Concerted action by two or more persons to accomplish some unlawful purpose.

SUBPOENA A mandate issued by a court to compel a witness to appear at trial.

Braswell v. United States

Business proprietor (D) v. Federal government (P)

487 U.S. 99 (1988).

NATURE OF CASE: Appeal from denial of motion to quash.

FACT SUMMARY: Braswell (D) contended he was not bound, as the custodian of corporate records, to comply with a subpoena for such records because the act of production would incriminate him in violation of his Fifth Amendment rights.

🏛 RULE OF LAW
The custodian of corporate records cannot resist a subpoena on the grounds that such production would violate his Fifth Amendment rights against self-incrimination.

FACTS: Braswell (D) conducted business as a sole proprietor. He subsequently incorporated the business by forming two separate corporations. He, as president of each, was served with a subpoena by a federal grand jury ordering him to produce company records. He moved to quash the subpoena on the grounds that the act of production constituted testimony which could be used against him. Thus, he argued, the subpoena violated his right against self-incrimination. The district court refused to quash the subpoena. The court of appeals affirmed, and the United States Supreme Court granted review.

ISSUE: Can the custodian of corporate records avoid a subpoena for such records on the grounds that production would constitute self-incrimination?

HOLDING AND DECISION: (Rehnquist, C.J.) No. The custodian of corporate records cannot resist a subpoena on the grounds that production of the records would constitute self-incrimination. Corporations are treated differently under the self-incrimination analysis. The collective entity rule, which applies to corporate defendants, dictates that custodians of corporate records hold them in a representative capacity, not a personal capacity. Thus, production is a fulfillment of corporate duties and is not a personal testimonial act. Thus, no Fifth Amendment violation would occur when compelling a corporate act. Affirmed.

▌ ANALYSIS

The Court recognized that a different result in this case would simply hinder any prosecution of "white collar crime." All an individual would have to do to avoid turning over incriminating documents would be to make sure they were created in a corporate capacity. If in this case the business had remained a sole proprietorship, the subpoena might have been quashed because the custodian would hold the documents in a personal capacity.

■══■

Quicknotes

COLLECTIVE BARGAINING Negotiations between an employer and employee that are mediated by a specified third party.

FIFTH AMENDMENT Provides that no person shall be compelled to serve as a witness against himself, or be subject to trial for the same offense twice, or be deprived of life, liberty, or property without due process of law.

SUBPOENA A mandate issued by a court to compel a witness to appear at trial.

■══■

Smith v. Richert

Alleged tax delinquent (D) v. Indiana Department of Revenue (P)

35 F.3d 300 (7th Cir. 1994).

NATURE OF CASE: Appeal from conviction for failing to permit an examination of records.

FACT SUMMARY: Smith (D) did not file income tax returns and refused to comply with a subpoena commanding production of income records.

RULE OF LAW
The required records doctrine with respect to self-incrimination does not apply to general records needed to determine tax liability.

FACTS: Smith (D) did not file Indiana tax returns for several years and the state's Department of Revenue (P) served him with a subpoena demanding the production of records necessary to determine his tax liability. An Indiana statute provided that any person subject to tax was required to keep records for purposes of determining their taxes. Smith (D) refused to comply with the subpoena on the ground that it violated his right against self-incrimination. He was convicted for failing to permit the examination of records required by the state. The conviction was affirmed. The court ruled that the records sought by the subpoena were required records and, thus, not self-incriminating. Smith (D) appealed.

ISSUE: Does the required records doctrine with respect to self-incrimination apply to general records needed to determine tax liability?

HOLDING AND DECISION: (Posner, C.J.) No. The required records doctrine with respect to self-incrimination does not apply to general records needed to determine tax liability. The Fifth Amendment protects the rights of individuals not to testify against themselves. The required records doctrine developed as an exception in the cases where a document was required to be kept as part of a regulated industry. Its only applicability now is when the act of production itself is testimonial and would be protected by the Fifth Amendment. In such instances, a person cannot resist the subpoena because compliance only shows acknowledgment that the regulatory program applies. However, this required records doctrine should only be used where an industry is closely regulated by the government. A statute that requires taxpayers to maintain general records is far too broad; taxpayers do not voluntarily enter into any implicit agreement to maintain documents for the government. Furthermore, production by Smith (D) of certain tax forms in this case would be testimonial and incriminating in that it would foreclose a defense that he omitted income because he had no record of it. Therefore, the district court should not have affirmed the conviction

on the basis that the documents sought by the subpoena were required records. Reversed and remanded.

ANALYSIS

The court pointed out that Indiana (P) could have agreed not to disclose at a prosecuting trial for willful non-payment of taxes that Smith (D) had provided the documents that established his tax liability. This immunity-like use of the information would have protected Smith's (D) Fifth Amendment rights, while still allowing the subpoena to go forward. The required records doctrine hasn't been used much since 1984, when the United States Supreme Court ruled that the compelled surrender of a self-incriminating document was not barred by the Fifth Amendment.

Quicknotes

FIFTH AMENDMENT Provides that no person shall be compelled to serve as a witness against himself, or be subject to trial for the same offense twice, or be deprived of life, liberty, or property without due process of law.

SUBPOENA A mandate issued by court to compel a witness to appear at trial.

Securities and Exchange Commission v. Dresser Industries, Inc.

Federal agency (P) v. Corporation (D)

628 F.2d 1368 (D.C. Cir. 1980).

NATURE OF CASE: Appeal from decision to enforce subpoena.

FACT SUMMARY: Dresser (D) claimed that a Securities and Exchange Commission (SEC) (P) subpoena should not be enforced because of a parallel criminal investigation into the same facts.

🏛 RULE OF LAW
In the absence of substantial prejudice to the rights of the parties involved, parallel civil and criminal proceedings are unobjectionable.

FACTS: In face of allegations that some U.S. companies had used corporate funds to bribe foreign officials, the SEC (P) investigated whether Dresser (D) had falsified its financial records to hide such payments. The Department of Justice was also conducting an investigation into possible criminal violations arising from illegal foreign payments. Both the SEC (P) and a grand jury issued subpoenas seeking information from Dresser (D). Dresser (D) appealed the district court's decision to enforce the SEC (P) subpoena.

ISSUE: In the absence of substantial prejudice to the rights of the parties involved, are parallel civil and criminal proceedings unobjectionable?

HOLDING AND DECISION: (Skelly Wright, C.J.) Yes. In the absence of substantial prejudice to the rights of the parties involved, parallel civil and criminal proceedings are unobjectionable. Only where the nature of the proceedings demonstrably prejudices substantial rights of the investigated party or of the government, may parallel investigations be blocked. Here, no indictment has been returned, no Fifth Amendment privilege has been threatened, and the SEC (P) subpoena does not require Dresser (D) to reveal the basis for its defense. The SEC (P) and Justice should be able to investigate possible violations simultaneously. Affirmed.

▶ ANALYSIS

Federal civil and regulatory laws frequently overlap with criminal laws. A stay of civil proceedings pending the outcome of the criminal charges is not usually required. Only where bad faith or malicious prosecution may exist, is such a stay mandatory.

■■■■

Quicknotes

FIFTH AMENDMENT Provides that no person shall be compelled to serve as a witness against himself, or be subject to trial for the same offense twice, or be deprived of life, liberty, or property without due process of law.

STAY An order by a court requiring a party to refrain from a specific activity until the happening of an event or upon further action by the court.

SUBPOENA A mandate issued by court to compel a witness to appear at trial.

■■■■

United States v. Kordel

Federal government (P) v. Corporate officers (D)

397 U.S. 1 (1970).

NATURE OF CASE: Appeal from reversal of convictions for violations of the Federal Food, Drug and Cosmetics Act.

FACT SUMMARY: Kordel (D), a corporate officer, was convicted of criminal offenses after being required to respond to civil interrogatories from the Food and Drug Administration (FDA).

🏛 RULE OF LAW
Agencies do not have to choose between criminal and civil proceedings or delay civil proceedings pending the outcome of a criminal trial.

FACTS: In June 1960, the FDA filed a suit against Detroit Vital Foods (Vital Foods), alleging that two of its products violated the Food, Drug, and Cosmetic Act. The company was served with interrogatories from the FDA. The Government (P) then notified Vital Foods that it would begin a criminal prosecution. Vital Foods asked the district court to stay the FDA civil proceedings or delay the interrogatories until after the criminal trial was finished. However, Vital Foods did not raise the issue of self-incrimination and the court denied their request. Kordel (D), a corporate officer, and other officers answered the interrogatories and subsequently were convicted of violating the Act. The court of appeals reversed their convictions on the ground that the Government's (P) use of the interrogatory responses in a nearly contemporaneous civil proceeding to obtain evidence was a violation of the right against self-incrimination. The Government (P) appealed.

ISSUE: Do agencies have to choose between criminal and civil proceedings or delay civil proceedings pending the outcome of a criminal trial?

HOLDING AND DECISION: (Stewart, J.) No. Agencies do not have to choose between criminal and civil proceedings or delay civil proceedings pending the outcome of a criminal trial. In the present case, the court of appeals found that the interrogatory responses were involuntary after the district court's order. However, the privilege of self-incrimination is a personal right. The individuals at Vital Foods could have invoked their privilege even though the corporation itself had no such right. Although it is possible that there would have been no one at Vital Foods who could have answered without subjecting himself to the risk of self-incrimination, and in such a case, a protective order might have been warranted. However, the record before us does not present this question. Additionally, it cannot be said that the government's conduct was so unfair as to require reversal. It would stultify the

enforcement of federal law to require an agency to choose between giving up criminal prosecutions or deferring civil proceedings pending the outcome of a criminal trial. Often the decision of whether to proceed criminally against those responsible depends on having a full civil record. Therefore, Kordel (D) and the other officers' convictions are reinstated. Reversed.

▶ ANALYSIS

The Court seemed concerned with the public interest in having the FDA remove offending products as soon as possible without having to worry about the implications for later criminal proceedings. The Court went out of its way to suggest that the attorneys for Vital Foods could have explored other options after the district court insisted that the interrogatories be answered. The Court did note that a company could elude answering discovery by assigning the responsibility to someone who would invoke the Fifth Amendment.

■=■

Quicknotes

FIFTH AMENDMENT Provides that no person shall be compelled to serve as a witness against himself, or be subject to trial for the same offense twice, or be deprived of life, liberty, or property without due process of law.

FOOD, DRUG, AND COSMETIC ACT Federal law regulating the transportation of food, drugs and cosmetics and interstate commerce.

PROTECTIVE ORDER Court order protecting a party against potential abusive treatment through use of the legal process.

STAY An order by a court requiring a party to refrain from a specific activity until the happening of an event or upon further action by the court.

■=■

United States v. LaSalle National Bank

Internal Revenue Service (P) v. Taxpayer's bank (D)

437 U.S. 298 (1978).

NATURE OF CASE: Appeal from denial of enforcement of administrative subpoena.

FACT SUMMARY: LaSalle (D) refused to comply with a subpoena for a customer's bank records from the Internal Revenue Service (IRS) (P).

🏛 RULE OF LAW
An IRS summons must be enforced if it is issued in good faith before a recommendation for criminal prosecution.

FACTS: The IRS (P) assigned Olivero, a special agent, to investigate the tax liability of Gattuso. Olivero issued summons for Gattuso's records at two banks, including LaSalle National Bank (D). The banks (D) refused to comply and the IRS (P) sought enforcement in district court. Olivero and other IRS (P) officials testified that there had been no decision or recommendation as to whether criminal charges were justified at the time of the summons. But Gattuso insisted that the investigation was purely criminal and the district court agreed that Olivero's motivation seemed to be for criminal proceedings. The court refused to enforce the administrative subpoenas and the court of appeals affirmed. The IRS (P) appealed.

ISSUE: Must an IRS summons be enforced if it is issued in good faith before a recommendation for criminal prosecution?

HOLDING AND DECISION: (Blackmun, J.) Yes. An IRS summons must be enforced if it is issued in good faith before a recommendation for criminal prosecution. The legislative history of the Internal Revenue Code shows that Congress intended to design a system with interrelated civil and criminal elements. Thus, tax fraud investigations were not categorized and any limitation on an IRS (P) summons should reflect this. The criminal and civil aspects of tax fraud cases only diverge when a recommendation for prosecution is sent from the IRS (P) to the Department of Justice. It would be an improper use of the summons power for the IRS (P) to gather evidence solely for a criminal investigation. Otherwise, the IRS (P) may issue summons as long as it is done in good faith for a legitimate purpose. The determination of whether an improper purpose was behind a summons is not dependent on the motivation of one agent, but depends on institutional good faith. There are layers of review built into the IRS (P) administration that temper against the motivations of one agent. In the present case, LaSalle (D) has not demonstrated anything that goes against good faith other than that agent Olivero may have already possessed the information sought in the summons.

Therefore, the summons should have been enforced. Reversed.

DISSENT: (Stewart, J.) The "institutional good faith" of the IRS (P) will be just as, if not more, difficult to decide as the purpose of an individual agent.

▶ ANALYSIS

The Court stated that the good faith standard does not permit the IRS (P) to become an information-gathering agency for other agencies, regardless of the status of the criminal case involved. This decision reflects a trend in the cases where most parallel proceedings are allowed. The Court noted that bad faith will rarely be found in cases of this type.

■══■

Quicknotes

GOOD FAITH An honest intention to abstain from taking advantage of another.

SUBPOENA A mandate issued by a court to compel a witness to appear at trial.

■══■

Public Access to Agency Processes

Quick Reference Rules of Law

The Bureau of National Affairs, Inc. v. United States Department of Justice

Publisher (P) v. Government agency (D)

742 F.2d 1484 (D.C. Cir. 1984).

NATURE OF CASE: Appeal from a denial of disclosure of requested documents under the FOIA.

FACT SUMMARY: The Bureau of National Affairs (BNA) (P) sought disclosure of appointment records and calendars of an assistant Attorney General under the Freedom of Information Act (FOIA).

RULE OF LAW
Only documents classified as agency records are subject to disclosure under the FOIA.

FACTS: BNA (P) sued to compel disclosure of daily agendas and appointment calendars of an assistant Attorney General. The daily agendas were prepared so that the individual's staff would know where to reach him, and were distributed to the staff daily. The appointment calendars were created for his personal convenience. The Department of Justice (D) contended the documents were not "agency records" and thus not subject to disclosure. The district court refused to compel production and the BNA (P) appealed.

ISSUE: Are only documents classified as agency records subject to disclosure under the FOIA?

HOLDING AND DECISION: (Mikva, J.) Yes. Only documents classified as agency records are subject to disclosure under the FOIA. Here, the telephone message slips clearly are not agency records because they contained no substantive information, they were used only by the official for whom they were taken, and distinguishing between personal and business purposes for the calls was often impossible. The daily agendas were agency records because they were generated on agency time primarily for the use of agency personnel for agency business. The calendars, however, were not agency records because they were kept for the personal convenience of the officials. BNA's (P) request for daily agendas is granted, its other requests are denied.

ANALYSIS

The court in this case recognizes an absence of legislative and judicial guidance in defining the scope of "agency records." Some guidelines have been suggested such as how the records were generated, by whom, for what purpose, and under whose direction. Also whether the agency possesses the documentation is a factor.

Quicknotes

FOIA, § 552 Expressly defines records which must be made available to the public.

United States Department of Justice v. Tax Analysts

Government agency (D) v. Publisher (P)

492 U.S. 136 (1989).

NATURE OF CASE: Appeal from order to comply with FOIA records request.

FACT SUMMARY: In July 1979, Tax Analysts (P) filed a Freedom of Information Act (FOIA) request asking the U.S. Department of Justice Department (D) to make available all district court tax opinions and final orders received by the Tax Division earlier that month, but the Department (D) denied the request.

🏛 RULE OF LAW
The FOIA confers jurisdiction on the district courts to enjoin an agency from withholding agency records and to order the production of any agency records improperly withheld.

FACTS: The Tax Division of the U.S. Department of Justice (Department) (D) represents parties in litigation, receives copies of all opinions and orders issued by the courts in such cases, and makes copies of these decisions for the Tax Division's staff attorneys. The original documents are sent to the official files kept by the Department (D). In July 1979, Tax Analysts (P), publisher of a weekly magazine which reports on legislative, judicial, and regulatory developments in the field of federal taxation to a readership largely composed of tax attorneys, accountants, and economists, filed a request under the FOIA asking the Department (D) to make available all district court tax opinions and final orders received by the Tax Division earlier that month. The Department (D) denied the request on the grounds that these decisions were not Tax Division records. The Department (D) appealed a lower court order to comply with the request.

ISSUE: Does the FOIA confer jurisdiction on the district courts to enjoin an agency from withholding agency records and to order the production of any agency records improperly withheld?

HOLDING AND DECISION: (Marshall, J.) Yes. The FOIA confers jurisdiction on the district courts to enjoin an agency from withholding agency records and to order the production of any agency records improperly withheld. Under the Act, "federal jurisdiction is dependent on a showing that an agency had (1) 'improperly' (2) 'withheld' (3) 'agency records.'" Each of these criteria must be met before a district court will have jurisdiction to devise remedies to force an agency to comply with the FOIA's disclosure requirements. The test as to whether requested materials qualify as "agency records" requires two steps. First, the requested materials must have been either "created or obtained" by an agency, and second, the agency must have been in control of the requested materials at the time the FOIA request was made. Under these two tests, the requested district court decisions constituted "agency records." Congress used the word "withheld" only in its usual sense. When a document is under an agency's control, and that agency denies an otherwise valid request for its production, the agency has "withheld" the document, despite public availability of the document outside of the agency. Finally, Congress sought "to insulate its product from judicial tampering and to preserve the emphasis on disclosure by admonishing that the 'availability of records to the public' is not limited, 'except as specifically stated.'" It follows from the exclusive nature of the exemption scheme in § 552(b) that agency records which do not fall within one of the exemptions are "improperly" withheld. None of the § 552(b) enumerated exemptions protects the district court decisions sought by Tax Analysts (P). Thus, the documents requested by Tax Analysts (P) were agency records improperly withheld by the Department (D), which must comply with the request for production made under the FOIA by Tax Analysts (P).

DISSENT: (Blackmun, J.) Tax Analysts (P) is in the business of selling summaries of these opinions and supplies full texts to major electronic databases. The result of this litigation is to impose the cost of obtaining the court orders and opinions upon the government and thus upon taxpayers generally, rather than on the requesting party.

▶ ANALYSIS

According to the dissent, the public, as taxpayers, is being asked to pay the cost of providing information to a commercial enterprise. It would appear that Justice Blackmun's fears of the taxpayers' bearing the expense of responding to FOIA requests is not unfounded, since even though the FOIA stipulates that each agency shall promulgate regulations specifying a uniform schedule of fees applicable to all document search and duplication, oftentimes these fees are waived. In his hornbook on Administrative Law, Professor William F. Fox, Jr., reveals that because—in addition to the many agencies that waive fees—fee schedules rarely reflect the actual costs of searching and retrieval, congressional inquiries indicate that the FOIA is costing agencies millions of dollars each year in processing expenses.

■═■

Quicknotes

FOIA, § 552 Expressly defines records which must be made available to the public.

■═■

National Parks and Conservation Association v. Morton

Government agency (D) v. Concessioner (P)

498 F.2d 765 (D.C. Cir. 1974).

NATURE OF CASE: Appeal in connection with nondisclosure of records.

FACT SUMMARY: Morton (P) wanted information about concessions operated in national parks.

🏛 RULE OF LAW

The Freedom of Information Act (FOIA) may be invoked for the benefit of a person who has provided commercial or financial information if it can be shown that public disclosure is likely to cause substantial harm to his competitive position.

FACTS: Morton (P) sought financial information concerning concessions operated in national parks. The district court held that this information was exempt under the FOIA, on the ground that this information was of the kind "that would not generally be made available for public perusal." Morton (P) appealed, contending that disclosure could not impair the concessioners' competitive position because they were monopolists and had no competition.

ISSUE: May the FOIA be invoked for the benefit of a person who has provided commercial or financial information if it can be shown that public disclosure is likely to cause substantial harm to his competitive position?

HOLDING AND DECISION: (Tamm, J.) Yes. The FOIA may be invoked for the benefit of a person who has provided commercial or financial information if it can be shown that public disclosure is likely to cause substantial harm to his competitive position. The district court's conclusion does not, by itself, support application of the financial information exemption of the FOIA. The district court must also inquire into the possibility that disclosure will harm legitimate private or governmental interests in secrecy. While Morton's (P) argument concerning the concessioners' monopoly is very compelling, the court is reluctant to accept it without first providing National Parks (D) the opportunity to develop a fuller record in the district court. It might be shown, for example, that disclosure of information about concession activities will injure the concessioners' competitive position in a noncompetitive enterprise. In that case, disclosure would be improper. "[R]emanded to the district court for [determination as to] whether public disclosure of the information in question poses the likelihood of substantial harm to the competitive positions of the parties from whom it has been obtained."

▶ ANALYSIS

This case came before the court of appeals again in 1976. The court emphasized that the defendant had to prove the

possibility of harm, and not its certainty, otherwise, "the costs of obtaining such detailed economic evidence ... might well preclude a small business from ever seeking to prevent disclosure." Gellhorn, W., Administrative Law, quoting 547 F.2d 673.

■═■

Quicknotes

FOIA, § 552 Expressly defines records which must be made available to the public.

MONOPOLY A privilege or right conferred upon an individual or entity granting it the exclusive power to manufacture, sell and distribute a particular service or commodity; a market condition in which one or a few companies control the sale of a product or service thereby restraining competition in respect to that article or service.

■═■

Critical Mass Energy Project v. Nuclear Regulatory Commission

Project (P) v. Government agency (D)

975 F.2d 871 (D.C. Cir. 1992).

NATURE OF CASE: Appeal from a grant of summary judgment in favor of the defendant in relation to a Freedom of Information Act (FOIA or Act) request.

FACT SUMMARY: Critical Mass Energy Project's (CMEP) (P) FOIA request for information voluntarily provided to the Nuclear Regulatory Commission (NRC) (D) by the Institute for Nuclear Power Operations (INPO) was denied on the basis that the information was protected from disclosure under the Act's confidential commercial information exemption.

🏛 RULE OF LAW
Financial or commercial information voluntarily provided to the government is confidential and exempt from disclosure if it would usually not be released to the public by the person who provided it.

FACTS: CMEP (P) sought to gain access through the FOIA to information voluntarily provided to the NRC (D) pursuant to a non-disclosure agreement by the INPO. CMEP (P) instituted its action after its request was denied on the ground that the information requested was not subject to disclosure under Exemption 4 of the FOIA because it contained confidential commercial information. While recognizing that disclosure might chill strictly voluntary reports, a divided appellate panel reversed and remanded to the district court. *Critical Mass I*, 830 F.2d 278. On remand, the district court ruled in favor of the NRC (D), but a different panel reversed and remanded again. After the district court granted summary judgment to the NRC (D), CMEP (P) appealed.

ISSUE: Is financial or commercial information voluntarily provided to the government confidential and exempt from disclosure if it would usually not be released to the public by the person who provided it?

HOLDING AND DECISION: (Buckley, J.) Yes. Financial or commercial information voluntarily provided to the government is confidential and exempt from disclosure if it would usually not be released to the public by the person who provided it. This exemption serves to encourage cooperation with the government by persons having information useful to officials. Unless persons having such information can be assured that it will remain confidential, they may decline to cooperate with officials, and the ability of the government to make intelligent well-informed decisions will be impaired. The above test is objective, and the agency invoking the exemption must meet the burden of proving the provider's custom. So long as the information requested here is provided voluntarily, and so long as it is of a kind that INPO customarily withholds from the public, it

must be treated as confidential. Accordingly, our decision in *Critical Mass I* is vacated, and the district court's grant of summary judgment for the NRC (D) is affirmed.

DISSENT: (Ginsburg, J.) No longer is there to be an independent judicial check on the reasonableness of the provider's custom and the consonance of that custom with the purposes of Exemption 4 and of the Act of which the exemption is part. The FOIA request at issue here is sought to advance public understanding of the nature and quality of the NRC's (D) oversight operations or activities. The public interest that the FOIA was enacted to serve is thus centrally at stake.

▶ ANALYSIS

Prior to the decision in this case, courts applied a two-part test to determine the applicability of Exemption 4 of the FOIA: whether disclosure was likely to (1) impair the government's ability to obtain information, or (2) cause harm to the supplier's competitive position. While overruling its decision in *Critical Mass I*, the court of appeals noted that the panel there adopted the First Circuit's conclusion that the exemption also protects a governmental interest in administrative efficiency and effectiveness. However, the court of appeals offered no opinion as to whether any other governmental or private interest might also fall within the exemption's protection.

■━■

Quicknotes

EXEMPTION Colloquial term usually used to refer to a deduction not keyed to actual expenditures, such as (mainly) the § 151 Deductions ("personal and dependency exemptions").

FOIA, § 552 Expressly defines records which must be made available to the public.

■━■

Chrysler Corporation v. Brown

Auto manufacturer (P) v. Labor department (D)

441 U.S. 281 (1979).

NATURE OF CASE: Appeal of court order mandating disclosure of certain documents.

FACT SUMMARY: Chrysler Corporation (P) contended that certain documents pertaining to it held by the government fell outside the Freedom of Information Act (FOIA) and, therefore, could not be disclosed pursuant to unrelated regulations.

RULE OF LAW
The FOIA does not give rise to a private right to prevent disclosure of documents pursuant to unrelated regulations.

FACTS: Pursuant to Executive Order, Chrysler Corporation (Chrysler) (P) had to prepare certain reports giving the status of Chrysler's (P) compliance with federal affirmative action programs. The Executive Order and Regulations of the Department of Labor (D) allowed for public inspection of these records. The Department of Labor (D) informed Chrysler (P) that a request for some of these records had been made. Chrysler (P) argued that the records contained trade secrets and, therefore, fell under Exemption 4 of the FOIA. The court of appeals held the documents subject to disclosure.

ISSUE: Does the FOIA give rise to a private right to prevent disclosure of documents pursuant to unrelated regulations?

HOLDING AND DECISION: (Rehnquist, J.) No. The FOIA does not give rise to a private right to prevent disclosure of documents pursuant to unrelated regulations. The FOIA, by its terms, is exclusively a disclosure statute. This is borne out by its provisions for judicial review, which allow a court to order disclosure but say nothing about withholding disclosure. Also, legislative history makes it clear that the FOIA was designed to create an avenue for disclosure pursuant to other laws. [The Court went on to hold that the Trade Secrets Act may prevent disclosure and remanded to the court of appeals for consideration of this issue.]

ANALYSIS

This was what had been labeled a "reverse-FOIA" suit. Suppliers of information to the government had argued, as did Chrysler (P), that disclosure broader than that allowed by the FOIA was impermissible. The argument was that the FOIA had superseded all other disclosure rules. This decision put that argument to rest.

Quicknotes

FOIA, EXEMPTION 4 Exempts trade secrets and privileges or confidential financial information from disclosure.

TRADE SECRET Consists of any formula, pattern, plan, process, or device known only to its owner and business which gives an advantage over competitors.

Public Citizen v. U.S. Department of Justice

Lobby group (P) v. Government agency (D)

491 U.S. 440 (1989).

NATURE OF CASE: Suit alleging violation of the Federal Advisory Committee Act (FACA).

FACT SUMMARY: Public Citizen (P) alleged that the American Bar Association's (ABA's) committees that reviewed the nominations for federal judgeships fell under FACA rules.

🏛 RULE OF LAW
FACA was not meant to apply to the American Bar Association's review of judicial nominees.

FACTS: The FACA was passed by Congress to provide public access and accountability to committees that advise the executive branch. According to FACA, it is to be applied to "any committee, board, commission . . . established or utilized by one or more agencies in the interest of obtaining advice or recommendations for the President." For many years prior to FACA, the ABA had reviewed potential nominees for appointment as federal judges and reported whether the nominee was qualified. These recommendations were very influential in the appointment process. Public Citizen (P), a public interest lobbying group, filed suit claiming that these ABA committee meetings should be open to the public since they fell within the purview of FACA. The issue reached the United States Supreme Court.

ISSUE: Was FACA meant to apply to the American Bar Association's review of judicial nominees?

HOLDING AND DECISION: (Brennan, J.) No. FACA was not meant to apply to the American Bar Association's review of judicial nominees. According to a straightforward reading of FACA, it is clear that the ABA committees on judicial nominees are "utilized" by the executive branch. However, it does not seem that Congress could have intended that any group of two or more people from which the President seeks advice would have to meet FACA requirements. The principal purpose of FACA was to enhance public accountability of advisory committees that were actually established by the executive branch. This could be done without expanding FACA's coverage to privately organized groups such as the ABA. The legislative history of FACA demonstrates that neither the House nor the Senate intended to bring all private advisory committees within FACA. Given its prominence, it is telling that it was omitted from a list of groups that would be covered by FACA. The words "or utilized" appear to have been added to the final statute in order to make sure that it covered quasi-public organizations. The literal reading of the law would have a far greater reach than Congress intended. Since the constitutionality of FACA would be arguable under a broad reading, it is appropriate to use a construction that will avoid such problems. Therefore, FACA should be read more narrowly and does not encompass such private groups as the ABA.

▶ ANALYSIS

The Court noted that the district court had declared FACA unconstitutional when it found that it applied to the ABA. Justices Kennedy, Rehnquist and O'Connor also agreed with this position. However, the majority seemed intent on somehow saving the law by looking past a literal reading of the statute.

■═■

Quicknotes

FEDERAL ADVISORY COMMITTEE ACT Law intended to open up executive branch advisory groups to the public and make them more accountable.

■═■

In re Cheney

Opponents of national energy policy (P) v.
Vice President of the United States (D)

406 F.3d 723 (D.C. Cir. 2005).

NATURE OF CASE: Suit for disclosure of documents related to a group formed to help the President of the United States establish a national energy policy.

FACT SUMMARY: The President assigned several federal officials to a "development group" to help him formulate a national energy policy. Two citizen organizations (P) sought documents related to the President's development group.

> ## 🏛 RULE OF LAW
> The Federal Advisory Committee Act does not require disclosure of committee documents if only federal officials compose the committee.

FACTS: President Bush established the National Energy Policy Development Group (NEPDG) to develop a national energy policy. Vice President Cheney (D) and other federal officials were named to the NEPDG. Two citizen groups, Judicial Watch (P) and the Sierra Club (P), filed separate suits against Cheney (D), among others, for declaratory and injunctive relief ordering that documents related to the NEPDG be disclosed. Both suits alleged that persons who were not federal officials regularly participated in the NEPDG, thereby giving such persons de facto membership on the NEPDG. The plaintiffs alleged further that the NEPDG was therefore an "advisory committee" whose documents were disclosable under the Federal Advisory Committee Act (FACA) because FACA's disclosure provisions exempted only groups composed solely of full-time or permanent part-time federal officials. The trial court dismissed most of the suits, leaving only a mandamus claim against Cheney (D) asking the court of appeals to order the trial court to order Cheney (D) to comply with FACA's disclosure provisions.

ISSUE: Does the Federal Advisory Committee Act require disclosure of committee documents if only federal officials compose the committee?

HOLDING AND DECISION: (Randolph, J.) No. The Federal Advisory Committee Act (FACA) does not require disclosure of committee documents if only federal officials compose the committee. Neither the NEPDG nor its so-called subgroups were "advisory committees," within the meaning of FACA, because only federal officials had a vote on the committee or could veto the committee's decisions. This strict construction of FACA is necessary because of the grave separation-of-powers problems in a case such as this one. Even if some persons who were not federal officials did assist the NEPDG, they did not vote on the NEPDG or have the ability to veto the committee's decisions; like congressional aides, such persons might have had extensive influence on the committee's decisions, but that influence alone does not make them de facto members of the committee. In this case, neither complaint alleged that a nonfederal official voted on the NEPDG or could have vetoed the committee's decisions. Accordingly, the NEPDG was not an "advisory committee" under FACA. Furthermore, Cheney (D) did not use his delegated authority to create "subordinate working groups," and Judicial Watch (P) made no allegation that an unofficial subgroup voted on the NEPDG or could have vetoed the committee's decisions. Therefore the subgroups were also not "agency committees" under FACA. Writ of mandamus denied.

▶ ANALYSIS

FACA's reporting requirements are onerous. The statute itself acknowledges separation-of-powers concerns, however, and FACA permits the President the latitude of establishing advisory bodies not governed by FACA, an option that President Bush exercised in this case. Separation-of-powers concerns then play another role in the court, where the "constitutional avoidance" canon of construction requires judges to make all reasonable efforts to avoid interpreting a statute as unconstitutional. See, e.g., *Clark v. Martinez*, 543 U.S. 371, 380-81 (2004). In this case, that canon of construction guided the court of appeals to read FACA as respecting the core functions of the highest office in a coordinate branch of government.

■═■

Quicknotes

DE FACTO In fact; in reality; actual. Existing in fact but not officially approved or engendered.

FEDERAL ADVISORY COMMITTEE ACT Law intended to open up executive branch advisory groups to the public and make them more accountable.

■═■

Northwest Forest Resource Council v. Espy

Trade organization (P) v. Government agencies (D)

846 F. Supp. 1009 (D.D.C. 1994).

NATURE OF CASE: Suit challenging the legality of an advisory committee under the Federal Advisory Committee Act (FACA).

FACT SUMMARY: The Forest Ecosystem Management Assessment Team (FEMAT) (D) was established by the executive branch to make recommendations with regard to forest uses, but there was a dispute as to whether it was covered by FACA.

RULE OF LAW
State employees without federal duties may not be considered officers of the federal government for purposes of FACA.

FACTS: FEMAT (D) was composed of many subteams and subgroups, encompassing as many as 700 people, in order to study uses of federal forests and identify the best solutions. An interagency group, the Forest Conference Executive Committee, was established to direct and supervise the work of FEMAT (D). At least five people who worked for FEMAT (D) were faculty members at state public universities. The Northwest Forest Resource Council (D), a trade group representing the timber industry, claimed that FEMAT (D) was an advisory committee that had to meet the requirements of FACA.

ISSUE: May state employees without federal duties be considered officers of the federal government for purposes of FACA?

HOLDING AND DECISION: (Jackson, J.) No. State employees without federal duties may not be considered officers of the federal government for purposes of FACA. That law defines an advisory committee as any group established by the executive branch to provide advice. There is no doubt that FEMAT (D) meets these general conditions. However, FACA does exempt certain groups if they are composed wholly of full-time officers or employees of the federal government. The agencies involved with FEMAT (D) claim that the outside faculty members should fit within this exception because they are state employees who could have been assigned a federal function. However, it is obvious that their presence precludes FEMAT (D) from fitting within the FACA exception. The argument that FEMAT (D) was not providing policy advice to the President is also clearly wrong. The record shows that the administration looked only at FEMAT (D) proposals in choosing a policy to implement. Therefore, FEMAT (D) was an advisory committee and its use violated FACA.

▶ ANALYSIS

Other courts have also rejected the contention that FACA should not apply to advisory committees that consist only of technicians who supply data. In another case, a court was faced with the legality of President Clinton's task force on health care reform. That group was composed of all full-time federal employees except for the First Lady. That court decided that the First Lady should be considered a federal employee for FACA purposes.

■═■

Quicknotes

FEDERAL ADVISORY COMMITTEE ACT Law intended to open up executive branch advisory groups to the public and make them more accountable.

■═■

Federal Communications Commission v. ITT World Communications, Inc.

Government agency (D) v. International telecommunications company (P)

466 U.S. 463 (1984).

NATURE OF CASE: Review of order challenging international conferences.

FACT SUMMARY: ITT (P) contended that certain international conferences attended by Federal Communications Commission (FCC) (D) members were covered by the federal Sunshine Act.

RULE OF LAW
The Sunshine Act applies only to discussions that effectively predetermine official actions.

FACTS: Three FCC (D) members attended a series of informal conferences with overseas telecommunications regulators. The FCC (D) had participated in the conferences in the hope that an information exchange might persuade European nations to encourage competition. ITT World Communications (P) filed a rulemaking petition with the FCC (D), contending that the meetings were within the scope of the Sunshine Act and should have been held in public. The court of appeals held that the Sunshine Act did apply to the conferences. The United States Supreme Court granted review.

ISSUE: Does the Sunshine Act apply only to discussions that effectively predetermine agency actions?

HOLDING AND DECISION: (Powell, J.) Yes. The Sunshine Act applies to discussions that effectively predetermine official actions. Section 552b(a)(2) of the Act defines "meetings" as "the deliberations of at least the number of individual agency members required to take action on behalf of the agency where such deliberations determine or result in the joint conduct or disposition of official agency business." Although the FCC (D) commissioners who attended the conferences did not constitute a quorum, they did have the power to approve common carrier applications, and therefore the Sunshine Act would normally apply to such conferences. However, the conferences did not result in any formal action by the FCC (D) regarding applications, nor did they result in any firm agency positions on any matter before the commissioners. Therefore the conferences were not meetings "of an agency" since they were not convened by the FCC (D) nor subject to its unilateral control. For these reasons, the Sunshine Act does not apply. Reversed and remanded.

▶ **ANALYSIS**

The Sunshine Act strikes a balance between the public's "need to know" and agency process. On the one hand,

"meetings" must be open. On the other hand, the term "meetings" is narrowly defined.

Quicknotes

SUNSHINE ACT § 552 Requires that meetings of agencies be open to the public.

Attorney's Fees

Quick Reference Rules of Law

Buckhannon Board and Care Home, Inc. v. West Virginia Department of Health and Human Resources

Assisted-living provider (P) v. State agency (D)

532 U.S. 598 (2001).

NATURE OF CASE: Suit to invalidate a state regulation for assisted-living providers.

FACT SUMMARY: An assisted-living provider sued a state agency to invalidate a state regulation for assisted-living providers. While the suit was pending, the state legislature eliminated the requirement. The trial court granted the state's motion to dismiss the suit for mootness and denied the assisted-living provider's request for an award of attorney's fees.

🏛 **RULE OF LAW**
The "catalyst theory" does not justify an award of attorney's fees under the Fair Housing Amendments Act of 1988 (FHAA) or under the Americans with Disabilities Act of 1990 (ADA) where a party achieves its desired result but the court enters no judgment on the merits or court-ordered consent decree.

FACTS: The West Virginia Office of the State Fire Marshal found that some residents who were cared for by Buckhannon Board and Care, Inc. (P) were not capable of "self-preservation" as required by state law. Buckhannon (P) sued the State of West Virginia (D) and several others, alleging that the "self-preservation" requirement violated the Fair Housing Amendments Act of 1988 (FHAA), 42 U.S.C. § 3601 et seq., and the ADA, 42 U.S.C. § 12101 et seq. While the suit was pending, the West Virginia legislature eliminated the "self-preservation" requirement. The State (D) then moved to dismiss Buckhannon's (P) suit on grounds of mootness. The trial court granted the motion, and Buckhannon (P) requested an award of attorney's fees, arguing that it was entitled to the award under the "catalyst theory" because the suit indirectly achieved Buckhannon's (P) desired result by encouraging the West Virginia legislature to eliminate the challenged requirement. The Fourth Circuit Court of Appeals, which had squarely rejected the "catalyst theory" in an earlier case, affirmed the trial court's denial of attorney's fees. Buckhannon (P) petitioned the United States Supreme Court for further review.

ISSUE: Does the "catalyst theory" justify an award of attorney's fees under the FHAA or under the ADA where a party achieves its desired result but the court enters no judgment on the merits or court-ordered consent decree?

HOLDING AND DECISION: (Rehnquist, C.J.) No. The "catalyst theory" does not justify an award of attorney's fees under the FHAA or under the ADA where a party achieves its desired result but the court enters no judgment on the merits or court-ordered consent decree.

The "American Rule" generally requires each side to bear its own litigation expenses, including attorney's fees, unless a statute explicitly permits an award of attorney's fees. Here, the FHAA and ADA both permit attorney's fees to a "prevailing party," and the question is therefore whether a party "prevails," within the meaning of these statutes, if a court does not grant the party some form of relief. Our case law has consistently held that a party is a "prevailing party," for fee-shifting purposes, only if the result bears a judicial imprimatur by entering a judgment or a court-ordered consent decree. Buckhannon's (P) several policy arguments thus have no weight, and Buckhannon (P) is not entitled to an award of attorney's fees in this case. Affirmed.

DISSENT: (Ginsburg, J.) Contrary to the clear majority of federal appellate courts, the Court today permits defendants to escape attorney-fee liability even when a plaintiff "prevails" under a less restrictive definition of the term.

▶ *ANALYSIS*

Buckhannon highlights a tension inherent in courts for dispute resolution. This decision encourages plaintiffs to make extra efforts to try to resolve their differences with defendants outside the judicial system, where legal fees are more likely to remain relatively low. At the same time, defendants often will not take plaintiffs' complaints seriously unless and until a judicial figure oversees the dispute's resolution. Although the prior law presented in the casebook excerpt seems to require judgment against the plaintiffs in this case, as a practical matter Justice Ginsburg is also surely correct that *Buckhannon* will "impede access to court for the less well heeled"—that is, for the parties most likely to need attorneys who will risk taking a meritorious case on only the mere likelihood that they will be able to collect fees after the case concludes.

Quicknotes

CONSENT DECREE A decree issued by a court of equity ratifying an agreement between the parties to a lawsuit; an agreement by a defendant to cease illegal activity.

JUDGMENT ON THE MERITS A determination of the rights of the parties to litigation based on the presentation evidence, barring the party from initiating the same suit again.

Barrios v. California Interscholastic Federation

Paraplegic coach (P) v. State athletic association (D)

277 F.3d 1128 (9th Cir. 2002).

NATURE OF CASE: Suit for alleged discrimination under federal and state law.

FACT SUMMARY: A state athletic association prevented a paraplegic baseball coach from coaching after he had been permitted to coach for seven years. The coach sued, and the parties eventually reached a private settlement agreement.

🏛 RULE OF LAW
A party is a "prevailing party" entitled to attorney's fees under the Americans with Disabilities Act (ADA) where a case concludes with a stipulated dismissal and a settlement agreement expressly entitling the party to an award of attorney's fees.

FACTS: From 1992 to 1999, Victor Barrios (P), who was paraplegic and used a wheelchair, coached baseball, without incident, at a California high school. In 1999, umpires inexplicably started prohibiting Barrios (P) from coaching games simply because he used a wheelchair. Through counsel, Barrios (P) made extensive efforts to resolve the matter informally, without filing suit against the California Interscholastic Federation (CIF) (D). The CIF (D), through its counsel, repeatedly assured Barrios's (P) counsel that Barrios's (P) use of a wheelchair was not a problem and that the umpires apparently did not understand the situation. Nevertheless, umpires continued to prevent Barrios (P) from coaching, even after he filed suit against the CIF (D). Out of court, the CIF's (D) counsel continued to assure Barrios's (P) counsel that all was well, although the CIF's (D) counsel also repeatedly refused to sign written stipulations memorializing his oral assurances about Barrios's (D) ability to continue coaching baseball. Eventually the parties did enter a long written settlement agreement that required the CIF (D) to pay Barrios (P) $10,000 in compensatory damages; the agreement also expressly reserved, for the trial court's determination, the issue of whether any party was a "prevailing party" for purposes of awarding attorney's fees. Barrios (P) moved for an award of attorney's fees and costs. Following the terms of the settlement agreement, the trial court entered a judgment and order. One month later, the CIF (D) moved to vacate the judgment, arguing that the parties had not agreed on whether a judgment or a stipulation of dismissal would be filed to terminate the case. Barrios (P) conceded that point but argued that a judgment was necessary for the agreed compensatory damages. The trial court vacated the original judgment and [despite also finding Barrios (P) to be the "prevailing party,"] denied Barrios's (P) request for attorney's fees. The parties then filed a stipulation for dismissal with prejudice, with the filing silent on the question of attorney's fees. Barrios (P) appealed.

ISSUE: Is a party a "prevailing party" entitled to attorney's fees under the Americans with Disabilities Act where a case concludes with a stipulated dismissal and a private settlement agreement?

HOLDING AND DECISION: (Tashima, J.) Yes. A party is a "prevailing party" entitled to attorney's fees under the ADA where a case concludes with a stipulated dismissal and a private settlement agreement. Ninth Circuit law holds that a legally enforceable settlement agreement is sufficient to confer "prevailing party" status. Like a judgment or consent decree, an enforceable settlement agreement materially alters the legal relationship between the parties such that a party can be said to "prevail" in the litigation. The United States Supreme Court's recent decision in *Buckhannon Board and Care Home, Inc. v. West Virginia Dept. of Health and Human Resources*, 532 U.S. 598 (2001), does not affect this case. In *Buckhannon,* the United States Supreme Court rejected the "catalyst theory" for awarding attorney's fees—as has the Ninth Circuit—but Barrios grounds his argument for "prevailing party" status on the settlement agreement, not on his having encouraged policy change. Moreover, *Buckhannon's* apparent restriction of "prevailing party" status to favorable judgments or consent decrees was not only dictum but also dictum that does not reach this Circuit's law on enforceable settlement agreements. Reversed and remanded.

▶ ANALYSIS

Students should approach *Barrios's* reading of *Buckhannon* with caution. *Buckhannon* can easily—perhaps even most justifiably—be read as directly holding that "prevailing party" status is available only when a court enters a favorable judgment or orders and adopts a consent decree. See, e.g., *Union of Needletrades, Industrial & Textile Employees v. INS,* 336 F.3d 200, 204-05 (2d Cir. 2003) (so reading *Buckhannon*).

■=■

Quicknotes

CONSENT DECREE A decree issued by a court of equity ratifying an agreement between the parties to a lawsuit; an agreement by a defendant to cease illegal activity.

JUDGMENT A determination of the rights among the parties by a court having jurisdiction over the matter.

■=■

Roberson v. Giuliani

Applicants for public assistance (P) v. City mayor (D)

346 F.3d 75 (2d Cir. 2003).

NATURE OF CASE: Suit challenging a city's disposition of applications for various forms of public assistance.

FACT SUMMARY: Applicants for public aid sued New York City (City) (D) to challenge its means of disposing of public-aid applications. The trial court entered summary judgment for the City (D) on one count, and the parties resolved the remaining six counts through a private settlement agreement over which the trial court retained enforcement jurisdiction.

RULE OF LAW
A trial court's retention of enforcement jurisdiction over a private settlement agreement is a sufficient judicial sanction to confer prevailing-party status on the plaintiffs.

FACTS: Roberson (P) and others sued the City (D) to challenge the manner in which the City (D) disposed of applications for various forms of public assistance. The trial court entered summary judgment for the City (D) on one count of the complaint, and the parties resolved the complaint's other six claims through a private settlement agreement. According to the agreement, Roberson (P) agreed to dismiss the remaining six counts in consideration of the City's (D) agreement to extensive modifications of its procedures. The agreement also reserved Roberson's (P) entitlement to attorney's fees for a later determination by the trial court. Roberson (P) eventually submitted a proposed dismissal order to the trial court, with that order expressly reserving to the court enforcement jurisdiction over the parties' private settlement agreement. Three months later, Roberson (P) moved for an award of attorney's fees, and the City (D) resisted, arguing that Roberson (P) was not a prevailing party. The trial court interpreted the recent decision in *Buckhannon Board and Care Home, Inc. v. West Virginia Dept. of Health and Human Resources*, 532 U.S. 598 (2001), as limiting prevailing-party status to instances in which a court enters a judgment or adopts and orders a consent decree. Accordingly, the trial court denied Roberson's (P) request for attorney's fees. Roberson (P) appealed.

ISSUE: Is a trial court's retention of enforcement jurisdiction over a private settlement agreement a sufficient judicial sanction to confer prevailing-party status on the plaintiffs?

HOLDING AND DECISION: (Feinberg, J.) Yes. A trial court's retention of enforcement jurisdiction over a private settlement agreement is a sufficient judicial sanction to confer prevailing-party status on the plaintiffs. Although

Buckhannon somewhat restricted the availability of prevailing-party status, that opinion's reference to judgments and consent decrees was only illustrative, not exhaustive. A majority of appellate courts have, therefore, read *Buckhannon* to permit other indications of judicial approval that are sufficient to confer prevailing-party status on plaintiffs. One such judicial imprimatur is a retention of enforcement jurisdiction like the one present in the dismissal order in this case. Such a retention of jurisdiction is similar to an approved consent decree: breaching the agreement would constitute a violation of a court order; at most, requiring compliance in this case would necessitate an intermediate order of specific performance, which would properly be followed by an enforceable finding of contempt upon noncompliance. Accordingly, Roberson (P) is a prevailing party for purposes of attorney's fees. Vacated and remanded.

ANALYSIS

As the *Roberson* court notes, the determination of prevailing-party status remains the same from one federal statutory scheme to another. Although this case decided the question with reference to the fee-shifting provisions at 42 U.S.C. § 1988, the analysis is the same as that engaged in by the U.S. Supreme Court under the Fair Housing Amendments Act of 1988, 42 U.S.C. § 3601 et seq., and the American with Disabilities Act, 42 U.S.C. § 12101 et seq., in *Buckhannon Board and Care Home, Inc. v. West Virginia Dept. of Health and Human Resources,* 532 U.S. 598 (2001).

Quicknotes

CONSENT DECREE A decree issued by a court of equity ratifying an agreement between the parties to a lawsuit; an agreement by a defendant to cease illegal activity.

SUMMARY JUDGMENT Judgment rendered by a court in response to a motion made by one of the parties, claiming that the lack of a question of material fact in respect to an issue warrants disposition of the issue without consideration by the jury.

Doe v. Boston Public Schools

Disabled student (P) v. Public school system (D)

358 F.3d 20 (1st Cir. 2004).

NATURE OF CASE: Suit to require a student with disabilities' placement in a private therapeutic school.

FACT SUMMARY: A student with severe mental disabilities negotiated with a public school system under the Individuals with Disabilities Education Act (IDEA) for placement in a private therapeutic school. The parties eventually resolved their differences purely through a private settlement agreement, and the trial court dismissed the student's subsequent complaint in which she requested an award of her attorney's fees.

🏛 RULE OF LAW
Plaintiffs suing under the IDEA who achieve their desired result through a private settlement agreement do not qualify as "prevailing parties" for purposes of attorney's fees if a court does not sanction the case's resolution.

FACTS: Jane Doe (P) was a student with severe mental disabilities in the Boston public school system (Boston) (D). Her father informally asked Boston (D), without judicial assistance, to place her in a private therapeutic school, but the parties could not agree on such a placement. They then could not resolve the matter through mediation or during a pre-hearing conference held before a scheduled administrative hearing on the case. Three months after the pre-hearing conference, and just before the scheduled hearing, Boston (D) proposed to place Doe (P) in a different private school from the one she originally requested, and Doe (P) agreed to the placement. After further administrative proceedings, Doe (P) filed a complaint in federal court for an award of her attorney's fees in the matter. The trial court dismissed her complaint because, the judge reasoned, she was not a "prevailing party" as defined by *Buckhannon Board and Care Home, Inc. v. West Virginia Dept. of Health and Human Resources*, 532 U.S. 598 (2001). Doe (P) appealed.

ISSUE: Do plaintiffs suing under the IDEA who achieve their desired result through a private settlement agreement qualify as "prevailing parties" for purposes of attorney's fees if a court does not sanction the case's resolution?

HOLDING AND DECISION: (Stahl, Sr. J.) No. Plaintiffs suing under the IDEA who achieve their desired result through a private settlement agreement do not qualify as "prevailing parties," for purposes of attorney's fees, if a court does not sanction the case's resolution. No court or administrative agency sanctioned the result achieved by Doe (P). Her result, accordingly, is only a private settlement agreement that lacks the judicial imprimatur required by *Buckhannon*. The Ninth Circuit's reading of *Buckhannon* in

Barrios v. California Interscholastic Federation, 277 F.3d 1128 (9th Cir. 2002), seems to contradict the U.S. Supreme Court's express disapproval of private settlements in *Buckhannon* and, thus, does not support a ruling for Doe (P) in this case. Doe (P) is, therefore, not a "prevailing party" under the IDEA, and she is not entitled to an award of attorney's fees. Affirmed.

▌ ANALYSIS

Note the crucial distinction between *Doe* and *Roberson v. Giuliani*, 346 F.3d 75 (2d Cir. 2003). In *Roberson*, the dismissal order expressly reserved enforcement jurisdiction to the trial court over the parties' settlement agreement. The Second Circuit therefore treated the dismissal order in *Roberson* as a consent decree that met the "judgment or consent decree" standard for determining prevailing-party status arguably announced in *Buckhannon*. In *Doe*, however, the purely private settlement agreement enjoyed no judicial sanction, and the First Circuit accordingly held that Doe (P) was not a prevailing party and, therefore, not entitled to an award of attorney's fees.

■═■

Quicknotes

CONSENT DECREE A decree issued by a court of equity ratifying an agreement between the parties to a lawsuit; an agreement by a defendant to cease illegal activity.

■═■

Pierce v. Underwood

[Parties not identified.]

487 U.S. 552 (1988).

NATURE OF CASE: Appeal of an award of attorney's fees.

FACT SUMMARY: A district court awarded attorney's fees to a party because it found that the Housing and Urban Development agency had taken a position that was not substantially justified.

🏛 RULE OF LAW
Attorney's fees may be awarded against a party whose position was not justified to a degree that would satisfy a reasonable person.

FACTS: The Equal Access to Justice Act (EAJA) allows for the awarding of attorney's fees to the prevailing party in litigation when the other party's position was not "substantially justified." In a suit against the Secretary of Housing and Urban Development (D), the case was settled on grounds very unfavorable to the agency and the trial court ruled that the Secretary's (D) position was not substantially justified because of the objective indicia of the case, including the terms of the settlement, and awarded attorney's fees. The Ninth Circuit Court of Appeals affirmed, finding that a position is "substantially justified" if it "had a reasonable basis both in law and fact." The Secretary (D) appealed to the United States Supreme Court.

ISSUE: May attorney's fees be awarded against a party whose position was not justified to a degree that would satisfy a reasonable person?

HOLDING AND DECISION: (Scalia, J.) Yes. Attorney's fees may be awarded against a party whose position was not justified to a degree that would satisfy a reasonable person. Courts should not try to substitute for the formula that Congress has laid out in the statute. Accordingly, the "substantially justified" test is the only one that matters. There are a few different meanings of the word "substantial" so the test is susceptible to different interpretations. However, in this field of law there are other tests that use similar phrases and we should use them in interpreting the language of the EAJA. It is clear from these other phrases that substantial justification was not meant to mean "justified to a high degree." Rather, it was meant to be interpreted as "justified in substance." This is essentially the same as the Ninth Circuit's formulation of "reasonable basis both in law and fact." The Court is less sure that the district court should have looked only at the objective indicia of the case to determine whether the Secretary's (D) position was substantially justified. The terms of a settlement may be the result of other factors than a poor legal position. It is better to look directly at the merits of the position taken. After considering the merits, the Court can

not find that the district court abused its discretion in finding that there was no substantial justification for the Secretary's (D) position. Affirmed.

▶ ANALYSIS

The Court noted that looking only at settlement terms to determine justification might discourage settlements in the future. The standard of review in looking at the award of attorney's fees is abuse of discretion. Accordingly, it is not easy for an appellate court to overrule the trial court's initial determination.

■■■

Quicknotes

ABUSE OF DISCRETION A determination by an appellate court that a lower court's decision was based on an error of law.

EQUAL ACCESS TO JUSTICE ACT Provides for the awarding of attorney's fees to a prevailing party, other than the government, when the opposing side took a position that was not substantially justified.

■■■

Martinez v. Secretary of Health & Human Services

Injured worker (P) v. Government agency (D)

815 F.2d 1381 (10th Cir. 1987).

NATURE OF CASE: Appeal from an award of attorney's fees.

FACT SUMMARY: The Government's (D) position in a disability benefits case was against the position adopted in the jurisdiction after the suit was filed.

🏛 RULE OF LAW

Private litigants are not entitled to attorney's fees from the government under the Equal Access to Justice Act (EAJA) if the governing law at the time was unclear or in flux.

FACTS: Martinez (P) was injured in a work accident in 1978 and began receiving disability benefits under the Social Security Act. An investigation led to the cessation of the benefits in 1981 and the termination was upheld by an administrative law judge. In 1983, Martinez (P) sought judicial review in district court and argued that termination of the benefits required evidence that his medical condition had improved and that failure to apply that standard commanded reversal. The Secretary of Health and Human Services (D) asserted that this was not the proper test. In 1984, in a separate case, the Tenth Circuit ruled that benefits could not be discontinued without a showing that the claimant's medical condition had improved. Based on this ruling, the district court ruled that Martinez (P) should have his benefits reinstated. Martinez (P) then applied for attorney's fees under EAJA. The Secretary (D) argued that the medical improvement standard was not adopted until after the litigation and thus there was substantial justification for their position. The district court agreed and denied attorney's fees. Martinez (P) appealed.

ISSUE: Are private litigants entitled to attorney's fees from the government under EAJA if the governing law at the time was unclear or in flux?

HOLDING AND DECISION: (Per curiam) No. Private litigants are not entitled to attorney's fees from the government under EAJA if the governing law at the time was unclear or in flux. The more clearly established the governing norms are, the less justified a position in litigation will be. Where there are contrary interpretations by district courts and no clear precedent on a particular issue, it would be unfair to say that one position is not substantially justified because the other position is later adopted as law. In the present case, other circuit courts had adopted the medical improvement standard, but the governing law in this circuit was less certain. There were some intimations that this standard would be used, but some district courts had ruled differently on the issue prior to our definitive 1984 ruling.

Accordingly, the Secretary (D) was substantially justified in taking an opposing position in the Martinez (P) litigation, which was prior to the 1984 decision. Therefore, the district court's ruling denying an award of attorney's fees is affirmed.

▶ ANALYSIS

In deciding this case, Justice McKay dissented, finding that the government was not substantially justified. This case stands for the proposition that the governing law must be fairly well settled before a court will find that an opposing position is not justified. Where there is any controversy or ambiguity, parties won't be punished for taking a position later ruled wrong.

Quicknotes

EQUAL ACCESS TO JUSTICE ACT Provides for the awarding of attorney's fees to a prevailing party, other than the government, when the opposing side took a position that was not substantially justified.

JUDICIAL REVIEW The authority of the courts to review decisions, actions or omissions committed by another agency or branch of government.

Friends of the Boundary Waters Wilderness v. Thomas

Public interest group (P) v. Government agency (D)

53 F.3d 881 (8th Cir. 1995).

NATURE OF CASE: Appeal from denial of attorney's fees.

FACT SUMMARY: The Chief of the United States Forest Service (D) argued that its position in a losing case was justified because a district court had agreed before being reversed on appeal.

🏛 RULE OF LAW
A party must show that its position was clearly reasonable and well founded in law and fact in order to prove substantial justification for an incorrect legal position in litigation.

FACTS: In 1978, Congress passed the Boundary Waters Canoe Wilderness Area Act providing that the termination of existing motor boat transport operations at a certain waterway was required unless it was determined that there was no "feasible" nonmotorized means available. In 1986, the Forest Service authorized continued motor boat operations of various portages because it found that it was not feasible to use nonmotorized portage wheels. The Friends (P) brought an administrative appeal of this ruling and the Chief of the Forest Service (D) affirmed. The Friends (P) filed suit in district court, which found that the Chief's (D) interpretation of the Act was reasonable and also affirmed. The Friends (P) appealed and the court of appeals reversed, finding that the Chief's (D) interpretation was contrary to the definition of "feasible." The Friends (P) applied for an award of attorney's fees under the Equal Access to Justice Act (EAJA) as the prevailing party, but the district court denied the award, finding that the Chief's (D) position was substantially justified given the ambiguity of the statute. The Friends (P) once again appealed.

ISSUE: Must a party show that its position was clearly reasonable and well founded in law and fact in order to prove substantial justification for an incorrect legal position in litigation?

HOLDING AND DECISION: (Gibson, Sr. J) Yes. A party must show that its position was clearly reasonable and well founded in law and fact in order to prove substantial justification for an incorrect legal position in litigation. In order for the government's position to be substantially justified, it must be justified to a degree that would "satisfy a reasonable person" and have "a reasonable basis both in law and fact." The most powerful indicator of the reasonableness of an ultimately rejected position is a decision on the merits and the rationale supporting that decision. The decision of the district court and dissenting judges may be considered. However, when the superior appellate court finds that a position was clearly contrary to the law, this must be given greater weight. In this case, this court concluded that the Chief's (D) position was contrary to clear congressional intent and the plain meaning of "feasible." Given this unequivocal rejection of the Chief's (D) position in the earlier litigation, it cannot now be said that the position was reasonable or well founded. Thus, the district court abused its discretion in concluding that the Chief (D) was substantially justified and the attorney's fees should have been awarded to the Friends (P). Reversed.

▶ ANALYSIS

The court also noted that the Chief (D) had not always interpreted the statute in the same way prior to the litigation with the Friends (P). One judge dissented from the majority position when the original litigation reached the court of appeals. This decision here is rather biting in that it implies strongly that the dissenting judge took a clearly unreasonable position in the dissent.

■=■

Quicknotes

ABUSE OF DISCRETION A determination by an appellate court that a lower court's decision was based on an error of law.

EQUAL ACCESS TO JUSTICE ACT Provides for the awarding of attorney's fees to a prevailing party, other than the government, when the opposing side took a position that was not substantially justified.

■=■

Pierce v. Underwood

[Parties not identified.]

487 U.S. 552 (1988).

NATURE OF CASE: Review of award of attorney's fees.

FACT SUMMARY: A district court awarded attorney's fees in excess of the statutory cap because of allegedly special circumstances.

> ## 🏛 RULE OF LAW
> For attorneys to be awarded fees under the Equal Access to Justice Act (EAJA) that exceed the statutory cap, they must be qualified for the proceedings in some specialized sense.

FACTS: When a lawsuit against the Secretary of Housing and Urban Development (D) was settled, attorneys for the plaintiff were awarded attorney's fees under the EAJA. The amount of the fees awarded was higher than the limit set by the statute. The district court based the amount of the award on an exception in the statute for cases involving allegedly special factors, such as the limited availability of qualified attorneys for the proceedings involved. The Government (D) appealed, claiming that no special factors were present in this case to warrant the higher award.

ISSUE: For attorneys to be awarded fees under EAJA that exceed the statutory cap, must they be qualified for the proceedings in some specialized sense?

HOLDING AND DECISION: (Scalia, J.) Yes. For attorneys to be awarded fees under EAJA that exceed the statutory cap, they must be qualified for the proceedings in some specialized sense. The exception should be applied only when attorneys have some distinctive knowledge or specialized skill related to the litigation in question, such as an identifiable practice specialty or knowledge of a foreign language. The factors considered by the court below were too generally applicable to be regarded as special reasons for exceeding the statutory cap. It was an abuse of discretion for the court to rely on those factors. Reversed.

▶ ANALYSIS

The district court had based its award on the novelty and difficulty of the issues, the undesirability of the case, the work and ability of counsel, the results obtained, and the customary fees and awards in other cases. The Court here found that none of those factors justified the higher award. The special factors to be considered for a higher award must not be of broad and general application.

Quicknotes

EQUAL ACCESS TO JUSTICE ACT Provides for the awarding of attorney's fees to a prevailing party, other than the government, when the opposing side took a position that was not substantially justified.

■═■

Pirus v. Bowen

Class representative (P) v. Department of Health and Human Services (D)

869 F.2d 536 (9th Cir. 1989).

NATURE OF CASE: Appeal of an award of attorney's fees.

FACT SUMMARY: The Government (D) complained that an award of attorney's fees should not have been enhanced past the statutory maximum rate.

🏛 **RULE OF LAW**
Attorneys with distinctive knowledge in a practice specialty are entitled to fees higher than the maximum rate under the Equal Access to Justice Act (EAJA) where those qualifications are necessary to the litigation and there are no other lawyers to take the case at the statutory rate.

FACTS: Pirus (P) brought a class action against the Secretary of the Department of Health and Human Services (D) on behalf of a class which was denied social security benefits. The district court granted summary judgment to Pirus (P) and the class. Pirus (P) then petitioned for an award of attorney's fees under EAJA. The court awarded the fees and determined that special factors justified an award of fees in excess of the EAJA maximum cap. The factors considered by the court were the attorney's expertise, the lack of other lawyers willing to take the case, and the unique ability of the attorneys in this particular area of the law. The Secretary (D) appealed.

ISSUE: Are attorneys with distinctive knowledge in a practice specialty entitled to fees higher than the maximum rate under EAJA where those qualifications are necessary to the litigation and there are no other lawyers to take the case at the lower rate?

HOLDING AND DECISION: (Norris, J.) Yes. Attorneys with distinctive knowledge in a practice specialty are entitled to fees higher than the maximum rate under EAJA where those qualifications are necessary to the litigation and there are no other lawyers to take the case at the statutory rate. The Supreme Court has decided that Congress intended for courts to deviate from the statutory cap only if the attorney had some distinctive knowledge or specialized skill needed for the litigation. Although the Supreme Court pointed out patent law as an example of a practice specialty and specialized skill, there is no reason to believe that this standard would not apply to other areas of the law. In the present case, Pirus's (P) attorneys developed a specialty in social security law and had expertise pertaining to the complex statutory scheme of the law. The district court found that this special expertise was needed in the case, which was highly complex and required substantial knowledge about a narrow area of the law. Accordingly, the

district court acted properly in awarding an enhanced fee. Affirmed.

▶ **ANALYSIS**

The reasoning of this decision seems to open up many types of cases to fee enhancements. In many, if not most, cases the prevailing party's attorneys will have some expertise in the legal area of the case.

■■■■

Quicknotes

EQUAL ACCESS TO JUSTICE ACT Provides for the awarding of attorney's fees to a prevailing party, other than the government, when the opposing side took a position that was not substantially justified.

■■■■

Chynoweth v. Sullivan

Benefits recipient (P) v. Government agency (D)

920 F.2d 648 (10th Cir. 1990).

NATURE OF CASE: Appeal from denial of enhancement of attorney's fees award.

FACT SUMMARY: Chynoweth (P) claimed her attorneys were entitled to a fee enhancement under the Equal Access to Justice (EAJA) because of their special expertise in Social Security disability law.

🏛 RULE OF LAW
The EAJA statutory cap on attorney's fees may be exceeded only in unusual situations where the legal services rendered require specialized training and expertise unattainable by an ordinary competent attorney.

FACTS: After winning a Social Security disability case, Chynoweth (P) petitioned the district court for attorney's fees of $130 per hour under EAJA. Chynoweth (P) claimed that her attorney was a specialist in Social Security Disability benefits law. The district court held that Chynoweth (P) was entitled to attorneys fees since the Secretary's denial of disability benefits was not substantially justified. However, the district court concluded that Chynoweth's (P) attorney was not entitled to a fee enhancement based on the absence of a special factor. Chynoweth (P) appealed this aspect of the award.

ISSUE: May the EAJA statutory cap on attorney's fees be exceeded only in unusual situations where the legal services rendered require specialized training and expertise unattainable by an ordinary competent attorney?

HOLDING AND DECISION: (Baldock, J.) Yes. The EAJA statutory cap on attorney's fees may be exceeded only in unusual situations where the legal services rendered require specialized training and expertise unattainable by an ordinary competent attorney. EAJA mandates a maximum rate unless a special factor justifies a higher fee. Expertise in a particular legal field alone does not justify the higher rate. Merely because some scholarly effort or professional experience is required to attain proficiency in a particular practice area does not automatically require a fee enhancement. Social Security law is not beyond the grasp of a typical competent practicing attorney. In the present case, the district court also made no findings that Chynoweth's (P) action was a particularly difficult case or that she would have been unable to obtain other competent representation at the statutory rate. Affirmed.

▶ ANALYSIS

Although this case would seem to turn mostly on the court's opinion that expertise with Social Security law is not a specialized skill, there may be more important factors. The court was reviewing the district court's denial of the fee enhancement under an abuse of discretion standard. Also, the district court obviously made no effort to put on the record facts about Chynoweth's (P) case that would make it seem difficult and unique.

Quicknotes

ABUSE OF DISCRETION A determination by an appellate court that a lower court's decision was based on an error of law.

EQUAL ACCESS TO JUSTICE ACT Provides for the awarding of attorney's fees to a prevailing party, other than the government, when the opposing side took a position that was not substantially justified.

Raines v. Shalala

Benefits recipient (P) v. Secretary of Health and Human Services (D)

44 F.3d 1355 (7th Cir. 1995).

NATURE OF CASE: Appeal from award of attorney's fees.

FACT SUMMARY: Raines's (P) attorney was awarded fees in excess of the Equal Access to Justice Act (EAJA) statutory cap in a Social Security benefits case.

🏛 RULE OF LAW
Attorney's fees in excess of the EAJA statutory maximum rate are only appropriate in unusual cases where the case requires someone with specialized training and expertise unattainable by a standard competent attorney.

FACTS: Raines (P) filed suit against Health and Human Services (D) for his entitlement to Social Security disability benefits and prevailed. Raines's (P) petition requested $175 per hour for attorney's fees, claiming that this was the prevailing market rate due to the limited availability of qualified Social Security lawyers. The district court awarded attorney's fees pursuant to EAJA, deciding that special factors were present in order to award fees in excess of the statutory cap. The court found that the attorney had expertise with a complex statutory scheme, familiarity with a particular agency, and understood the needs of a particular class of clients. Health and Human Services (D) appealed, claiming that if such practice specialties were routinely found to be special factors, fee awards subject to the statutory cap would be rare.

ISSUE: Are attorney's fees in excess of the EAJA statutory maximum rate only appropriate in unusual cases where the case requires someone with specialized training and expertise unattainable by a standard competent attorney?

HOLDING AND DECISION: (Ripple, J.) Yes. Attorney's fees in excess of the EAJA statutory maximum rate are only appropriate in unusual cases where the case requires someone with specialized training and expertise unattainable by a standard competent attorney. The United States Supreme Court has clearly held that a fee enhancement under EAJA cannot be based simply on the limited availability of qualified attorneys. The nature of the case must also make it necessary to have an attorney with a specialized skill in an identifiable practice specialty. This special skill requirement means something not easily acquired by a reasonably competent attorney or a special non-legal skill such as knowledge of a foreign language. Additionally, it will be an exceptional or unusual situation when the special factors will apply. The test applied by the district court in the instant case was a bit too lenient. Although Raines's (P) attorney was undoubtedly very proficient in the area of Social Security benefits law, this isn't the type of skill and expertise that is unattainable by a competent attorney through diligent study. Furthermore, the principal issues arising in Raines's (P) case are issues that arise not infrequently in disability litigation. Accordingly, the award in excess of the statutory cap was improper and must be reversed and remanded.

▶ ANALYSIS

The weight of authority in attorney fee cases pursuant to the EAJA declines to award fees in excess of the statutory cap. Indeed, "[i]f expertise acquired through practice justified higher reimbursement rates then all lawyers practicing administrative law in technical fields would be entitled to fee enhancements." *F.J. Vollmer Company, Inc. v. Magaw*, 102 F.3d 591 at 598 (D.C. Cir. 1996). To receive a fee award exceeding the statutory cap, an attorney must have an identifiable practice specialty such as patent law, or knowledge of foreign law or language. See, *Pierce v. Underwood*, 487 U.S. 552 (1988).

■=■

Quicknotes

EQUAL ACCESS TO JUSTICE ACT Provides for the awarding of attorney's fees to a prevailing party, other than the government, when the opposing side took a position that was not substantially justified.

■=■

Common Latin Words and Phrases Encountered in the Law

A FORTIORI: Because one fact exists or has been proven, therefore a second fact that is related to the first fact must also exist.

A PRIORI: From the cause to the effect. A term of logic used to denote that when one generally accepted truth is shown to be a cause, another particular effect must necessarily follow.

AB INITIO: From the beginning; a condition which has existed throughout, as in a marriage which was void ab initio.

ACTUS REUS: The wrongful act; in criminal law, such action sufficient to trigger criminal liability.

AD VALOREM: According to value; an ad valorem tax is imposed upon an item located within the taxing jurisdiction calculated by the value of such item.

AMICUS CURIAE: Friend of the court. Its most common usage takes the form of an amicus curiae brief, filed by a person who is not a party to an action but is nonetheless allowed to offer an argument supporting his legal interests.

ARGUENDO: In arguing. A statement, possibly hypothetical, made for the purpose of argument, is one made arguendo.

BILL QUIA TIMET: A bill to quiet title (establish ownership) to real property.

BONA FIDE: True, honest, or genuine. May refer to a person's legal position based on good faith or lacking notice of fraud (such as a bona fide purchaser for value) or to the authenticity of a particular document (such as a bona fide last will and testament).

CAUSA MORTIS: With approaching death in mind. A gift causa mortis is a gift given by a party who feels certain that death is imminent.

CAVEAT EMPTOR: Let the buyer beware. This maxim is reflected in the rule of law that a buyer purchases at his own risk because it is his responsibility to examine, judge, test, and otherwise inspect what he is buying.

CERTIORARI: A writ of review. Petitions for review of a case by the United States Supreme Court are most often done by means of a writ of certiorari.

CONTRA: On the other hand. Opposite. Contrary to.

CORAM NOBIS: Before us; writs of error directed to the court that originally rendered the judgment.

CORAM VOBIS: Before you; writs of error directed by an appellate court to a lower court to correct a factual error.

CORPUS DELICTI: The body of the crime; the requisite elements of a crime amounting to objective proof that a crime has been committed.

CUM TESTAMENTO ANNEXO, ADMINISTRATOR (ADMINISTRATOR C.T.A.): With will annexed; an administrator c.t.a. settles an estate pursuant to a will in which he is not appointed.

DE BONIS NON, ADMINISTRATOR (ADMINISTRATOR D.B.N.): Of goods not administered; an administrator d.b.n. settles a partially settled estate.

DE FACTO: In fact; in reality; actually. Existing in fact but not officially approved or engendered.

DE JURE: By right; lawful. Describes a condition that is legitimate "as a matter of law," in contrast to the term "de facto," which connotes something existing in fact but not legally sanctioned or authorized. For example, de facto segregation refers to segregation brought about by housing patterns, etc., whereas de jure segregation refers to segregation created by law.

DE MINIMIS: Of minimal importance; insignificant; a trifle; not worth bothering about.

DE NOVO: Anew; a second time; afresh. A trial de novo is a new trial held at the appellate level as if the case originated there and the trial at a lower level had not taken place.

DICTA: Generally used as an abbreviated form of obiter dicta, a term describing those portions of a judicial opinion incidental or not necessary to resolution of the specific question before the court. Such nonessential statements and remarks are not considered to be binding precedent.

DUCES TECUM: Refers to a particular type of writ or subpoena requesting a party or organization to produce certain documents in their possession.

EN BANC: Full bench. Where a court sits with all justices present rather than the usual quorum.

EX PARTE: For one side or one party only. An ex parte proceeding is one undertaken for the benefit of only one party, without notice to, or an appearance by, an adverse party.

EX POST FACTO: After the fact. An ex post facto law is a law that retroactively changes the consequences of a prior act.

EX REL.: Abbreviated form of the term "ex relatione," meaning upon relation or information. When the state brings an action in which it has no interest against an individual at the instigation of one who has a private interest in the matter.

FORUM NON CONVENIENS: Inconvenient forum. Although a court may have jurisdiction over the case, the action should be tried in a more conveniently located court, one to which parties and witnesses may more easily travel, for example.

GUARDIAN AD LITEM: A guardian of an infant as to litigation, appointed to represent the infant and pursue his/her rights.

HABEAS CORPUS: You have the body. The modern writ of habeas corpus is a writ directing that a person (body) being detained (such as a prisoner) be brought before the court so that the legality of his detention can be judicially ascertained.

IN CAMERA: In private, in chambers. When a hearing is held before a judge in his chambers or when all spectators are excluded from the courtroom.

IN FORMA PAUPERIS: In the manner of a pauper. A party who proceeds in forma pauperis because of his poverty is one who is allowed to bring suit without liability for costs.

INFRA: Below, under. A word referring the reader to a later part of a book. (The opposite of supra.)

IN LOCO PARENTIS: In the place of a parent.

IN PARI DELICTO: Equally wrong; a court of equity will not grant requested relief to an applicant who is in pari delicto, or as much at fault in the transactions giving rise to the controversy as is the opponent of the applicant.

IN PARI MATERIA: On like subject matter or upon the same matter. Statutes relating to the same person or things are said to be in pari materia. It is a general rule of statutory construction that such statutes should be construed together, i.e., looked at as if they together constituted one law.

IN PERSONAM: Against the person. Jurisdiction over the person of an individual.

IN RE: In the matter of. Used to designate a proceeding involving an estate or other property.

IN REM: A term that signifies an action against the res, or thing. An action in rem is basically one that is taken directly against property, as distinguished from an action in personam, i.e., against the person.

INTER ALIA: Among other things. Used to show that the whole of a statement, pleading, list, statute, etc., has not been set forth in its entirety.

INTER PARTES: Between the parties. May refer to contracts, conveyances or other transactions having legal significance.

INTER VIVOS: Between the living. An inter vivos gift is a gift made by a living grantor, as distinguished from bequests contained in a will, which pass upon the death of the testator.

IPSO FACTO: By the mere fact itself.

JUS: Law or the entire body of law.

LEX LOCI: The law of the place; the notion that the rights of parties to a legal proceeding are governed by the law of the place where those rights arose.

MALUM IN SE: Evil or wrong in and of itself; inherently wrong. This term describes an act that is wrong by its very nature, as opposed to one which would not be wrong but for the fact that there is a specific legal prohibition against it (malum prohibitum).

MALUM PROHIBITUM: Wrong because prohibited, but not inherently evil. Used to describe something that is wrong because it is expressly forbidden by law but that is not in and of itself evil, e.g., speeding.

MANDAMUS: We command. A writ directing an official to take a certain action.

MENS REA: A guilty mind; a criminal intent. A term used to signify the mental state that accompanies a crime or other prohibited act. Some crimes require only a general mens rea (general intent to do the prohibited act), but others, like assault with intent to murder, require the existence of a specific mens rea.

MODUS OPERANDI: Method of operating; generally refers to the manner or style of a criminal in committing crimes, admissible in appropriate cases as evidence of the identity of a defendant.

NEXUS: A connection to.

NISI PRIUS: A court of first impression. A nisi prius court is one where issues of fact are tried before a judge or jury.

N.O.V. (NON OBSTANTE VEREDICTO): Notwithstanding the verdict. A judgment n.o.v. is a judgment given in favor of one party despite the fact that a verdict was returned in favor of the other party, the justification being that the verdict either had no reasonable support in fact or was contrary to law.

NUNC PRO TUNC: Now for then. This phrase refers to actions that may be taken and will then have full retroactive effect.

PENDENTE LITE: Pending the suit; pending litigation under way.

PER CAPITA: By head; beneficiaries of an estate, if they take in equal shares, take per capita.

PER CURIAM: By the court; signifies an opinion ostensibly written "by the whole court" and with no identified author.

PER SE: By itself, in itself; inherently.

PER STIRPES: By representation. Used primarily in the law of wills to describe the method of distribution where a person, generally because of death, is unable to take that which is left to him by the will of another, and therefore his heirs divide such property between them rather than take under the will individually.

PRIMA FACIE: On its face, at first sight. A prima facie case is one that is sufficient on its face, meaning that the evidence supporting it is adequate to establish the case until contradicted or overcome by other evidence.

PRO TANTO: For so much; as far as it goes. Often used in eminent domain cases when a property owner receives partial payment for his land without prejudice to his right to bring suit for the full amount he claims his land to be worth.

QUANTUM MERUIT: As much as he deserves. Refers to recovery based on the doctrine of unjust enrichment in those cases in which a party has rendered valuable services or furnished materials that were accepted and enjoyed by another under circumstances that would reasonably notify the recipient that the rendering party expected to be paid. In essence, the law implies a contract to pay the reasonable value of the services or materials furnished.

QUASI: Almost like; as if; nearly. This term is essentially used to signify that one subject or thing is almost analogous to another but that material differences between them do exist. For example, a quasi-criminal proceeding is one that is not strictly criminal but shares enough of the same characteristics to require some of the same safeguards (e.g., procedural due process must be followed in a parole hearing).

QUID PRO QUO: Something for something. In contract law, the consideration, something of value, passed between the parties to render the contract binding.

RES GESTAE: Things done; in evidence law, this principle justifies the admission of a statement that would otherwise be hearsay when it is made so closely to the event in question as to be said to be a part of it, or with such spontaneity as not to have the possibility of falsehood.

RES IPSA LOQUITUR: The thing speaks for itself. This doctrine gives rise to a rebuttable presumption of negligence when the instrumentality causing the injury was within the exclusive control of the defendant, and the injury was one that does not normally occur unless a person has been negligent.

RES JUDICATA: A matter adjudged. Doctrine which provides that once a court of competent jurisdiction has rendered a final judgment or decree on the merits, that judgment or decree is conclusive upon the parties to the case and prevents them from engaging in any other litigation on the points and issues determined therein.

RESPONDEAT SUPERIOR: Let the master reply. This doctrine holds the master liable for the wrongful acts of his servant (or the principal for his agent) in those cases in which the servant (or agent) was acting within the scope of his authority at the time of the injury.

STARE DECISIS: To stand by or adhere to that which has been decided. The common law doctrine of stare decisis attempts to give security and certainty to the law by following the policy that once a principle of law as applicable to a certain set of facts has been set forth in a decision, it forms a precedent which will subsequently be followed, even though a different decision might be made were it the first time the question had arisen. Of course, stare decisis is not an inviolable principle and is departed from in instances where there is good cause (e.g., considerations of public policy led the Supreme Court to disregard prior decisions sanctioning segregation).

SUPRA: Above. A word referring a reader to an earlier part of a book.

ULTRA VIRES: Beyond the power. This phrase is most commonly used to refer to actions taken by a corporation that are beyond the power or legal authority of the corporation.

Addendum of French Derivatives

IN PAIS: Not pursuant to legal proceedings.

CHATTEL: Tangible personal property.

CY PRES: Doctrine permitting courts to apply trust funds to purposes not expressed in the trust but necessary to carry out the settlor's intent.

PER AUTRE VIE: For another's life; during another's life. In property law, an estate may be granted that will terminate upon the death of someone other than the grantee.

PROFIT A PRENDRE: A license to remove minerals or other produce from land.

VOIR DIRE: Process of questioning jurors as to their predispositions about the case or parties to a proceeding in order to identify those jurors displaying bias or prejudice.

Casenote Legal Briefs